Rupturing African Philosophy on Teaching and Learning

"Against a global and South African background of increasing calls for the decolonisation of knowledge, this book provides a refreshing account of a pedagogic rupturing as a decolonising exertion. Instead of ridding itself of all that might be 'colonialist', this book – through adopting an African philosophical lens – argues for deliberative inquiry and reflexive openness, not only in relation to pedagogical encounters, but as enactments of just humaneness."

—Nuraan Davids, *Associate Professor of Philosophy of Education, Stellenbosch University, South Africa*

Yusef Waghid • Faiq Waghid
Zayd Waghid

Rupturing African Philosophy on Teaching and Learning

Ubuntu Justice and Education

palgrave
macmillan

Yusef Waghid
Education Policy Studies
Stellenbosch University
Stellenbosch, South Africa

Faiq Waghid
Centre for Innovative Learning Technology
Cape Peninsula University of Technology
Cape Town, South Africa

Zayd Waghid
Faculty of Education
Cape Peninsula University of Technology
Cape Town, South Africa

ISBN 978-3-319-77949-2   ISBN 978-3-319-77950-8   (eBook)
https://doi.org/10.1007/978-3-319-77950-8

Library of Congress Control Number: 2018937234

© The Editor(s) (if applicable) and The Author(s) 2018
This work is subject to copyright. All rights are solely and exclusively licensed by the Publisher, whether the whole or part of the material is concerned, specifically the rights of translation, reprinting, reuse of illustrations, recitation, broadcasting, reproduction on microfilms or in any other physical way, and transmission or information storage and retrieval, electronic adaptation, computer software, or by similar or dissimilar methodology now known or hereafter developed.
The use of general descriptive names, registered names, trademarks, service marks, etc. in this publication does not imply, even in the absence of a specific statement, that such names are exempt from the relevant protective laws and regulations and therefore free for general use.
The publisher, the authors and the editors are safe to assume that the advice and information in this book are believed to be true and accurate at the date of publication. Neither the publisher nor the authors or the editors give a warranty, express or implied, with respect to the material contained herein or for any errors or omissions that may have been made. The publisher remains neutral with regard to jurisdictional claims in published maps and institutional affiliations.

Cover illustration: © Oleksandr Drypsiak / Alamy

Printed on acid-free paper

This Palgrave Macmillan imprint is published by the registered company Springer International Publishing AG part of Springer Nature.
The registered company address is: Gewerbestrasse 11, 6330 Cham, Switzerland

Foreword A

In California, Stanford University's recent "MacArthur genius" invents a powerful MOOC (massive open online course) that teaches introductory economics with the course title "Using big data to solve economic and social problems".[1] Students learn about inequality and the course invites them to design practical solutions to real problems facing the poor such as health care, education and migration. This inventive technology at one of the world's leading universities allows for open access to advanced learning about inequality, is offered without cost, and therefore presents students with quality, affordable education. Professor Raj Chetty is an expert on "Big Data" and so students also gain knowledge of cutting-edge methods of data analysis to make sense of complex social problems and to act on them as activists backed up with real-time evidence of problems and concrete skills for how to tackle those problems.

In South Africa, Cape Town university professors in collaboration with an international partner have also designed an impressive MOOC that introduces students to African Philosophy of Education, in which they are equipped with powerful concepts from within their own environment to understand and act on the world around them. Their problem sets concern subjects such as student protests, military rule in Africa, geno-

---

[1] https://qz.com/1103806/a-pioneering-economics-class-is-tackling-social-justice-issues-with-big-data-and-women-and-minorities-are-enrolling-in-droves/.

cide, terrorism and the education implications of such phenomena on the content. The content for such engagement is various strands within African philosophies generally and philosophies of education, in particular. Through engagement with this rich conceptual language drawn from various African leaders—such as Nelson Mandela and Desmond Tutu—and African philosophy—such as *ubuntu*—students are equipped to make sense of these social dilemmas familiar to the continent. The MOOC is the subject of this fascinating new book titled *Rupturing African Philosophy on Teaching and Learning: Ubuntu Justice and Education* (*Rupturing*, in this review, for short).

What is the difference between these 'massive online courses' offered from Palo Alto and Cape Town? At first glance, both MOOCs tackle problems of injustice in their respective societies—from housing inequality in the USA to the unaffordability of tuition fees for poor students in South Africa. Both provide free access to online education and specific competencies for analysing and changing familiar social problems. Both make some very bold claims, though somewhat more modestly in the California case, about the impacts of these technological innovations on students and their learning. And yet these two creative platforms for teaching university students are fundamentally different in how they present their political claims for the change they seek.

The Stanford MOOC works in the best tradition of what Americans call a liberal arts education. It offers broad access to the best ideas available in the stock of human knowledge and engages students practically in conception and action on those ideas. The problems are social and their resolutions are technological. The language deployed is simple and accessible and the tools for engagement drawn from evidence that informs rational action.

The Cape Town MOOC is explicitly political in its orientation and links some of its case work and language to South Africa's student protest movement of 2015–16 through references to *decolonisation* and *coloniality*. Its work is an attempt to give prominence in university curricula, which is still largely based on European intellectuals, their concepts and methods, to African scholars and their thoughts as these relate to social problems on this continent. The language is conceptually dense with familiar and fresh concepts concerning the human condition. Students are invited not only to engage with these concepts but teachers are expected to engage this "disruptive pedagogy" to change their minds as individuals and their social conditions as activists.

This book does well to deal with three common criticisms of the quest to seek knowledge within the "ethno-narratival" archives of African reservoirs of knowledge. First, it does not fall into the trap of ethnic chauvinism, the position that there is something uniquely or essentially African that merits an engagement with philosophy in isolation of international streams of thought in this field. This is important in the strident atmosphere of South African student politics in which Africanisation is sometimes posed in rigid contradistinction to the Europeanisation of the curriculum; the global development of knowledge production has long become much more complex and cosmopolitan than these old polarities still insist on. In this respect, the book takes forward the enduring debate on knowledge, power and identity in the wake of cataclysms such as colonialism and apartheid.

Second, the book avoids not only the pitfalls of African chauvinism but the common retreat into an African romanticism about the present past. Difficult subjects are taken on such as military rule and genocide as subjects for philosophical inquiry. The narrative of the evil West posited against the good African finds no refuge in a scholarship that insists on truth as its standard of pedagogical engagement. How does philosophy in and from Africa speak to problems of its own making? To simply dismiss these continental problems as a reflexive consequence of Western imperialism is to both dull the intellectual senses and disable a necessary activism that should flow from a critical philosophy in Africa.

And thirdly, the book places social problems within the context of ideology and power. This opens up difficult questions that the liberal arts orientation of the curriculum in capitalist America would rather avoid—namely, that problems of inequality are not simply an unfortunate aberration inside a political economy that distributes access and opportunity fairly across the populace. If only the individual worked hard enough or pulled themselves up by their bootstraps or simply showed up—anything is possible; even that founding myth of American society has recently floundered on the hard realities of a globalising economy.

The book draws attention, rather, to the social and material conditions that create and sustain inequality. By implication, the solutions to these dilemmas are not simply technical but social; not merely instrumental but political; not individual but communitarian. This book offers transformation with a soul so that what results is not simply a "big data" solution to intractable problems but a large-hearted response to these problems through perhaps the most recognisable precept if not practice of philosophy in South Africa, *ubuntu*. For here, the solution to inequality is not merely to rectify but to restore through an approach that is moral, compassionate, inclusive, humane and interdependent.

In these and other respects, *Rupturing* breaks new ground as the first online course on African philosophy of education to emerge from this continent.

Education Policy Studies   Jonathan D. Jansen
Distinguished Professor
Stellenbosch University

Foreword B

One significant societal sphere of the application of the worldwide increasing importance of Information and Communication Technologies (ICT) is the domain of education, with various dimensions, implications and possibilities for the different levels and types. There are considerable cross-national variations of the application depending on the levels of broader technological capacities and the nature of the demand for education. As African countries in general have more prevailing limitations in educational supply, from the basic issues of inadequate facilities to accommodate simple access for all to tackling effectively the issues of severe attrition to the low percentage of access to higher education. In search of cost-effective methods and tools to respond to high demand, help equalise educational opportunity at all levels of the systems including tertiary, African countries have been increasingly exploring and adopting distance learning using ICT. While in this context the advantages tend to be highlighted, there has been a debate about concerns for the various usages of the technology for teaching. Among such issues has been the actual or potential impact on the sustainability and integrity of the teaching profession. While various dimensions and nuances have been articulated, it is fair to argue that the discourse has been structured in the polar and nearly mutually exclusive framework of capital-intensive versus labor-intensive policies and practices in the present and future of education amid the fast-paced technological possibilities for delivery of education.

In this very groundbreaking, daring, insightful and provocative manuscript, *Rupturing African Philosophy on Teaching and Learning: Ubuntu Justice and Education*, Yusef Waghid, Faiq Waghid and Zayd Waghid unequivocally situate their project outside this focus of the debate. They situate their theoretical and conceptual parameters from the onset, arguing that their goal is not to take a position on the discourse regarding, in this case, the use of massive open online courses (MOOCs). They clarify that, instead, their aim is to make a case for "an African philosophy of education which has been espoused through a Massive Open Online Course (MOOC)". In an article entitled "Implementing the Online Learning Community in Africa: A Unisa Case Study" J. F. Heydenrych, P. Higgs, and L. J. Van Niekerk (2003) articulated in a concise way the question of the desirability and even the necessity and possibility for utilising an African collective learning mode to the application of technology. In a similar spirit is the recognition that MOOCs have been irreversibly introduced in the education landscape and delivery in Africa. In this proposed book the authors argue that a deliberate approach informed by "African philosophy of education" ought to be part of the education delivery of education via MOOCs in Africa.

With a compelling and authoritative introduction of the subject matter and goal, the authors present nine well-structured and enthralling chapters. Chapter 1 has a didactic feature aiming to articulate a "plausible" understanding of African philosophy of education whose strands vary from what they refer to as "ethno-philosophy" to " a communitarian" philosophy of education, which must be, in its totality, taken into consideration in offering the framework for relevant understanding and reconceptualisation, thus departing from the hitherto misunderstanding and mischaracterisation of the assumed "ethno-centrism" and "communitarian practices". Instead of boxing African philosophy of education in its assumed shortcomings, the authors endeavour to articulate its values for "pedagogic justice" defined by its intrinsic capacity "deliberative engagement, responsibility towards one another, and the cultivation of humanity". In other words, the authors contend that African philosophy of education is far from being randomly set and applied. Rather, it is firmly and consistently framed by the tenet of *ubuntu*.

In Chap. 2, the authors articulate the ways in which teaching and learning that depart from the aforementioned usual misconceptions unravel possibilities for renewal of the pedagogic and curriculum conceptual framework and practices. The deliberate and purposeful rupture in teaching and learning has the capacity to offer context for the actualisation of "ethics of responsibility and humanity in pedagogic encounters", promoting equality of educational opportunities. The new learning and teaching space is close to the forum envisioned in Freire's *Pedagogy of the Oppressed* as the participants of this learning and teaching context become empowered agents who, in the process, acquire and share mutually beneficial competences that can enrich and enhance "cosmopolitan agendas of our pedagogic actions".

In Chap. 3 they engage more directly and forcefully *ubuntu*, emphasising the embedded dimension of justice and the logical connection of African philosophy of education to the concept articulating "restorative compassionate and moral justice". According to the authors, *ubuntu* justice constitutes the foundation and offers the rationale for the envisioned transformation that African philosophy of education can provide with the aim of promoting actions guided by pedagogy that deliberately breaks from the accepted practices and bears testimony to the liberatory concerns of such a philosophy of education. They articulate that collective fulfilment in the process and at the end of restoration leads to the enhancement of a common humanity that is dependent on the recognition of the need to acknowledge "one another's vulnerabilities compassionately...[and] moral autonomy ...". In sum, they continue, by enacting an African philosophy of education, it is not simply desirable or even necessary to achieve *ubuntu* justice, as a foundation for the actualisation of common humanity, but rather to set in motion a permanent corrective measure.

In Chap. 4 they tackle the deliberative, responsible and risk-oriented action that can be adopted and nurtured through an African philosophy of education. Rupture is neither sufficient nor an end in itself and cannot organically create new practices. Deliberate actions shaping the new pedagogic practices and guided towards the cultivation of pedagogic justice are necessary. In the teaching and learning space, educators and students can through rupturing engender risks with the possibility that cooperative human action might foster deliberative and responsible pedagogic encounters, thus constructing a curriculum strategy to promote deliberation, responsibility and risk-taking. While pedagogic rupturing may not be considered as an indispensable pedagogic online initiative that can, on its own, contain the potential to create and sustain responsible and responsive pedagogic encounters, the authors argue that any pedagogic action that invokes notions of deliberation, responsibility and risk-taking, as is the case with the MOOC on Teaching for Change, can cause rupture and engender emancipatory forms of human action.

Chapter 5 is devoted to the articulation of why pedagogic rupturing in African philosophy of education has not been actualised and remains in potentiality regarding pedagogic rupturing. The authors point out, as an illustration, that pedagogic rupturing remains in potentiality, especially considering that all contribute to that to the ongoing essence of education, as it cannot be conclusive and exhaustive. Hence, among curriculum initiatives that awaits being uncovered and learned involve that which give fuller meaning to the possibilities associated with African philosophy of education. They argue that pedagogic rupturing offers the possibility for actualising the ideas of a constantly ongoing pedagogic encounter of continued quest.

Chapter 6 focuses on MOOC and contains relevant information with regard to some of the practical aspects of the constraints in its design and implementation in relation to African philosophy of education. It further engages the notion that in *ubuntu* justice through an African philosophy of education, cosmopolitan justice is also cultivated as a human action. The co-authors submit that cosmopolitan justice is indeed imbedded in *ubuntu* justice, which has the potential of being actualised in spaces where autonomous, deliberative and reflexive pedagogic action takes place. They further argue that *ubuntu* justice can be actualised on the condition that an African philosophy of education is recognised, which is another way of asserting the existential interdependence of African philosophy of education and *ubuntu* justice. As indicated above, this relationship is reflected in the ways that deliberative engagement, autonomous action, and reflexive encounters are actualised.

Chapter 7 offers illustrative possibilities through the narratives/stories of the three co-authors, sharing their experiences in how pedagogic rupturing with its emphasis on *ubuntu* justice became a defining experience for the respective pedagogic actions. From their experiential encounter, they assert that pedagogic justice and by implication *ubuntu* justice is intrinsically connected to the process of enacting the transformative capacity of education as a means and object of actions towards "decolonization" and "decoloniality". They contend that in an African philosophy of education lie the transformative capabilities in the potential for the reconfiguration of democratic citizenship education in which *ubuntu* justice becomes both a sufficient condition for pedagogic change and an enabling condition to trigger and sustain pedagogic change. It was argued earlier that both teaching and learning framed in African philosophy of education offer a space for action and the transformation of learners and teachers, in a Freirean framework. Thus, tapping into their experiences and reflective engagements, the authors affirm that there is a mechanism through which educators and students are moved by open, critical and reflexive pedagogic moments. They articulate the mutually transformative process that affects all involved and thus produces the reflective actualisation among the educators in a similar way that the learners are formally set and expected to experience the value added of this learning experience.

In Chap. 8 the authors make a connection between the notion of *ubuntu* justice and the idea of a democratic education, particularly in the context of institutional evolution and particularly in the case of institutions of higher learning, especially the university. Viewed by these co-authors as essentially and permanently evolving or, to use their term, remaining "in-becoming", the university offers transformative hope, regardless of its specific condition at difficult historical moments leading some analysts to refer to it as being "in ruins". With this conception of positive dynamics imbedded in the nature of the university, knowledge acquired in it also shares some of the attributes of the "university-in-becoming" and thus cannot be considered "complete and sufficient to advance humanity". Eric Ashby eloquently articulated this notion in his seminal book *Universities: British, Indian, African; a study in the ecology of higher education.* (Cambridge: Harvard University Press, 1966, p. 3) in which he argues that an institution "must be sufficiently stable to sustain the ideal which gave it birth and sufficiently responsive to remain relevant to the society which supports it. The university is a medieval institution which fulfills both these conditions". Thus, the authors rightly point out that in essence a university must always be ready to help address the most formidable challenges of every historical moment.

In Chap. 9 they articulate the justification for linking pedagogic rupturing to the practice of decoloniality, which they consider capable of engendering human actions with the promise of empowering people in the education process, whereby curriculum inquiry responds to the challenges of a decolonised education system. Decoloniality has the potential, capacity and mission of dislodging the foundation of societal and institutional actions that produce injustice and any dehumanising acts that are inherently part of colonial hegemony. A decolonial curriculum will, therefore, ensure an openness that is necessary for the understanding of African philosophy of education in the broader context of democratic citizenship.

In the postscript, the authors provide some concrete articulations of aspects of the practices that are associated with pedagogic rupturing and constructive disruption. They emphasise dimensions of their inquisitive pursuit in the effort towards the registration of MOOC as a curricular activity through which an African philosophy of teaching and learning can be acknowledged and established. They articulate a critical, deliberative, open and reflexive inquiry unfolded in pedagogic encounters in reference to some of the dialogical junctures that contributed towards responsible and responsive actions. For them, African philosophy of teaching and learning came to be enacted in a real online pedagogic initiative referred to as pedagogic rupturing.

Yusef Waghid, Faiq Waghid and Zayd Waghid, as co-authors with a solid mastery of the technical and technological expertise in the functioning of the MOOCs and optimal interface with philosophical knowledge as well as pedagogical factors in teaching and learning, have embarked on a fascinating and timely contribution in their purposeful disruption of the conventional assumption about African philosophy of education consistently grounded on the *ubuntu* paradigm. They offer a solid theoretical framework for a forward-looking interrogation of practices that have been erroneously informed by misconceptions and lack of understanding of the liberatory possibilities for collective advancement in adopting learning and teaching with a promise of African philosophy of education. The co-authors of this volume cover areas of critical importance to learning and teaching toward social progress. They provide a major theoretical intervention with a practical case that illustrates a way forward.

This volume will, without any doubt, fill an existing negative gap in triggering a critical examination of the assumptions and practices towards exploring an African-grounded philosophy of education and pedagogy of commitment for transformative action. The interface of the increasing use of the technology in educational processes and the quest for cross-sectional "decolonial" activism is timely. The forward-looking constructive rupture encompasses the potential for critical examination of the received and normalised routine practices which were created and have been sustained by a history of a unilateral setting and an imposition of norms founded on hegemony that constitute society at large and specifically in institutions of higher learning. This book will be welcomed by scholars in various disciplines, students and activists inside and outside of academia, policy makers, grassroots organisations and, more generally, the various teaching and learning communities, whether they have already been impacted by the MOOCs and other traditional models of face-to-face teaching and learning in brick-and-mortar institutions at national and across-national contexts.

Cornell University, Ithaca, NY   N'Dri T. Assié-Lumumba

Preface

This book is not a manuscript in defence of massive open online courses (MOOCs). Rather, it is a text in which we argue in support of an African philosophy of education which has been espoused through a massive open online course (MOOC). Throughout this book, we draw on our design, development, production and delivery experiences of a new MOOC on an African philosophy of education, in order to elucidate its pedagogic implications. The MOOC, entitled "Teaching for Change: An African Philosophical Approach", is Africa's first on philosophy of education, and is aimed at cultivating pedagogic justice. The idea of pedagogic justice lends and opens itself to considerations beyond the immediate constraints of an online initiative, and puts into play notions of potentiality, which are yet to be realised through the lens of an African philosophy of education.

Our view of an African philosophy of education is constituted by the following aspects. Firstly, such a philosophy of education has an ethno-narratival perspective whereby we invoke meanings of the discourse embedded in the practices of folklore, customs, cultures, habits, traditions and other indigenous ways of thinking, acting and being. Secondly, an African philosophy of education has a communitarian outlook—that is, the arguments in and about such a philosophy of education are situated in the proffering and exchange of reasons according to which understandings of education are justified. Thirdly, philosophy of education as

xvii

practised on the African continent is inherently attuned to the cultivation of *ubuntu* justice—that is, a form of justice that has moral, compassionate and restorative bias. One way of ensuring that *ubuntu* justice becomes manifest is by drawing renewed attention to an African philosophy of teaching and learning.

Moreover, considering that the afore-mentioned notions of an African philosophy of education are linked to the cultivation of *ubuntu* justice, we posit that conceptions of decolonisation and decoloniality might be possible through curricula amendments and changes. One way of actuating such changes through the curriculum—as will be discussed in this book—is through the enactment of a MOOC on "Teaching for Change: An African Philosophical Approach." In this sense, this book gives an account of an African philosophy of education with a communitarian—that is, human interdependent and co-argumentative—perspective. We proffer that deliberative inquiry, reflexive openness and disruptive thought are pedagogic ways in which a decolonised and decolonial understanding of African thought and practice could be enacted. And, Teaching for Change can be considered an online pedagogic curricular initiative through which an *ubuntu* notion of an African philosophy of education could be espoused, intertwined with notions of pedagogic justice that are both democratic and cosmopolitan. Democratic justice draws on deliberative stances of human engagement with the intent to cultivate just action, whereas cosmopolitan justice lends itself to the application of reflexivity and openness about educational matters concerning Africa, constantly in search of renewed understandings of human action. Together, democratic justice and cosmopolitan justice constitute pedagogic justice, which we argue is an instance of the broader concept of *ubuntu* justice.

More specifically, an African philosophy of education, we contend, involves identifying major philosophical problems on the African continent concomitantly with an examination of their consequences for education as a humane experience. By implication, it is not unusual that our book connects with issues of decolonisation and decoloniality, in particular showing how pedagogic justice is commensurate with the transformative potential Teaching for Change. The title of the book also reflects claims of education, most noticeably a liberatory form of education.

With reference to philosophical problems vis-à-vis the themes of agricultural production, student protests, reconciliation and nation building, and terrorism, we show that pedagogic justice has much to offer attempts to undermine and subvert problems associated with the afore-mentioned societal dilemmas. In nine intertwined chapters with a postscript, we tackle the notion of an African philosophy of education and pedagogic justice as an instance of *ubuntu* justice, especially concluding why *ubuntu* justice is conceptually linked to the enactment of decoloniality.

By implication, whereas our vehicle for pedagogic activity is Teaching for Change, our pronouncements on an African philosophy of education are premised on our engagement with what constitutes claims in and about education in Africa. Similarly, we are more interested in showing how pedagogic justice as an instance of *ubuntu* justice manifests in pedagogic activities than in making a case for the plausibility of MOOCs. Our interest in rupturing emanates from our concern that, unless pedagogic encounters are looked at differently, including the possibility that teaching and learning can be conceived as otherwise, we would not invoke deliberative, cosmopolitan and just actions, which came to be associated with the pedagogic activities of Teaching for Change. Thus, this book attempts to deepen understandings of some of the thoughts and practices of an African philosophy of education and concomitantly makes a case for more empowering forms of teaching and learning. It is through more imaginative forms of teaching and learning that an African philosophy of education can begin to rupture societal, political, moral and environmental dilemmas on the African continent. In a way, this is a book on an African philosophy of teaching and learning that holds the potential to rupture unjust and inhumane actions on the continent of Africa, most noticeably involving Africa's educational predicament. We have organised the book as follows:

In **Chap. 1,** a plausible understanding of an African philosophy of education is rendered. We contend that such a philosophy of education fluctuates between an extensively ethno-philosophy of education on the one hand, and a communitarian philosophy of education on the other. We argue that neither strands of African philosophy of education can be unduly dismissed as they offer plausible ways by which education on the African continent ought to be understood and reconceptualised.

xx   Preface

Immediately, we rupture (mis)understandings of African philosophy of education that are considered too ethnocentric, on the one hand, and perhaps too trivial on communitarian practices, on the other. Consequently, this chapter offers an account of a complementary view of an African philosophy of education and its implications for pedagogic justice—that is, mostly teaching and learning. The conceptual link between an African philosophy of education and pedagogic justice is constituted by notions of deliberative engagement, responsibility towards one another and the cultivation of humanity.

Chapter 2 discusses an analysis of teaching and learning as pedagogic moments in relation to an African philosophy of education. It shows how teaching and learning can be enhanced through the implementation of unconstrained pedagogic initiatives as instances of curriculum renewal. Teaching and learning through Teaching for Change hold the promise of evoking the potentialities of participants whereby they act responsibly and humanely towards one another. We argue that an ethics of responsibility and humanity in pedagogic encounters establishes equal opportunities for participants to speak with candour and clarity, to scrutinise one another's diverse points of view in an open and reflexive manner and to provoke one another to act anew—that is, with a sense of imaginativeness. In this way, the critical, reflexive and cosmopolitan agendas of our pedagogic actions might be enhanced.

Chapter 3 focuses on the notion of *ubuntu* justice and the reasons why an African philosophy of education connects the concept of *ubuntu* justice with restorative, compassionate and moral justice. It is our view that *ubuntu* justice can be considered the *raison d'être* of an African philosophy of education and that the effects of pedagogic initiatives through Teaching for Change bear testimony to the liberatory concerns of such a philosophy of education. By accentuating restoration through enhancing one another's humanity, recognising that people have to take into account one another's vulnerabilities compassionately, and acknowledging one another's moral autonomy, the possibility is always there to act profoundly with *ubuntu* justice. The point of this chapter is that *ubuntu* justice is possible through the enactment of an African philosophy of education. It is not that *ubuntu* justice is already there, for that in itself would be an acknowledgement that justice has been actualised already. In our view, an actualisation of *ubuntu* justice is neither possible nor desirable. Rather, such a form of justice as we show through our pedagogic encounters should always be considered possible and in-becoming.

Chapter 4 examines how deliberative, responsible and risk-oriented action can be cultivated through an African philosophy of education. We show how the afore-mentioned pedagogic practices can contribute towards the cultivation of pedagogic justice. Through deliberative and responsible pedagogic encounters, educators and students could engender risks through Teaching for Change with the possibility that cooperative human action might be enhanced. In this way, Teaching for Change can be viewed as a curriculum strategy to engender deliberation, responsibility and risk taking. Of course, our argument is not that Teaching for Change is an indispensable online pedagogic initiative that alone has the potential to cultivate responsible and responsive pedagogic encounters. Rather, we contend that any pedagogic action that invokes notions of deliberation, responsibility and risk taking, as has been the case with Teaching for Change, could rupture such emancipatory forms of human action.

Chapter 5 makes an argument for why an African philosophy of education remains in potentiality. Our argument in defence of potentiality vis-à-vis Teaching for Change is linked to the idea that education cannot be conclusive and exhaustive and that curriculum initiatives, such as Teaching for Change, are always in potentiality. Simply put, pedagogic encounters remain in-becoming as there is much more to learn and always more that we encounter and have to respond to, that is, there remains more to learn and more to find out. Furthermore, if an African philosophy of education does not remain in-becoming, the possibility that it can offer relentless alternatives to educational discourses might just be impeded. Instead, our argument in defence of Teaching for Change is an acknowledgement that ideas and practices in and about education, remain in the making. Pedagogic encounters shown to be reflexive and open to criticism do show a propensity to being resolute in the quest to cultivate what is still not there.

Chapter 6 identifies and examines some of the constraints in designing and implementing a MOOC on African philosophy of education. In turn, it offers possibilities as to how Teaching for Change could contribute

xxii   Preface

towards cultivating cosmopolitan justice in and through education. We argue that cosmopolitan justice is an instance of *ubuntu* justice, which remains possible with an enactment of autonomous, deliberative and reflexive pedagogic encounters. The thrust of our argument in this chapter is that *ubuntu* justice could be worked towards if the possibility of an African philosophy of education is recognised. An African philosophy of education and *ubuntu* justice are thus inextricably connected—that is, the one cannot do without the other. In addition, the relationship between an African philosophy of education and *ubuntu* justice manifests in the ways that deliberative engagement, autonomous action and reflexive encounters are realised. Simply put, the argument of this chapter is that *ubuntu* justice, through an African philosophy of education, is witnessed to be present on account of cosmopolitan human action.

Chapter 7 offers an account of three narratives (our stories) about how Teaching for Change, more specifically its emphasis on *ubuntu* justice, influenced our own pedagogic actions. We aver that pedagogic justice—and, by implication, *ubuntu* justice—has some connection with what it means to enact decolonisation and decoloniality in and through education. Our contention is that an African philosophy of education has the potential to reconfigure democratic citizenship education in such a way that *ubuntu* justice becomes not only a sufficient condition for pedagogic change, but also an enabling condition to bring about pedagogic change. In a way, this chapter shows how educators are equally moved by open, critical and reflexive pedagogic moments in much the same way as they bear testimony to the actions of students. Once again, highlighting the experiences of educators and their responsiveness to students as well as their responsibility towards just human action, shows the mutuality and collaboration involved in pedagogic encounters. In this way, we discount teaching and learning as merely one-way pedagogic activities. Instead, teaching and learning are mutually attached and attuned to one another—the one cannot do without the other.

Chapter 8 links the notion of *ubuntu* justice with the idea of a democratic education imaginary. In line with Ron Barnett's three-pronged analysis of the university as an institution with possibilities, particulars and universals, we make a case for a university as a responsible African institution-in-becoming, thereby challenging the view that a university can ever be "in ruins". For a university to be "in ruins" would be an acknowledgement that such a university has already been actualised and there is just no way that it (the university) can transcend its "ruins". Instead, we hold a different view. Our argument is in defence of a university that remains in-becoming thus opening the doors for more deliberative reflexivity and openness in and through pedagogic encounters. The idea of a university-in-becoming is connected to the argument that a university experience should never be associated with something that depicts humans as having acquired an education that is complete and sufficient to advance humanity. Not at all. A university human being is always on the edge, ready to be thrown in at the deep end where he or she can find a way to make sense and to respond to even the most daunting challenges of the day.

In **Chap. 9**, we elucidate why Teaching for Change can be linked to the practice of decoloniality. More specifically, we make an argument for pedagogic encounters to be linked to an enactment of decoloniality. Decoloniality, we posit, could engender just human actions that show the promise of empowering people as they endeavour to make curriculum inquiry responsive to the challenges of a decolonised education system. Decoloniality undermines the injustice, humiliation and other forms of manipulative coercion that have characterised colonial hegemony and exclusion. A decolonial curriculum, we argue, is an extended way in which a renewed, imaginative understanding of an African philosophy of education could be worked towards. In this, the notion of democratic citizenship education as a corollary of African philosophy of education would be reimagined.

In the **postscript**, we delineate some of the practices associated with the pedagogic encounters of Teaching for Change. We focus on the lines of inquiry we pursued in getting Teaching for Change registered as a curricular activity through which an African philosophy of teaching and learning manifested. We particularly show how critical, deliberative, open and reflexive inquiry unfolded in pedagogic encounters with reference to some of the dialogical junctures that contributed towards responsible and responsive actions. Our conclusion with a postscript is premised on an understanding that an African philosophy of teaching and learning came to be enacted in a real online pedagogic initiative referred to as Teaching for Change.

Stellenbosch, South Africa
Cape Town, South Africa

Yusef Waghid
Faiq Waghid
Zayd Waghid

Acknowledgements

In **Chap. 8**, we draw on revised and expanded versions of two previously published articles which have been relied on and in which our tentative ideas on disruptive pedagogic encounters have been reported: Waghid, Y. (2017). A university without ruins: Some reflections on possibilities of an African university. *South African Journal of Higher Education*, *31*(3): 1–5; and, Waghid, Y. & Waghid, F. (2017). Can MOOCs contribute towards enhancing disruptive encounters in higher education? *South African Journal of Higher Education*, *31*(1): 1–13.

The MOOC on Teaching for Change has been offered through FutureLearn at: https://www.futurelearn.com/profiles/4014011. We remain grateful to FutureLearn and Stellenbosch University for the opportunity to present Teaching for Change. We are cognisant of participants' comments in relation to our responses on discussion posts, but do not have to refer to the posts because we articulate our arguments on the basis of pedagogic justifications, rather than drawing on comments made by participants. Of course, comments posted are valuable to ascertain whether learning took place. However, we are more concerned about the possibilities that an African philosophy of education and *ubuntu* justice offer a discourse of teaching and learning. For the sake of corroboration and justification, we acknowledge some of the posts but our arguments are not primarily based on the discussions reflected on the posts. In sum, participants offered understandings and meanings of an African philosophy of education (as indicated in discussion posts) and *ubuntu* justice in order to corroborate their learning that remains in potentiality, and from which we also learned.

Contents

1 Towards an Understanding of African Philosophy of Education — 1

1.1 Introduction: Giving Thought to an African Philosophy of Education — 1

1.2 Towards a Plausible View of African Philosophy of Education — 8

1.3 On Exploring Some of the Goals of African Philosophy of Education — 10

1.4 Exploring Different Approaches to African Philosophy of Education — 13

1.5 Summary and Implications for Online Learning — 22

References — 25

2 A Curriculum Response to Pedagogic Dilemmas: Towards Enhancing Teaching and Learning — 27

2.1 Introduction — 27

2.2 Responding to the Excluded Students or the Democratic Dilemma — 27

2.3 Responding to the Unimaginable or the Cosmopolitan Dilemma — 30

xxvii

xxviii Contents

	2.4	Responding to Curriculum Unresponsiveness or the Coloniality Dilemma	33
	2.5	Summary: Contextualising Online Education	36
	References		37

3 African Philosophy of Education and *Ubuntu* Justice — 39
   3.1 Introduction — 39
   3.2 Moral Justice — 40
   3.3 Compassionate Justice — 43
   3.4 Restorative Justice — 45
   3.5 Summary: Teaching for Change and the Cultivation of *Ubuntu* Justice — 48
   References — 49

4 Cultivating Pedagogic Justice Through Deliberation, Responsibility and Risk-Oriented Action Commensurate with an African Philosophy of Education — 51
   4.1 Introduction — 51
   4.2 Deliberation Through the Virtue of Conversational Justice: Cultivating Pedagogic Justice — 54
   4.3 Responsibility Through the Virtue of Truthfulness: Pursuing Pedagogic Justice — 60
   4.4 Risk-Oriented Action Through the Virtue of Courage: Towards Pedagogic Justice — 65
   4.5 Pedagogic Justice Through Deliberation, Responsibility and Risk-Oriented Action — 68
   4.6 Summary — 72
   References — 73

5 Cultivating Assemblages of Learning: From Teaching to Learning and Back to Teaching — 75
   5.1 Introduction — 75
   5.2 Mapping an Assemblage — 75

5.3	Pedagogic Intensification	76
5.4	Summary: Towards a Metamorphic Pedagogy	79
References		82

6 Designing and Implementing a Course on African Philosophy of Education: Cultivating Cosmopolitan Justice

83

6.1	Introduction	83
6.2	Reconstituting African Philosophy of Education	84
6.3	African Philosophy of Education and Cosmopolitan Justice	87
6.4	Cosmopolitan Justice and Teaching for Change	89
6.5	Towards Equal and Disruptive Pedagogic Encounters	99
6.6	Summary	110
References		111

7 Reflexive Thoughts on Teaching for Change: Democratic Education Reimagined

113

7.1	Introduction	113
7.2	Yusef Waghid on Cosmopolitan Reflexivity	114
7.3	Faiq Waghid on Democratic Equality	116
7.4	Zayd Waghid on Education as Disruption	119
7.5	Democratic Education Expanded	120
7.6	Summary	124
References		124

8 A Democratic University Without Ruins: Some Reflections on the Possibilities and Particularities of an African University

127

8.1	Introduction: Departing from Bill Readings's *University in Ruins*	127
8.2	Barnett's "Three Planes" of Understanding a University	128
8.3	An African University and the Enactment of Responsibility	131

xxx Contents

8.4 Disruptive Pedagogic Encounters	133
8.5 Summary	143
References	144

9 Decolonised Education: Cultivating Curriculum Renewal and Decoloniality 147

9.1 Introduction	147
9.2 Towards an Understanding of Decolonisation	148
9.3 Rethinking Democratic Citizenship Education	151
9.4 Decolonised Education and the Enactment of Just Pedagogic Encounters	155
9.5 Towards Decolonised Curriculum Renewal	159
9.6 Summary: Decolonisation or Decoloniality?	161
References	163

Postscript: Reflecting on Ruptured Pedagogic Moments in Teaching for Change 165

Index 183

1

Towards an Understanding of African Philosophy of Education

1.1 Introduction: Giving Thought to an African Philosophy of Education

On having been introduced to massive open online courses (MOOCs), we contrived to devise, develop and implement an online course that would be both relevant and responsive to our pedagogy, more specifically, teaching and learning encounters. As it happened, African philosophy of education became the central focus in relation to which we could situate our educational research interests. We chose the idea of an African philosophy of education premised on the following three considerations. First, we envisaged focusing on a MOOC that would attract students to other ways of knowing, doing and being. Put differently, we considered a MOOC on African philosophy of education because we endeavoured to bring to masses of students a pedagogic discourse which could foreground the African condition. Second, having been initiated into dominant Western discourses of thinking and acting, we thought it apposite to introduce a platform of learning (and teaching for that matter) that foregrounds less dominant discourses, which often have to endure caricature on the part of those who hold a view of education prejudiced

© The Author(s) 2018
Y. Waghid et al., *Rupturing African Philosophy on Teaching and Learning*,
https://doi.org/10.1007/978-3-319-77950-8_1

towards Western studies. Third, our interest in African philosophy of education has been stimulated by a notion of *ubuntu* (human interconnectedness and co-existence) through which justice for all might be possible. It is, therefore, not surprising that we selected the figure of the late President Nelson Mandela of the first democratic South Africa as our backdrop to the publicity of the MOOC. As has been argued elsewhere, Mandela's educational contribution is constituted by at least three aspects: an education for non-violence guided by deliberative engagement and compassionate and reconciliatory actions, exercising responsibility towards others and cultivating a reasoned community of thinking (Waghid 2014a: 4).

Literature on African philosophy of education is much in vogue, as is evident from at least three major volumes on the subject: *The African philosophy reader* (Coetzee and Roux 2003), *A companion to African philosophy* (Wiredu 2004), and *African ethics: An anthology of comparative and applied ethics* (Murove 2009). One of the reasons that African philosophy of education is gaining prominence in scholarly texts today is because it has been criticised for existing mostly in the oral tradition, while most philosophical works are documented in texts (Waghid 2014b). Instead of refuting the criticism that the oral tradition dominates African philosophy of education, inasmuch as Socrates' ideas were documented in the dialogues of Plato (both Greek philosophers of ancient times), we rather refer to literature on African philosophy of education to explain the concept. Although we have not specifically identified a notion of African philosophy of education, we have nevertheless used the concept to elucidate a philosophy of education that is other than what we have encountered in our learning. Our notion of an African philosophy of education emanates from our engagement with scholarly texts in and about education in Africa. In addition, our inferences most often rely on what we think an African philosophy of education foregrounds, instead of drawing on elucidations of the practice. Small wonder that many critics of an African philosophy of education take issue with an enunciation of the concept, as they contend that such a concept is not known to Africa. This in itself, we argue, is contentious considering that any philosophy of education represents a situatedness connected with the idea of where the particular philosophy of education has manifested. In this way,

Towards an Understanding of African Philosophy of Education 3

to talk about an African philosophy of education is related to the ideas that frame such a philosophy of education and, in our case, we draw on ideas espoused by African scholars and those whose ideas we aver resonate with African thought and practices. Thereafter, we consider how this concept of an African philosophy of education will influence educational relationships among people. We focus specifically on how constitutive features of the concept guide pedagogical actions such as teaching and learning. Later on, we also look again at the notion of democratic citizenship education as another way in which African philosophy of education has guided ideas in and about democracy, citizenship and education in multiple ways.

Our own interest in the texts of African philosophy of education is guided by an initiation into an Anglo-Saxon analytic philosophy of education, which focused overwhelmingly on the quest for meaning and understanding in and about the texts that informed educational change in post-apartheid South Africa. Our exposure to African philosophy of education gained much prominence vis-à-vis the seminal thoughts of the Ghanaian philosopher Kwasi Wiredu (an African now living in Florida in the United States). By far the most poignant claim that Wiredu makes in terms of an understanding of African philosophy of education, is that which is connected to the integration of a plurality of views. Wiredu's claim—that one would not necessarily compromise one's African identity if one draws on other "truths" outside of one's own African tradition of thought (Wiredu 2005)—had a major influence on our own scholarship in the field of African philosophy of education. His recognition of a plurality of "truths" influenced a particular understanding of an African philosophy of education, to which we are drawn. In his words,

> Any African effort to construct a philosophy for contemporary living by combining the insights of traditional philosophy with those originating from elsewhere is an effort in the Africanisation of philosophical studies. (Wiredu 2005: 17)

What is significant about his integrationist perspective of an African philosophy of education are the following. First, he couches such a philosophy of education as one that invokes "contemporary living" experiences. This claim in itself is significant in the sense that Wiredu (2005) immediately opens the doors to an idea that is in consonance with what is "contemporary". Being attuned to contemporary living experiences today is not the same in a different time and space. For this reason, he immediately announces the open-endedness associated with a philosophy of education linked to Africa. Second, Wiredu (2005) is adamant that what is traditional philosophy is insightful. In other words, he recognises that in indigenous philosophy, there are discernments that are worthwhile considering. The point is that, in articulating an African philosophy of education, he recognises the importance of what is indigenously linked to Africans. Third, he does not discount philosophical thought from "elsewhere". This in itself is recognition that not everything about African philosophy of education should be attributed to African scholars but that discerning thoughts from others—albeit Western scholars—are not necessarily to be held incongruent with what constitutes an African philosophy of education. By implication, an African philosophy of education invokes traditional and non-traditional thoughts in enduring educational practices.

Moreover, whereas our interest in African philosophy of education is guided by an attempt at Africanising philosophy of education, the discourse also offers opportunities for those interested in enacting justice in and through their educational experiences (the focus of Chap. 3 of this book). In Chap. 3, our focus will be on some of the reasons why philosophy of education from an African perspective potentially offers possibilities for just human relations in and through pedagogic encounters, and more specifically through teaching and learning in a university setting. The rationale of Chap. 3, namely that an African philosophy of education engenders just action, also underscores the notions of decolonisation and decoloniality—ideas that have gained much prominence in African academic circles, most notably nowadays in South African universities. Inspired by the #FeesMustFall movement, decolonisation and decoloniality have often been associated incorrectly with the rejection of everything other than African, as if African philosophy of education is absolute and untainted by any form of otherness as has been espoused earlier. The notion of decolonisation, on the one hand, argued for in this book, is tantamount to a pedagogic response that connects educational encounters with the attainment of just human action. On the other hand, decoloniality, which will be elucidated in Chap. 7, has some bearing on the transformative pedagogic discourses along the lines of attempts at deculturating such discourses from the overwhelming neo-colonial hegemonies.

For now, we further examine what constitutes an African philosophy of education. Like any philosophy of education (Anglo-Saxon, Continental, Chinese, Arabian and Buddhist), African philosophy of education is an activity, that is, something that is being done in the pursuit of something that could render plausible acts of knowing, being and doing. When one offers reasons for one's actions—an activity of the mind—one offers some justification (evidence) for acting in a particular way. This idea of performing some cognitive activity for some moral purpose (a matter of what is good for oneself, others and society) is what is called philosophy of education. In addition, when we prioritise African interests (such as decolonisation and decoloniality, economic growth and democratisation), African philosophy of education is practised. Let us look at the following ways in which African philosophy of education is expressed:

First, Wiredu (2005: 8) states that African philosophy of education involves harmonising individual and societal interests; embarking on "reflexive imagination", such as putting oneself in the shoes of others; and respecting human and non-human life. When doing philosophy of education in this way, universal (global) and particular (local) knowledge is produced that is of relevance to Africa's advancement (Wiredu 2005: 18). When one intertwines individual and societal concerns, an individual's interests are considered constitutive of that of a society and, in turn, the interests of a society are reflective of an individual's concerns. This does not mean that an individual and society act in exactly the same way, as such actions are neither possible nor perhaps desirable. Rather, the actions of an individual and society are at least commensurable to the extent that both actions are reflective of one another. With such a commensurability between individual and societal actions, it becomes reasonably possible to imagine someone else's vulnerabilities and forbearances reflexively. For instance, in many African societies, respect for human and non-human life is considered as important for the individual as it would be for the society as a whole. Also, when an individual shows some discontent towards other humans and non-humans, it becomes the responsibility of society to ensure that their collective interests towards humans and non-humans are safeguarded. Failure to do so often results in animosity and disgust for the other. Thus, important to Wiredu's (2005) understanding of an African philosophy of education is his accentuation of reflexive imagination. To be reflexive implies looking again and again at something such as a word, sentence, paragraph or problem in a particular situation. In addition, even if one has inferred a particular understanding based on one's reflection, the possibility should always be there for a new thought or idea on the basis of looking again, that is, being reflexive. This kind of reflexivity, one presumes, would enable one to conjure up new thoughts and perspectives about a particular situation. Furthermore, Wiredu (2005) accentuates the importance of imagining oneself. To imagine is not just to accept things as they are. Rather, it involves looking at things without knowing beforehand what they would be. That is, looking at things as if they could be otherwise. By implication, following Wiredu, one immediately gets an understanding that an African philosophy of education is about reflexive imagination. Only then would one get deeper meanings and understandings of particular problems with which the African continent is confronted. Likewise, what is also significant about the notion of reflexive imagination is Wiredu's (2005) claim that such an act is inextricably connected to the achievement of something morally worthwhile. Hence, Wiredu's insistence that reflexive imagination ought to be about enacting a responsibility to both human and non-human actions.

Second, Assié-Lumumba (2005: 23) posits that African philosophy of education endeavours to cultivate a self-determining, free and decent citizenry, which fuses (merges) fitting aspects of other cultures with one's own culture, and where individuals strive to remain in relation to other human beings. In the first place, a self-determining or autonomous citizenry would at least function in an atmosphere of co-belonging. That is, through philosophy of education, Africans are perceived as co-existing humans in a spirit of freedom and decency. Any violation of their freedom and decency is tantamount to acting inhumanely, which is what an African philosophy of education would detest. Yet, recognising one

Towards an Understanding of African Philosophy of Education 7

another's humanity is what is important for Africans to the extent that they not only respect one another's cultural differences, but also show a willingness to integrate aspects of another's culture into their own. In this way, by showing respect for one another's culture, Africans not only demonstrate their willingness to co-belong but more significantly to remain in relation to one another. This means that Africans recognise at once that people should be considered as existing relationally and that there is, therefore, no need to undermine one another's co-existence, at least not in a condescending way. As a corollary of the recognition of such humane (respectful and decent) living, African philosophy of education ought to be considered a discourse that could cultivate humanity along the lines of intercultural recognition and relationality. The point about decency or civility is that when people are so vehemently in contradiction with one another's practices, they always show a willingness to want to engage with one another's otherness. Civility holds people together to the extent that there is always an opportunity to listen to what the other has to say irrespective of how deeply troubling one might consider another's perspective and way of living. To remain civilly engaged depends on the respect that people have for others' rights to be and act differently because coexistence does not require that people should all be the same. On the African continent, there are many ethnicities with multifarious cultures. This means that people will invariably be different and, at times, they will exhibit contrasting ways of being. By implication, people's educational experiences will also be diverse. Following the latter point, the willingness of people to remain in conversation with one another is what gives such an understanding of African philosophy of education its distinctive feature of recognising multiple differences. Such a philosophy of education does not misrecognise the autonomies of others to hold on to their preferred ways of being and not to what others want them to be. People are different; yet, on the basis of their civility—that is the recognition that difference is always a possibility and that people should recognise such differences—they do not misrecognise one another's ways of being and acting.

The upshot of the aforementioned view of African philosophy of education is that enacting such a discourse would imply that people are intent on fusing knowledge in such a way that they deliberately integrate the past with the present. This is so because human living is considered relational and through fusion of what transpired in the past with the present, the possibility of improving people's lives could be an act of becoming. The latter implies that African people's attachment to the past and their attenuation of present human conditions are considered deeply intertwined or fused with the aim of producing more just forms of living—that is, forms of living that are not only more just, but also other forms of just living as yet not yet conceived but which remain civil. Such an understanding of African philosophy of education brings the recognition of human autonomy, acknowledgement of difference and possibly the fusion of different perspectives on life and knowledges, into profound relationality—a concept couched as *ukama* (relational) in the African Shona language (Ndofirepi and Shanyanana 2015). The point is that showing civility through human co-existence and recognition of the importance of fusing knowledges, is what makes the concept of *ukama* relevant to African communities. This is so because the sense of an autonomous self is constructed in relation to communitarian social constructions, thus bringing into play a concept of community in Africa that can be understood as interactions and interconnections rather than individuated human action (Ndofirepi and Shanyanana 2015: 428). This brings us to a discussion of an understanding of African philosophy of education.

1.2 Towards a Plausible View of African Philosophy of Education

Drawing on the views of both Wiredu (2005) and Assié-Lumumba (2005), our own understanding of African philosophy of education is based on a three-pronged approach. First, through reflection (that is, looking for reasons and thinking about them) we identify major problems on the African continent that seem to hamper Africans' ways of being and living. Second, we justify or validate (through the offering of reasons) the existence of such problems. Third, we determine what the consequences of these problems are to educational experiences. While performing the aforementioned approach, we remain cognisant of bringing individual and social interests into conversation with one another, identifying people's vulnerabilities and thinking about ways of addressing these, advocating what can possibly advance African people's self-determination and freedom, and fusing what is considered universal (and perhaps global and dominant) and appropriate with what counts as local or indigenous and credible.

For example, we consider military rule as a major problem in some parts of the African continent. Next, we justify why military rule is a problem by linking this form of dictatorship to the coercion of citizens. In other words, the reasons we account for such an occurrence relate to the prevention of people's political freedom and participation by a military regime. To this effect, a political dictatorship prevents the masses from exercising their political rights to vote, for instance. The reason offered is that military rule is a political dictatorship that excludes people's right to free and fair elections or political participation. By implication, some of the consequences of a military dictatorship for education are that students could be prevented from questioning and challenging the state, and even challenging curriculum matters at universities for that matter. Furthermore, scholars might be censored and in some instances silenced if they speak out against the state, or students might even be curtailed from dissent at universities. In both the latter instances, education would be constrained because education, in the first place, should allow people to criticise, oppose and disagree, and at the same time, people would be included in an educational experience. One cannot expect students, for instance, to engage in pedagogic encounters if they are not expected to show dissent or to proffer points of view that might be in disagreement with what their educators or fellow students have to say. What makes their pedagogic encounters credible is that they engage with the possibility of agreement and/or dissent. When the latter is no longer possible, pedagogic encounters would be highly constraining.

Moreover, what an African philosophy of education affords us, is to respond educationally to addressing major problems on the continent. This would imply that we have to justify the reasons that constitute the problems and then set out to dismantle or deconstruct them. It is not sufficient merely to clarify problems without justifying them. Clarification and justification of claims are complementary, and articulations are defensible only if they are both elucidated on and justified—in this instance, reasons would have been proffered in defence of the claims being made. Likewise, one way of deconstructing a problem is to examine its implications for education. In this regard, deconstruction involves looking at problems as they could be otherwise. In other words, one does not merely elucidate problems as one thinks such problems ought to be. Rather, one looks deeper to the extent that one also looks for, or more appropriately said, constructs meanings beyond one's common understanding of the specific problems. That is, one looks beyond the margins for those meanings that are not obvious except when one delves deeper. In the light of deconstructing meanings, the idea of ascertaining how educational relations are affected by particular human problems on the African continent is what constitutes our notion of an African philosophy of education; in other words, a notion of African philosophy of education that is more than what is presented currently. Consequently, understanding, reflecting on, deconstructing and considering the implications of human problems for education and endeavouring to resolve such problems educationally would be tantamount to doing African philosophy of education. The point we are making, is that African philosophy of education is not some existing dogma or text of information and knowledge that depicts a certain understanding of the concept. Rather, doing African philosophy of education involves moments of reflection, coming to insightful inferences and deconstructing understandings of meanings associated with problems on the African continent. Thereafter, one examines the implications of such an analysis of problems for education. Next, we examine some of the goals of such a philosophy of education.

1.3   On Exploring Some of the Goals of African Philosophy of Education

By now, African philosophy of education can be conceived as both a way of thinking and a way of doing. Such an approach involves understanding, reflecting on and deconstructing problems on the African continent, and then examining the educational implications of such problems. As a way of thinking, on the one hand, such an approach offers a framework of criticism whereby one listens, reflects, reasons and questions. On the other hand, thinking also draws on the experiences of people within their environments or contexts. In this sense, African philosophy of education consists of criticism and attendance to lived experience. As a way of doing, African philosophy of education involves making one's thinking responsive to problems on the African continent. Of course, the latter action does not undermine the claim that thinking in itself is a form of doing. However, thinking can be enacted in different ways, and being responsive to problems on the continent is one way of enacting thinking. In addition, embarking on reflective scrutiny and deconstruction invariably involves looking deeper and more than once. The implication of such a way of thinking—reflecting and deconstructing—that connects with resolving problems on the continent is that African philosophy of education—the form of thinking and by implication acting—is pragmatic in the sense that it could contribute to the political, economic, cultural and ethical development of the people of Africa (Higgs 2012: 42). To come back to our earlier discussion of African philosophy of education, one finds that such a philosophy insists that, first, people's individual and collective (social) interests are brought into harmony with one another—that is, people do things collectively. Second, people recognise one another's vulnerabilities by putting themselves into one another's shoes. Third, people become self-determining or autonomous beings in the sense that they can do things for themselves. Fourth, people fuse the global understandings with the local views or vice versa. Let us examine these goals of African philosophy of education in relation to criticism, lived experience and (human) responsibility.

Concerning the task of an African philosophy of education to offer a framework of thinking and rethinking, consider the participation of some women in food production in Africa. Using criticism, one would examine the farming knowledge of these women regarding food production. On the basis of determining their lived experiences in terms of harvesting food crops and how their knowledge of farming contributes to sustaining the agricultural economy responsibly, all three practices (criticism, lived experience and responsibility) of such a philosophy of education have been considered, which could make the achievement of people's integrated individual and societal interests possible. Similarly, their (women) autonomous actions in the pursuit of recognising people's vulnerabilities and forbearances, as well as fusing global and local understandings of particular societal matters are a vindication of the achievement of some of the goals associated with an African philosophy of education. The implication of the actions of such women is that their individual knowledge of farming is combined in the collective interest of their society. They (re)imagine what it would mean for their society to suffer hunger and famine by identifying the vulnerabilities of those others in their communities who experience famine. In a self-determining way, they fuse their local understandings of farming with (perhaps) the knowledge of those people who had prior ownership of the land. In this way, women's local knowledge of crops, trees and soil is used in a complementary way with their former—perhaps colonisers'—knowledge of farming as they endeavour to advance agricultural development on the African continent (Jagire 2014). This example of analysing the agricultural practices of certain women is a specific way in which African philosophy of education can be used. Central to such a philosophy of education is that the practices of African people are guided by the human understandings that constitute their actions. In turn, such peoples draw on their own contextualised knowledge in relation to other external understandings of knowledge to respond to specific problems at hand. As has been said before, an analysis of their actions in the pursuit of solving Africa's problems is what can be understood as an African philosophy of education because together with an identification of problems, an examination of the educational implications for society is also given priority. The point we are making is that practising an African philosophy of education does not only have a methodology, that is a way of reflecting on and deconstructing problems on the African continent. Practicing such a philosophy of education is also at the level of method whereby one examines the educational implications of such problems. Of course, an African philosophy of education is also connected to striving towards goals. However, these goals are not ends in themselves for that would mark the end of practising an African philosophy of education. Rather, the ends of such a philosophy of education are connected to cultivating ways in which the problems can be resolved without ever declaring that these ends are completed and there would be no further need to look at other understandings of goals that should always be forthcoming. This brings us to a discussion of different approaches to African philosophy of education, in particular how such approaches are considered in enacting and realising some of the current goals constitutive of an African philosophy of education.

1.4 Exploring Different Approaches to African Philosophy of Education

If one considers that African philosophy of education involves reflecting on and deconstructing problems on the African continent and examining the implications of such problems for education, we turn our attention to two different and interrelated approaches to African philosophy of education.

Any approach to practicing education involves pointing to guiding rules that underscore the practice of education. First, ethno-philosophy of education draws on sources of knowledge such as customs (traditions), lifestyles, myths (folklore), languages, beliefs, artefacts and histories of different African cultures. In other words, by using oral stories, poetry, songs, legends and proverbs, for example, as sources of knowledge, one examines the consequences of such knowledge for educational experiences. Drawing on the work of Sefa Dei (2014), it is quite interesting to note how oral narratives uncover past lineages, the migration of specific extended families and communities, inspirational tales, popular cultural belief systems, or knowledge of local fauna (wildlife), flora (vegetation) and ecology (environmentalism) that may be of consequence to educational relations. For instance, we are reminded by Sefa Dei (2014) why and how cultural sayings and knowings allow learners to grow mentally, spiritually and morally into adulthood, as oral culture, proverbs, riddles, cultural songs, myths and folklore often emphasise the importance of social values in African life (Sefa Dei 2014: 175). We specifically think of our own initiation into memorising sayings—such as 'cleanliness is next to godliness' and 'good deeds are the result of good intentions'—that shaped our moral conduct and identity in relation to purity of body and mind. Similarly, as an instance of ethno-philosophy of education, the Ghanaian philosopher, Kwame Gyekye, uses the concepts and proverbs of his Akan culture to explain the social relationships between individuals and their communities (Gyekye 1995). Dzobo (1992: 95) also uses African (more specifically Yoruba) proverbs to respond to the question, "What is knowledge?" by saying, "Knowledge is like a baobab tree and so no person can embrace it with both arms" [another way of saying that knowledge grows and grows and there is no end to what a person can know] and "He who knows all knows nothing" [a way of emphasising intellectual curiosity and openness, that is, there is always more to know]. The point about using proverbs and other knowledge constructs is that an articulation of knowledge does not happen independently from one's identity—in other words, who we are and what we become. Our connections with knowledge are constituted by our own reflections on and deconstructions of such knowledge. Simply put, such knowledge has to make sense to us, unless we embark on merely remaining compliant with that with which we are confronted. Unfortunately, such a form of learning is undesirable as it negates any form of reflective and deconstructive meaning-making. Of course, we are not making an argument against rote learning per se. We rather opine that rote learning on its own is insufficient as it does not encourage reflectiveness and less so deconstructive thought. In addition, although ethno-philosophical concepts at times require putting to memory many proverbs or sayings, learning does not end with memorisation. Instead, learning in the African sense can be more meaningful if opportunities for reflection and deconstruction become possible. In the main, recourse to ethno-philosophy of education involves the application, that is, reflection and deconstruction of traditional—cultural, ethnic and historical—African worldviews, as explained in the thoughts of Kwame Gyekye (1997: 34), who claims, "[philosophical] intellectual enterprise is essentially a cultural phenomenon". In the latter regard, the philosophy we interpret and extend to reflective openness and deconstructive scrutiny without which practicing an ethno-philosophy of education would not be entirely possible. In other words, cultural, ethnic and historical practices should always be subjected to a form of inquiry, which we associate with ethno-philosophy of education.

Towards an Understanding of African Philosophy of Education   15

Not putting ethno-understandings and concepts to scrutiny cannot be associated with an African philosophy of education. What makes African ethno-philosophy of education philosophical is that such a philosophy of education in the first place ought to be linked to practices of reflection and deconstruction.

Second, on critical African philosophy of education, the Beninese philosopher Paulin Hountondji (1996) describes African philosophy of education as criticism that involves open, reflective and deliberative engagement with texts of the African experience. Quite inexplicably, he delinks criticism from the insights of African sages who offer cultural reasons for their communal worldviews, as if "wise" thought—following Odera Oruka (1990), the Kenyan scholar, does not require reflection, that is, thinking and rethinking about the African experience. If Hountondji (1996) wants to de-mythologise African philosophy of education from its partial reliance on the oral tradition of sage wisdom, then he does not do well in his defence of criticism, as criticism itself is open to clarifying and explaining cultural reasons, for example for addressing Africa's problems of inhumanity and underdevelopment. Briefly then, when one does critical African philosophy of education, one embarks first on a process of criticism, that is, one is open to and reflective about the reasons (explanations and justifications) one offers. Second, one uses explanations that justify a reliance on one's cultural connections, and third, one shows how one's justifications (defensible reasons) could respond to educational predicaments on the African continent. In the main, critical African philosophy of education uses both criticism and cultural wisdom (sagacious thought) to address the educational problems of the African experience. Our emphasis on critical African philosophy of education has some connection with practising criticism and dissent in philosophical inquiry. In other words, taking reasons into controversy and proffering alternative views about various issues or problems on the African continent would be one way of doing critical African philosophy of education. However, what makes such a philosophy of education critical is that one's criticism and dissent have an emancipatory action in mind. That is, what one proffers on account of criticism and dissent ought to have some liberatory concern such as making claims in defence of decolonisation, decoloniality and democratisation. What makes an

African philosophy of education critical is that the problems in and about African issues are examined vis-à-vis a concern for empowerment of people and their expected emancipation. If critical African philosophy does not have such a liberatory intent, such a philosophy of education would not have been practiced.

This brings us to a discussion of how critical African philosophy of education can be practised. The 2015 student protests against the hike in university fees in South Africa brought into focus the stark reality of inequality and poverty in the country. Inasmuch as the proposed fees hike by universities posed an immediate problem to those students who need to acquire a university qualification in order to be being taken up in the competitive labour market economy, it also highlighted the entrenched levels of inequity that drive university studies. Although the state has a National Student Financial Aid Scheme (NSFAS) to support poor students, the disqualification of many students from funding as a result of being too rich for aid but too poor to pay fees contributes largely to the exclusion of many students from university education. In this way, university education in the country remains inaccessible for many, and the historical injustice of exclusion continues.

The question is, how would critical African philosophy of education help to respond to the crisis in university education? Through criticism, one would get to know the reasons behind the protests. One might say that the high costs of university education and minimal (if any) state support prevent students from furthering their education. Moreover, the heavy-handed attitudes of security firms and police provoked some students, and thus contributed to the protests being marred (at times) by violent responses. In other words, if one understands why the protests started and why some incidents of violence happened during the protests, one can respond positively to address the protests—that is, applying criticism. Moreover, by looking at the historical and cultural backgrounds of students one would begin to get a better idea of the reasons why many students will be denied access to universities should more financial support not be forthcoming. Similarly, if one were to look at the reasons why police provocation perhaps resulted in some violence incidents, then one would be better placed to respond to and remedy the unfavourable situation. Historically, some police have responded brutally and insensitively

Towards an Understanding of African Philosophy of Education   17

to protest action in South Africa, and understanding the mentality behind this would be useful in perhaps curbing the incidents of violence—in other words it is a matter of examining the cultural and historical reasons. Likewise, understanding student protests and police involvement in a reflexive way has some connection with seeing the reasons behind such actions, namely protestations and policing. The openness in which one evaluates such human actions has a bearing on how plausible the reasons one comes up are in understanding the situation. However, not examining the liberatory implications of human actions, such as student protestations vis-à-vis policing, would not position one desirably to enact critical African philosophy of education. In sum, responding to the students' demand for no fee hike would address the immediate problem of student protests. However, in the long run, the state, business and universities have to do more to address inequity and student exclusion from higher education. Our own take on the matter is that the resources of privileged institutions and their financial assets should be utilised better to address the problem of access to quality higher education. If consideration is given to the latter, one can infer that some of the emancipatory implications of human actions have been considered. In this way, one would have practised critical African philosophy of education.

In relation, in relation to a communitarian notion of African philosophy of education, we begin by saying a word on the notion of "culture". The word "culture" derives from the practice of cultivating land—a process of helping crops to grow by giving them the needed care and attention (Gyekye 1997: 107). In this sense, culture refers to the nurturing of people's thinking and acting. This implies that culture includes people's values, beliefs and social practices; their habits and customs, and ways of conduct (etiquette); people's works of art (music, dancing, sculpture and painting); and their oral and written science, philosophy and literature (Gyekye 1997). In short, culture is a complex of shared meanings in terms of which people interpret their lived experiences. Moreover, people can share a set of common values, practices and ways of seeing the world. However, the same people can also differ in their culture, such as speaking the same language yet not sharing common religious or political beliefs. In this sense, culture is not homogenous or unified. People often experience a sense of belonging together based on their cultural commonalities and differences. They share a mutual attachment to one another and thus share a citizenship derived from a common history, territory and destiny. Similarly, they exercise their rights and responsibilities as citizens in relation to one another. So, people's citizenship is determined by their sense of belonging together, and the exercise of their rights and responsibilities towards one another.

In African cultures, citizenship is described as a form of communalism that considers the individual as integral to the group. In the words of John Mbiti (1970: 108):

> Whatever happens to the individual happens to the whole group, and whatever happens to the whole group happens to the individual. The individual can only say, 'I am, because we are; and since we are, therefore I am.'

Although this view in itself clarifies the individual's interconnectedness to the whole group, it does not imply that individuals' autonomous expressions of themselves are constantly taken up in communal practices. Kwame Gyekye (1992) clarifies individual autonomy in relation to communal practices as follows:

Premise I: Communalism or human interdependence is constituted by social relationships in which individual persons do not function in isolation from each other. Thus, if one is communally related to others, one is in conversation with others. That is, one does not enact one's role in an atomistic, narcissistic way. Simply put, communality is tantamount to a relationship with others of mutuality.

Premise II: Communalism recognises the individual's rights – the right to equal treatment, property, free association and freedom of speech, but privileges the individual's duty or responsibility towards others (community) over the exercise of the individual's rights. Of course, one does not always have to give up one's individual rights. However, when the rights of the community are given preferential treatment, one is said to be acting in communion with others.

Argument based on I & II: Although an individual's rights are not misrecognised – that is, the individual is an autonomous, self-determining being, it is the individual's responsibility or duty towards the well-being of the self and the community that is considered as more important than the exercise of individual rights. Communal rights, unless they undermine the moral and ethical concerns of a community, hold sway over the individual's concerns and rights.

What follows is that the *ubuntu* maxim, "I am, because we are; and since we are, therefore I am", can be extended to "I am, because we are; and since we are, therefore I am"—and, since I am, therefore we are.

Ubuntu, a central feature in this book, is an African ethic of care that literally means human interdependence and humaneness (Waghid and Smeyers 2012). In the isiXhosa language spoken in the Western Cape, a province of South Africa, we say "a person is a person through other people"—*ubuntu ngumuntu ngabanye abantu*. In this regard, the humaneness in *ubuntu* is explained through the personhood of someone who exercises his or her responsibility of caring for others (humaneness) and that a person's interdependence with others is confirmed through his or her relations with other people (human interdependence). When a person acts humanely towards others, he or she cares for others—a matter of exercising his or her responsibility towards fellow human beings. Likewise, when a person engages with others, he or she belongs with them in a spirit of human cooperation and peaceful coexistence. Considering that *ubuntu* emphasises both the person's responsibility and belonging without giving up all his or her rights, such person enacts his or her citizenship through *ubuntu*. In short, *Ubuntu* involves enacting (living out) one's individual rights, but not necessarily at the expense of one's responsibility to others, responsibility towards the community and loyalty (patriotism) to the community, without abandoning one's exercise of rights. The rights of the community take preference over individuality, as one always expresses one's loyalty to others—that is, one's responsibility to others—in an atmosphere of *ubuntu*, more specifically in community.

By way of an example, a citizen seems to be confronted with a government that cannot aptly deal with the Boko Haram (against Western education) militant group that kidnaps young girls, who are then indoctrinated with a particular version of radical Islam. Does such a person have religious and political rights to speak out against the actions of Boko Haram? Of course, as an internalisation of *ubuntu*, such person has the right and freedom of expression to voice his or her dissatisfaction with the group. Equally, the person could express his or her dismay with the unsuccessful attempts by government to engage the group in negotiations about the release of the girls. Is it that person's responsibility to do something about the influence of Boko Haram? *Ubuntu* suggests that he or she has a humane responsibility to condemn the callous acts of the radical group and that, concomitantly, he or she should contribute towards educating co-citizens (perhaps as a university scholar) against the misguided decision to dismiss Western education as satanic on the grounds that knowledge is universal, yet contextualised in terms of where one lives. Not everything about Western education can therefore be dismissed as irrelevant to knowledge production. In this way, he or she would perform a duty of care towards his or her co-citizens. Likewise, should such a person just condemn Boko Haram and hope that they disappear from African society? If one considers the teachings of Boko Haram as being contrary to the advancement of African ways of being and living, then he or she is obliged to engage with Boko Haram's understanding of the world and how it works. This means he or she does not marginalise them further, as that would breed only more contempt and our efforts to co-exist might be dented further. As a fellow citizen, he or she should recognise that there are views that are entirely different from his or her own and that the only way in which he or she could begin to co-exist and foster human interdependence is through mutual engagement with one another's differences and commonalities. This of course depends on whether the group also wants to engage others. In other words, there is no point of aspiring towards collective engagement if one party does not show the willingness to want to engage. In this way, engagement is conditional upon the mutual willingness of different and perhaps contending parties to want to engage.

In addition, deliberative engagement with others does not only mean that one ought to reach agreement. Of course, showing dissent is also a possibility. However, the opportunity should always be there that the engagement would be reflexive enough to derive at some plausible understanding and that the confidence in the possibility of an agreement should not be abandoned. In other words, agreement should not be a condition for engaging with others. That in itself is tantamount to unfree engagement. That is, one would be coerced to come to some sort of consensus. Agreement should emanate from the encounters of deliberative engagement rather than being considered a precondition for engagement. The latter in itself would already mark the end of deliberative engagement.

The aforementioned example of living out one's rights, responsibilities and a sense of belonging is one way in which *ubuntu* (human interdependence and co-existence) citizenship could be enacted. Fulgence Nyengela (2014: 4) posits that *ubuntu* is a postcolonial ethic that allows the marginalised 'subaltern' (subordinate) to speak because *ubuntu* is positively inclined towards empowering the excluded through conversational dialogue. Also, if one considers, as has been argued for previously, that an African philosophy of education aims to address major problems in African societies and then to examine their implications for education, one might claim that the disengagement of fellow Africans on what is considered good for Africa is a major problem. The idea of cultivating an *ubuntu* citizenship seems to be a purpose of such a philosophy of education. The implications of an *ubuntu* citizenship for education are as follows: Africans ought to realise that human co-existence and interdependence could be achieved through forms of mutual and deliberative engagement. This implies that, as co-Africans, we have to listen to what the other has to say, even if the other's views are abominable (detestable and atrocious). This means that one has to be prepared to listen to the other, even though one might dislike what the other has to say. After having listened to the other, one is expected to appraise the other—that is, to offer a reason why one thinks the other is wrong and should be challenged. Equally, one should also recognise any good point (that which is defensible) the other makes. If one is persuaded by the other, one should adapt or modify one's point of view in the light of the more convincing point of view. Or, one could abandon one's own view if one finds the other's view more palatable (agreeable). In this way, one exercises respect for the other and his or her otherness. In addition, when one shows respect in this way, the possibility that the engagement is ongoing will increase, as one's disagreement with the other does not mean that one entirely disconnects from the other; one still co-belongs. What follows is that the cultivation of *ubuntu* citizenship brings about deliberative or engaging ways of doing: listening, reflecting, agreeing, disagreeing and then talking back to the other (assessing). Therefore, using an African philosophy of education could engender *ubuntu* citizenship, which lends itself to educational ways of doing, such as listening, reflecting and assessing.

It is the notion of *ubuntu* citizenship that could potentially rupture xenophobic attitudes and behaviours towards fellow Africans, and fellow humans for that matter. For once, such a form of citizenship recognises that all humans are equal and deserve to be respected irrespective of their profound differences. Xenophobia towards people is often instigated by a kind of dismissiveness and repugnance towards those others one might not consider equal enough to enjoy the same living conditions to which one might be exposed. It is a form of racial and cultural intolerance shown towards others whom one perhaps loathes on the grounds of one's own prejudices towards others. *Ubuntu* citizenship recognises all others as worthy of respect, and any undignified behaviour shown towards others would be considered repugnant for human co-living. An African philosophy of education is most suitable to undermine xenophobic behaviours towards others for the sole reason that such a way of thinking and doing considers the recognition of equal citizenship a necessary condition for human co-belonging.

1.5 Summary and Implications for Online Learning

In this chapter we have given an account of an African philosophy of education and have shown how three interrelated approaches of the concept can engender plausible human action: first, we have argued how an African ethno-philosophy of education can be responsive to culturally different human action, in particular drawing on indigenous/traditional knowledge sources to account for defensible human action; second, critical African philosophy of education can engender open, reflective and deliberative engagement with Africans' lived experiences; and third, communitarian African philosophy of education can cultivate an *ubuntu* notion of

Towards an Understanding of African Philosophy of Education   23

citizenship whereby people can be taught to live together through mutual respect and co-belonging. The aforementioned three strands of African philosophy of education were thought to be apposite to address the practice of Teaching for Change. Whereas our interest in Teaching for Change is guided by an attempt at Africanising philosophy of education, the course also offers opportunities for those interested in enacting an *ubuntu* justice in and through their educational experiences. Our focus on Teaching for Change is linked to the reasons why philosophy of education from an African perspective potentially offers possibilities for just human relations in and through pedagogic encounters, and more specifically through teaching and learning in a university setting. Consequently, in Teaching for Change we have chosen the following four themes: giving thought to African philosophy of education; exploring different approaches to African philosophy of education; towards a communitarian understanding of African philosophy of education; and African philosophy of education and the achievement of *ubuntu* justice. In these themes, we examine at least three different understandings of African philosophy of education, namely, African ethno-philosophy of education, African critical and African communitarian philosophy of education. In the main, we endeavour to answer questions such as: What makes up (constitutes) an African philosophy of education? Why should an African philosophy of education be considered as credible? How can an African philosophy of education help us to think justly about education?

What we have done through Teaching for Change is to offer our understanding of what constitutes an African philosophy of education. This in itself has been a nuanced pedagogical action on the grounds that we opened ourselves up to critical scrutiny by others; and, this scrutiny has happened. Some of our participants were intent on wanting to know how distinctly different our account of an African philosophy of education differs from another philosophy of education that argues for the cultivation of justice. Our response is, that an African philosophy of education is uniquely African on the grounds that our proffering and arguments in defence of such a philosophy of education involves ascertaining what problems the African situation is confronted with and what the educational ramifications of such problems are for the continent. In this way, we have attempted to articulate a particular understanding of an African philosophy of education.

Our main interest is to evoke the potentialities of others (participants in Teaching for Change, and even readers of this manuscript) to articulate their own understanding of an African philosophy of education which can be in disagreement with our understanding as well. By implication, we posit that an African philosophy of education remains in potentiality as there is always more to know about such a philosophy of education and how it manifests in practices on the continent of Africa.

However, what we consider as a plausible notion of the practice of doing African philosophy of education involves an open reflectiveness about the notion and how it potentially impacts human ways of thinking, acting and being. Practising African philosophy of education ought to orientate oneself towards reflectively analysing, that is, looking for insights to again and again, major problems on the African continent irrespective of how atrocious and daunting such problems might turn out to be. The idea of gaining some insight into the problems that beset the African continent would not only (and hopefully we might add) sharpen one's responses to the seriousness of the problems—such as, poverty, genocide, human trafficking, gender-based violence, patriarchy and climate change—but also offer one the philosophical or analytical know how to deal with and examine adequately the ramifications of such problems for educational discourses. What makes our philosophy of education uniquely African is that the situatedness of the problems we identify invariably impact education and its arrangements differently from the ways in which an analysis of other world problems might guide the educational concerns of those who engage with it and remain affected by it. It is here that Teaching for Change can be considered a relevant discourse through which pedagogic lenses are used to look at some of Africa's problems more analytically, deconstructively and contextually. What the implications of such a philosophical endeavour might be can be varying. However, what such a practice would most poignantly realise is a pathway towards resolving problems more meaningfully on the continent alongside the educational malaises where meaningfulness refers to aspects of empowerment and emancipation. Finally, what Teaching for Change offers is an opportunity for more analysis, reflection and deconstruction. However, this time the analysis could be more reflective and contextual and invariably impact educational discourses differently.

References

Assié-Lumumba, N. T. (2005). African Higher Education: From Compulsory Juxtaposition to Fusion by Choice—Forgoing a New Philosophy of Education for Social Progress. In Y. Waghid (Ed.), *African(a) Philosophy of Education—Reconstructions and Deconstructions* (pp. 19–53). Stellenbosch: Department of Education Policy Studies.

Coetzee, P. H., & Roux, A. P. J. (Eds.). (2003). *The African Philosophy Reader* (2nd ed.). London: Routledge.

Dzobo, N. K. (1992). The Image of Man in Africa. In K. Wiredu & K. Gyekye (Eds.), *Person and Community* (pp. 123–136). Washington: The Council for Research in Values and Philosophy.

Gyekye, K. (1992). Person and Community in Akan Thought. In K. Wiredu & K. Gyekye (Eds.), *Person and Community* (pp. 101–122). Washington: The Council for Research in Values and Philosophy.

Gyekye, K. (1995). Indeterminacy, Ethnophilosophy, Linguistic Philosophy, African Philosophy. *Philosophy, 70*(273), 377–393.

Gyekye, K. (1997). *Tradition and Modernity: Philosophical Reflections on the African Experience*. New York/Oxford: Oxford University Press.

Higgs, P. (2012). African Philosophy and the Decolonization of Education in Africa: Some Critical Reflections. *Educational Philosophy and Theory, 44*(S2), 37–55.

Hountondji, P. (1996). *African Philosophy: Myth and Reality*. Bloomington/Indianapolis: Indiana University Press.

Jagire, J. M. (2014). Indigenous Women Science Teachers of Tanzania. In A. Asabere-Ameyaw, J. Anamuah-Mensah, G. Sefa Dei, & K. Raheem (Eds.), *Indigenist African Development and Related Issues: Towards a Transdisciplinary Perspective* (pp. 163–180). Rotterdam/Boston/Taipei: Sense Publishers.

Mbiti, J. S. (1970). *African Religions and Philosophy*. London: Heinemann.

Murove, M. F. (Ed.). (2009). *African Ethics: An Anthology of Comparative and Applied Ethics*. Scottsville: University of Kwazulu-Natal Press.

Ndofirepi, A., & Shanyanana, R. N. (2015). Rethinking *ukama* in the Context of Philosophy for Children in Africa. *Research Papers in Education, 31*(4), 428–441.

Nyengela, F. (2014). Cultivating Ubuntu: An African Postcolonial Pastoral Theological Engagement with Positive Psychology. *Journal of Pastoral Psychology, 24*(2), 4–35.

Oruka, H. O. (1990). *Sage Philosophy: Indigenous Thinkers and Modern Debate on African Philosophy*. Leiden/New York: E.J. Brill.

Sefa Dei, G. (2014). Indigenizing the Curriculum: The Case of the African University. In G. Emeagwali & G. J. Sefa Dei (Eds.), *African Indigenous Knowledge and the Disciplines* (pp. 165–180). Rotterdam/Boston/Tapei: Sense Publishers.

Waghid, Y. (2014a). Philosophical Remarks on Nelson Mandela's Education Legacy. *Educational Philosophy and Theory, 46*(1), 4–7.

Waghid, Y. (2014b). *African Philosophy of Education Reconsidered: On Being Human.* London: Routledge.

Waghid, Y., & Smeyers, P. (2012). Reconsidering *ubuntu*: On the Educational Potential of a Particular Ethic of Care. *Educational Philosophy and Theory, 44*(S2), 6–20.

Wiredu, K. (Ed.). (2004). *A Companion to African Philosophy.* Oxford: Blackwell.

Wiredu, K. (2005). Philosophical Considerations on the Africanisation of Higher Education in Africa. In Y. Waghid (Ed.), *African(a) Philosophy of Education—Reconstructions and Deconstructions* (pp. 6–18). Stellenbosch: Department of Education Policy Studies.

2

A Curriculum Response to Pedagogic Dilemmas: Towards Enhancing Teaching and Learning

2.1 Introduction

Teaching for Change represents a snapshot of our response to the predicament about teaching and learning in Africa. In this chapter, we endeavour to highlight some of the challenges we have identified and then set out to offer our response to the dilemmas about teaching and learning in higher education through Teaching for Change. The challenges we enumerate are based on our engagement with higher education discourses. These challenges to teaching and learning at universities include the predicament of the silenced or 'subaltern' of which Gayatri Spivak (2008) reminds us; the predicament of not being open to what is new and perhaps unimaginable; and the predicament of pedagogic or curriculum unresponsiveness.

2.2 Responding to the Excluded Students or the Democratic Dilemma

By far the most important challenge that faces universities on the African continent today, is that offered by teaching and learning. The colonial annexation succeeded by neoliberal concerns of producing a particular

© The Author(s) 2018
Y. Waghid et al., *Rupturing African Philosophy on Teaching and Learning*,
https://doi.org/10.1007/978-3-319-77950-8_2

type of student or worker who would be attentive to the competitive globalised labour market economy has excessively challenged universities to come up with strategies to engender the "ideal" student with clearly demarcated graduate attributes. Some of these graduate attributes are related to becoming an enlightened and critical person, a technologically adept worker and a globally informed citizen. Of course, at first, there can be nothing pernicious about producing students who are enlightened, critical, technologically savvy, and global-minded—that is, students who can contribute towards the development and success of Africa. However, looking closer again, mostly at many of the universities in Africa, in particular their preoccupation with producing graduates with delineated attributes, one gets the impression that teaching and learning in higher education have taken on some predetermined approaches on what students should be, rather than what they can become. There is a difference between being fixated on which attributes students ought to become skilled at—a matter of socialisation, on the one hand, and what students present on account of being initiated into particular practices, on the other. To be socialised into a predetermined array of skills is different from being initiated into practices whereby students might learn a set of competencies and skills.

To be socialised into pre-arranged competencies and skills is tantamount to being introduced to a set of competencies and skills that could put one in a position to do certain things. For instance, a student being socialised in terms of how to do a search on words, might end up doing it well on the grounds of having been told which procedures to adhere to in doing such a word search. The student might end up doing the search so well that doing word searches might become monotonous without the student being challenged to think about the word, in particular what the word could mean in a particular context. He or she is then so set on mechanically looking up descriptions and established explanations that he or she does not feel the need to think about the words him- or herself. Socialisation occurs when students merely take for granted that what they are introduced to is sufficient enough without any further efforts at contemplating the word or concept to which they are introduced. In a way, socialisation implies that students are told what to do without them necessarily having to think through what they encounter. Simply put, socialisation happens when students are urged to internalise this or that concept without them having to do much to think about the concept. The concept is what it is on account of that with which the student has been socialised. Here, I specifically think of learning whereby students are not expected to think about the concepts and practices to which they are introduced. In this way, students have become mere recipients of information—that is, they have been socialised into familiarising themselves with established meanings. In all likelihood, such students have been indoctrinated into an inherited tradition of thoughts and practices. The point is that being socialised into occupying the position of an enlightened, critical citizen is different from being initiated into being a citizen who is always in the process of becoming enlightened and critical. We surmise that universities are intent on producing graduates with certain established attributes and, hence, they seemingly socialise students into predetermined attributes.

However, to be initiated into a practice of meaning-making whereby one is required to reflect deeply on words or concepts, brings into play actions such as searching for meanings to which one has not been introduced before or meanings other than those that have been clarified to one. Initiation, unlike socialisation, involves constructing or reconstructing meanings of which one has not thought before because one is encouraged to think deeper about words and not just to accept at face value what one has been presented with. Whereas socialisation involves getting to acquaint oneself with meanings without any form of interrogation of such meanings, initiation requires one to consider meanings and to think through and about them for the purpose of constructing, and even deconstructing, meanings. In this way, initiation is a critical discourse of meaning-making on the grounds that new meanings are produced and deeper insights of such meanings are conjured up. The point is that one is initiated into a discourse of meaning-making whereby one's understanding of meanings is extended and even thought about differently. Initiation is thus a more critical activity of meaning-making, which brings more insights to the fore without just relying on meanings that have been thought out for one prior to having been socialised with such meanings. For Richard Rorty (1999: 117), initiation begins when socialisation recedes, which —in a different way—signifies the commencement of criticism. Initiation, or what Rorty (1999) refers to as individuation, actually helps "students realise that they can reshape themselves – that they can rework the self-image foisted on them by their past, the self-image that makes them competent citizens, into a new self-image, one that they themselves have helped to create" (Rorty 1999: 118). In a different way, socialisation familiarises students with what is established and considered as inculcated truths. Initiation or individuation is "a matter of inciting doubt and stimulating imagination, thereby challenging the prevailing consensus" (Rorty 1999: 118).

In our view, students are excluded from learning when they are expected to socialise themselves with pre-established truths only. In other words, as literate beings, students are socialised into an inherited corpus of ideas and practices without them having the freedom and openness to question and scrutinise. When students are not initiated into learning, they do not develop the capacities to inquire freely, to experiment, and to alter existing understandings (Rorty 1999: 124). In addition, when the latter happens, students are invariably excluded from learning. They are unable to invent new forms of human freedom and to take liberties never taken before. This is so because their learning will be stunted. That is, learning does not involve socialisation alone; it also involves initiation into narratives not cultivated previously. By implication, they (students) would have been silenced and they remain excluded—a predicament which is somewhat common in African higher education today. Next, we examine how learning would unfold without having the unexpected, unimaginable in mind.

2.3 Responding to the Unimaginable or the Cosmopolitan Dilemma

Nowadays, higher education institutions (HEIs) are very much attuned to protecting the knowledge traditions that are familiar to them. With specific reference to the South African higher education situation and with regard to its knowledge traditions, one gets a snapshot of how the pedagogic practices of teaching and learning have manifested in universities on the continent of Africa. According to the Council on Higher Education

(CHE) (2016: 143) in South Africa, teaching and learning have been considered as key to address societal inequalities, a solution to the country's dire need for skills development, a means to economic growth and "the path that holds out the most hope for individual social mobility and financial security" (CHE 2016: 145). In the public sector alone, at least 10% of the country's youth enter higher education, which confirms that widening access to participation and responding to equity has not yet been achieved (CHE 2016: 145). Of importance to this discussion is that 45% of all contact students and 55% of all students (contact plus distance education students) will not graduate, thus raising concerns about teaching and learning, in particular their seeming inability to address the high drop-out and low through-put rates of students (CHE 2016: 146). The point being accentuated is that, if 55% of all students who gain access to higher education do not graduate, the scholarship and practices of teaching and learning in universities have to be held liable. Although the CHE (2016: 169) report suggests that individual approaches to learning have been replaced by social ones, the approaches nevertheless failed to have a significant influence on curriculum and classroom practice.

One of the reasons being touted for enhancing a social approach to learning is for students to engage in deliberative encounters and for the cultivation of critical citizenship through teaching and learning (CHE 2016: 170). The CHE (2016: 170) argues that teaching and learning ought to become more concerned with criticism as "a matter of enhancing the possibility of dissent and of a diversity of interpretations, of complicating what is taken for granted and pointing to what has been overlooked in establishing identities". In this way, it is argued, teaching and learning would increasingly become a matter of connecting with theoretical understandings in the enactment of pedagogical practices— an aspect that is very much under-enacted in universities and which ought to be considered if teaching and learning were to salvage their social justice project (CHE 2016: 171). Our advocacy of teaching and learning in the pursuit of what has been overlooked in cultivating identities is in defence of action, in the words of Maxine Greene (1978: 18), critical reflection, because the one who is submerged, who cannot see, "is likely to be caught in *stasis*, unable to move". Critical reflection about what we know and adhere to in our university curriculum is a kind of reflective thinking whereby we create openings and demands for social change (Greene 1978: 18). Becoming critical and reflective about our established traditional practices would allow us not only to protect our knowledge traditions but more importantly to see things differently. Henry Giroux (2007: 3) posits that seeing things differently is tantamount to students and educators engaging "in a culture of questioning, a pedagogy of critical engagement, and a democratic politics of civic responsibility". Put differently, seeing things differently means that universities should be viewed as places of critical and engaged teaching and learning whereby reflective knowledge traditions are created to become more empowering with the possibility of cultivating students and educators who can "speak and act thoughtfully in defense of the university as a democratic public sphere" (Giroux 2007: 10). Only when teaching and learning stimulate educators and students "to be left free to look out upon their own landscapes", to be critically aware, "they may be able to overcome passivity and the temptation to withdraw [from learning]" (Greene 1978: 20). If the latter happens, and based on the CHE report about the state of higher education in South Africa the possibility of this occurring is there, then teaching and learning would have succumbed to the instrumental controls of unreflective education.

If one then considers that teaching and learning represent a commitment to the future, it remains the responsibility of educators to:

> [M]ake sure that the future points the way to a more socially just world, a world in which the discourses of critique and possibility in conjunction with the values of reason, freedom, and equality function to alter … the grounds upon which life is lived. (Giroux 2007: 181)

In this way, critical teaching and learning would not be merely concerned with offering students new ways to think reflectively but also be concerned with:

> [providing students with] skills and knowledge necessary for them to expand their capacities both to question deep-seated assumptions and myths that legitimate the most archaic and disempowering social practices that structure every aspect of society and take responsibility for intervening in the world they inhabit. (Giroux 2007: 182)

If the latter occurs, teaching and learning would not be at risk, but rather remain responsive to action that stifles questioning and conceptions of knowledge that are declared as finished products.

2.4 Responding to Curriculum Unresponsiveness or the Coloniality Dilemma

If university teaching and learning do not appeal to the public interest, but only for reasons of a consumerist and instrumentalist kind, then we concur with Giroux and Searls-Giroux (2004: 277) that higher education ought to be reclaimed back as the task of revitalising such a public sphere. We would argue that if enclaves of colonised curricula are going to become increasingly entrenched in teaching and learning spaces on the African continent, in particular those pedagogic spaces that restrain student engagement and struggle to open up opportunities to cultivate democratic citizenship education, then university education ought to be reclaimed. One way of reclaiming the teaching and learning spaces of university education is to view learning as an individual process that enables mature autonomous action, as well as a social practice capable of influencing and improving democratic civic life (Giroux and Searls-Giroux 2004: 280). In this regard, it is worth quoting Giroux and Searls-Giroux at length (2004: 285):

> Higher education [must] become not just a place to think, but also a space in which to learn how to connect thinking with doing, critical thought with civic courage, knowledge with socially responsible action, citizenship with the obligations of an inclusive democracy ... Knowledge must become the basis for considering individual and collective action, and it must reach beyond the university to join with other forces and create new public spaces in order to deal with the immense problems posed by neoliberalism and all those violations of human rights that negate the most basic premises of freedom, equality, democracy, and social justice. Higher education is also one of the few spheres in which freedom and privilege provide the conditions of possibility for teachers and students to act as critical intellectuals

and address the inhumane effects of power, forge new solidarities across borders, identities, and differences, and also raise questions about what a democracy might look like that is inclusive, radically cosmopolitan and suited to the demands of a global public sphere.

Our interest is in teaching and learning as a decolonial response to un-freedom, inequality and un-democracy. In response to the curriculum challenges of colonialism and coloniality—mostly associated with an imposition of coercive and unequal power relations between those in authority and those subjugated in society—an affinity to scepticism as a decolonial way of acting and being seems to be a way that teaching and learning can be reimagined. When live out their teaching students, they are not oblivious of their doubts about students and, in turn, students' doubts about them are equally not unheeded (Cavell 1979: 432). The point is that educators should not trust students unconditionally or blindly, as that would imply that educators are no longer answerable to students. Educators trust students to exercise their critical abilities and to reason; however, they cannot blindly trust them to assess their own judgements. The latter would imply that students' judgements would not have to be subjected to others' scrutiny, and the possibility that some of their judgements might be indefensible and weak might be flouted. Such a lack of scepticism also presumes that students' positions on this or that matter might not be questioned. In this way, educators would not live out their scepticism, as they would abandon their answerability to students. Raising doubts sceptically about others' points of view is not to misrecognise or abandon that with which one is confronted. Rather, educators acting with scepticism do so with an acknowledgement that others have something worthwhile to say. However, what others (students) have to say is not treated with disrespect and a lack of strangeness in the sense that what they have to say is not judged without a consideration that there might be other alternative perspectives. If this happens, learning would not take place, because learning depends on educators and students taking responsibility for their judgements with an acknowledgement that both can be proved wrong. Also, for the latter to happen, students' views have to be confronted with scepticism—that is, without raising doubts about others' points of view learning would cease to exist. Indoctrination, on the other hand, would occur because reasons would be accepted without critical scrutiny.

Moreover, acting with scepticism is also a matter of acknowledging humanity in the other, on which the basis of such an acknowledgement lies with oneself. When an educator acknowledges his or her student by showing that he or she (the educator) has learned something from the student, that is, when an educator acknowledges his or her humanity by revealing him- or herself to the student as a human being—that is, one acknowledges the student to be human, and simultaneously one's capacity to see human from inhuman. An educator acknowledging the humanity of a student, therefore, recognises the importance of not humiliating the student. Doing so would be misrecognising the humanity within the student. In this regard, the educator would know what it means to treat students inhumanely, by conducting him- or herself in a way that would inhumanely affront the dignity of the student. In other words, following Cavell (1979: 378), "it makes sense to speak of seeing human beings as human beings, then it makes sense to imagine that a human being may lack the capacity to see human beings as human beings". The point about recognising one another as human beings in teaching and learning encounters is connected to the possibility that such actions could be belligerent, distressful, courageous and, at times, even unsettling. Yet, recognising one another as human beings, educators and students, although being cognisant of their capacities to act inhumanely, endeavour to resist such possibilities—that is, to act hurtfully, disrespectfully and inhospitably. Put differently, as humans, they refrain from acting in an un-cosmopolitan way. When educators and students act humanely towards one another, the possibility is always there that their actions would counteract injustices and cruelties that might manifest in previously colonised societies. For example, such vices that Western imperialism brought to colonised parts of the world such as South Africa might be thwarted in the sense that benefits of teaching and learning could be realised in societies intent on cultivating humaneness. Following Seyla Benhabib (2006: 151), the possibility that societal benefits would dawn on previously colonised parts of the world, such as resistance to war, hostility and plunder on the African continent, could be an indirect outcome of responsive— we would argue, decolonial—teaching and learning at universities.

2.5 Summary: Contextualising Online Education

What started as an initiative to promote our institution's advocacy for online teaching and learning in the context of credible university education associated with a leading South African HEI, soon turned out to be a pedagogical initiative aimed at cultivating at least three aspects of a transformative understanding of teaching and learning. First, Teaching for Change is intended to be not only about socialising students into understandings of African philosophy of education as if they (participants) are merely passive recipients of knowledge who need to be provided with concepts and examples of practices. This in itself is a form of unlearning. Rather, with Teaching for Change, students are encouraged to initiate themselves into authoring their own narratives on what constitutes an African philosophy of education. Those students who insisted that they be told what is so distinctive about an African philosophy of education can be said to be still in the process of internalising and authoring their justifications on what such a philosophy of education is all about. The point is, teaching and learning have both socialising and initiating dimensions without which such pedagogical actions would not take place.

Considering that teaching and learning are underscored by criticism, moments of dissent and the autonomy of both educators and students to act towards carving out for themselves and others a better future, Teaching for Change offers students and educators opportunities to expand their capacities to question, to assume responsibility, and to look at meanings as they could be otherwise vis-à-vis the cultivation of a just world. Finally, at the core of doing Teaching for Change, educators and students are summoned to act humanely towards one another. By doing so, they position themselves (educators and students) more favourably and pedagogically to counteract injustices and cruelties that might continue unabatedly in African communities. Using Teaching for Change might offer educators and students the transformative reasons to enact more just human relations on the African continent and elsewhere. We contend that scepticism, criticism and recognising one another's humanity would be advantageous towards the cultivation of just pedagogic encounters such as are enveloped within Teaching for Change. In the next chapter, we elucidate the rationale of Teaching for Change.

References

Benhabib, S. (2006). *Another Cosmopolitanism*. Oxford: Oxford University Press.

Cavell, S. (1979). *The Claim of Reason: Wittgenstein, Scepticism, Morality and Tragedy*. New York/Oxford: Oxford University Press.

CHE (CHE). (2016). *South African Higher Education Reviewed: Two Decades After Democracy*. Pretoria: CHE.

Giroux, H. A. (2007). *The University in Chains: Confronting the Military-Industrial-Academic Complex*. Boulder: Paradigm Publishers.

Giroux, H., & Searls-Giroux, S. (2004). *Taking Back Higher Education: Race, Youth, and the Crisis of Democracy in the Post-civil Rights Era*. New York/London: Palgrave Macmillan.

Greene, M. (1978). *Landscapes of Learning*. New York/London: Teachers College Press.

Rorty, R. (1999). *Philosophy and Social Hope*. London: Penguin Books.

Spivak, G. (2008). *The Trajectory of the Subaltern in My Work*. Accessed from: https://www.youtube.com/watch?v=2ZHH4ALRFHw

3

African Philosophy of Education and *Ubuntu* Justice

3.1 Introduction

The main concern of an African philosophy of education is to be responsive to the African human condition, which is characterised by high levels of inequality and poverty, human suffering and inhumanity. The eradication of the aforementioned concerns goes along with the quest for justice, which, in the context of Teaching for Change, is of three kinds: moral justice, compassionate justice, and restorative justice. In this chapter, we examine the political and ethical thoughts of three luminaries—Nelson Mandela, Wangari Maathai and Desmond Tutu—in the cultivation of political and social democracy in order to ascertain why the aforementioned forms of justice are inextricably connected to an enactment of African philosophy of education. Thereafter, with specific reference to Teaching for Change, we show how students responded to these three forms of justice, in particular the idea of *ubuntu* justice that emanates from an understanding of moral justice, compassionate justice and restorative justice.

Our main focus in Teaching for Change is to initiate students into the *raison d'être* of African philosophy of education or, more poignantly, an African philosophy of teaching and learning. It is our contention that an

© The Author(s) 2018
Y. Waghid et al., *Rupturing African Philosophy on Teaching and Learning*,
https://doi.org/10.1007/978-3-319-77950-8_3

understanding of that which constitutes African philosophy of education would prompt in students and ourselves as educators the motivation and academic urgency to come to terms for what African philosophy of education is all about. It is not sufficient just to remain cognisant of the pedagogic procedures of analysis and reflection about the problems on the African continent and then to inquire about their educational ramifications. This is itself enabling—that is, one would do African philosophy of education. However, it would be insufficient as any pedagogic activity ought to have some humane purpose—and this cannot be exclusively related to understanding and interpretation. It also has to be connected to the cultivation of—and by implication, contributing to—the enhancement of just human living in relation to the context in which people happen to enact their forms of living. In a way, practising African philosophy of education is inextricably linked to the cultivation of humanity. In our analysis of the politico-economic and socio-cultural actions of three of Africa's most significant people—Mandela, Maathai and Tutu—we managed to get a lucid and justifiable understanding of the purposes of African philosophy of education. The point of doing African philosophy of education is connected to the enactment of some morally worthwhile pursuit related to the idea of *ubuntu* justice. Simply put, doing African philosophy of education is inextricably connected to the pursuit of *ubuntu* justice. Our reason for making this link is driven by an inherent understanding that post-colonial education on the African continent cannot be delinked from the pursuit of decolonisation and decoloniality as the latter forms of post-colonial action are ways in which striving for *ubuntu* justice becomes a reality for those engaged with and affected by the notion of an African philosophy of education. What makes an African philosophy of education what it is, is connected with an enactment of *ubuntu* justice. We now examine three constitutive features of *ubuntu* justice as enacted in the lived experiences of Mandela, Maathai and Tutu.

3.2 Moral Justice

Immediately after the late President Nelson Mandela became South Africa's first democratically elected president in 1994, he rendered a speech that emphasised the significance of moral justice in the quest to build a new democratic society. Mandela's concern for the achievement of moral justice lies in his appeal for equality, freedom and justice for all. Inequality and poverty can only be addressed if people make it their moral concern that justice for all implies that all people ought to be treated equally and that their freedom has to be recognised. In this way, moral justice is the same as exercising one's moral responsibility towards others. For Mandela, this implied liberating people from poverty, deprivation, suffering, gender and other forms of discrimination—all related to the achievement of moral justice. If humans are not all considered equal, then the possibility is always there for a people to discriminate against and ridicule those considered unequal.

Disrupting inequality on the basis of a plea for equality lies at the heart of what it means to treat someone with moral justice. Put differently, to ensure moral justice depends on people's willingness and responsibility to enact their equality. The basis of people's equality in a moral sense is intertwined with people's humanity (Munyaka and Motlhabi 2009: 66). People are equal on the basis of their humanity—an idea that connects with the concept of *ubuntu* (literally, respect for persons). What follows from the aforementioned is that the notion of moral justice is related to an enactment of people's humanity, which implies that they give recognition to one another's equality. Thus, moral justice is concomitantly linked to the cultivation of *ubuntu* on the grounds that *ubuntu* is intertwined with the recognition of people's equality and, by implication, their humanity.

What Teaching for Change recognised is that *ubuntu* (respect for persons) is constitutive of moral justice as people's equality is highlighted in order to counteract any possibility of poverty, inhumanity and suffering. Without such an understanding and enactment of moral justice, inequality and inhumane treatment of others are highly possible. Mandela's opposition to apartheid was instigated by a dissatisfaction with and abhorrence to the inhumanity and inequality that characterised apartheid legislation, which simply misrecognised that justice should be applicable to all moral beings. If human beings do not all experience *ubuntu*, the possibility is always there for injustice and inhumanity to undermine the equality that ought to exist among humans. In his riveting autobiography, *Long walk to freedom,* Mandela (1994: 751) links the exercise of one's equality with one's freedom, and states the following in relation to justice and the cultivation of humanity:

> It is during those long and lonely years that my hunger for the freedom [and equality] of my own people became a hunger for the freedom of all people, white and black. I knew as well as I knew anything that the oppressor must be liberated just as surely as the oppressed. A [wo]man who takes away another [wo]man's freedom is a prisoner of hatred, [s]he is locked behind the bars of prejudice and narrow-mindedness. I am not truly free [and equal] if I am taking away someone else's freedom, just as surely as I am not free when my freedom is taken from me. The oppressed and the oppressor alike are robbed of their humanity.

We infer from Mandela's claim of moral justice that without freedom and equality, humanity is not possible. Equally, the exercise of hatred and resentment toward others human beings is made easier in the absence of moral equality and freedom, which lie at the core of moral justice. When moral justice holds sway, violence and antagonism towards human beings will be deterred and people will hopefully see and honour one another's humanity. If such an understanding of moral justice manifests in the lived experiences of people, the possibility that *ubuntu* justice will be present is highly likely. For instance, analysing the problem of genocide in Africa in order to ascertain how such an atrocious form of human behaviour undermines human co-existence and co-belonging is at the core of African philosophy of education. However, being cognisant of the educational implications of genocide and of the effect that such a heinous crime could instil in others the desire to hate and annihilate other humans cannot be counteracted without the possibility that humans ought to engage justly. The point is that, without a recognition of *ubuntu* justice, there would be no point in doing African philosophy of education. *Ubuntu* justice also undermines any form of human action that might generate into "a kind of barbarism, where war, brutality, torture, misery, superexploitation, all sorts of draconian measures against the poor, … racism, extreme environmental devastation threatening whole populations and even the globe …" (McLaren and Jaramillo 2007: 6).

This brings us to a discussion of another form of *ubuntu* justice, namely compassionate justice.

3.3 Compassionate Justice

The idea of compassionate justice can most appropriately be expounded on in relation to the seminal thoughts of the founder of the Green Belt Movement (Maathai 2009) in Kenya since 1977, and Nobel Peace Prize laureate of 2004, Wangari Muta Maathai. In her book, *The challenge for Africa*, Maathai (2009: 189) aptly reminds us of our human responsibility to protect peoples all over the world from genocide, crimes against humanity, war crimes and ethnic cleansing. For her, only the willingness to engage with one another and the sharing of power and resources equitably on the continent of Africa can produce lasting change (Maathai 2009: 189). More specifically, her work with the Green Belt Movement anchored her protestations against human rights violations, poor governance, corruption, land grabbing and deforestation (Maathai 2009: 209). What is evident from Maathai's claims for justice (*ubuntu* justice we might add) is the recognition that something is wrong, and that the vulnerabilities people suffer specifically on the African continent can only be remedied if those vulnerabilities are acknowledged in the first place and something can be done to change it. Very much like Martin Luther King Jr. and Nelson Mandela, Maathai (2009: 201) advocates against violence, which tragically for her, begets violence. She particularly spoke out against stirring up people along ethnic lines to attack one another, and paying young people to commit atrocities such as to kill people and burn down their houses at the time of her writing in war-ravaged Kenya (Maathai 2009: 201). In other words, Maathai recognised that one way of combatting violence is to recognise African people's vulnerabilities and then to do something about remedying it. It is not enough merely to be aware of people's subjugation to acts of violence, but rather that something needs to be done about the eradication of violence. Our approach throughout this book and in Teaching for Change is to make the pedagogic more political and, echoing McLaren and Jaramillo (2007: 6), "the political more pedagogically critical [and reflexive]".

Put differently, Maathai's argument for compassionate justice is extended to her recognition that the militia wars for control of the Congo Basin forests in central Africa, with its abundant reserves of charcoal, gold, copper, diamonds, cobalt, zinc and other minerals, enhanced the possibility of people's exposure to diseases such as Ebola, HIV/AIDS and malaria and that, unless efforts to conserve the forests are put into place, human vulnerability would increase. That is, unless the pedagogic could inspire people to act more politically and by implication, transformatively, change in society would not happen. The point is that recognising those aspects that cause human vulnerability should be identified and then something should be done to prevent such vulnerabilities. In a way, compassionate justice needs to be shown towards all Africa's peoples and the environment (Maathai 2009: 269), which means that efforts will have to be put in place to address people's vulnerabilities, in particular against exploitation and corruption.

In sum, compassionate justice according to Maathai (2009: 288) is a struggle against that which causes injustice because, in her words:

> [I]f the soil is denuded and the waters are polluted, the air is poisoned, wildlife is lost, and the mineral riches are mined and sold beyond the [African] continent, nothing will be left that we can call our 'own'. It is through compassionate justice that Africans can feel secure and at peace with one another on the grounds that people's vulnerabilities would be attended to and human exploitation would be combated. (Maathai 2009: 289)

It is compassionate justice that can put an end to violence, demonisation, exploitation and genocide. Thus, without fighting corruption and promoting integrity among humans on the continent through counteracting the abuse of political power and exploitation—a matter of living with *ubuntu*—Africans will remain "vulnerable to anyone who wishes to exploit us" (Maathai 2009: 289). Without exercising compassionate justice, people are said to be inhumane and by implication would lack *ubuntu* (Munyaka and Motlhabi 2009: 65). Again, compassionate justice is a manifestation of *ubuntu*, conceived as that virtue necessary to avoid harm, misery and pain being inflicted upon all Africans, but of course, in this case, the marginalised and exploited masses (Munyaka and Motlhabi 2009: 71). This brings us to a discussion of another form of justice that connects with *ubuntu*.

3.4 Restorative Justice

Another significant contribution to justice on the African continent, more specifically the formation and enactment of restorative justice, is eloquently articulated by Archbishop Desmond Tutu. Tutu's appeal for restorative justice is evident from his claim that "A broken person needed to be helped to be healed" (Tutu 1994: 2). Of course, his idea of restorative justice does not deny retribution, as punishment must be meted out according to the crime and the law has to follow its course. His defence of restorative justice is grounded in an enactment of responsibility towards others through love, compassion and civility. In his monumental book, *No future without forgiveness*, Tutu (1994: 84) posits that people who have been wronged have the right to know who the perpetrators of the injustices against them are, and then they (that is, the victims) have to face an acknowledgement in their presence that they had been wronged. In this regard, the title of the book accentuates the importance of forgiveness in the restoration of justice. Without forgiveness, Tutu (1994) avers, reconciliation and the restoration of a community would be impossible. Put differently, it is forgiveness that stimulates people to act anew.

Moreover, what is important about Tutu's notion of restorative justice is the connection of the concept with *ubuntu*. For Tutu (1994: 35), a person with *ubuntu* is not only open and available to others, but also one who opposes the humiliation of and oppression of others. Such a person would assume a responsibility for restoring just human action through the agency of forgiveness and reconciliation (Tutu 1994). The very idea of offering forgiveness is connected to the process of starting again—that is, oppressed people should not alienate the oppressors on the grounds that they have been wronged. Rather, reconciliation should ensue if both oppressor and oppressed are prepared to start again. In this case, forgiveness is not just a one-off, but rather, a declaration not to repeat a crime committed against someone else. It is an acknowledgement that people should live together without oppressing one another. Forgiveness is an act of new re-beginnings.

It is possible to conceive of an African philosophy of education invoking three forms of justice: moral, compassionate and restorative. Collectively, these three forms of justice can be couched under the name of "*ubuntu* justice*", because *ubuntu* involves the cultivation of moral, compassionate and restorative responsibility. More clearly, *ubuntu* justice denotes an enactment of human autonomy in recognition that humans are not alone and should always be attached to other humans through their collective humanity. The possibility should always be there for humans to recognise their it refers to vulnerabilities and to change it irrespective of how trying the conditions might be. In this way, the possibility that a society or a community could be restored to new re-beginnings would be highly likely. When this occurs, *ubuntu* justice remains in potentiality.

One example of the practical enactment of a notion of *ubuntu* justice is the Truth and Reconciliation Commission (TRC) of South Africa (Bell 2002). The TRC hearings commenced in June 1994 with the intention to evoke the truth and offer reconciliation, by listening to the testimonies of both the victims and perpetrators of apartheid crimes. Within the TRC context, the victim was often not the direct target of the perpetration, but rather a family member who had lost someone under horrific circumstances, and was seeking answers about the last moments of that family member's life. This particular establishment of a dialogical exchange allowed the victim to share his or her pain, while the perpetrator not only offered remorse, but provided some insight about why, how and where the perpetration took place. The purpose of the TRC was to elicit "truth telling" about past atrocities and, for 18 months, the Commission, headed by Emeritus Archbishop Desmond Tutu, listened to the testimonies of those who wanted amnesty and those seeking reparation and healing. In this sense, the pursuit of the TRC was not punitive, but through an *ubuntu* justice, it sought to grant perpetrators amnesty and immunity from prosecution for apartheid crimes committed against humanity. The TRC did not encourage revenge and retribution, but rather offered reconciliation and forgiveness as ways to cultivate a new democratic South African society. This African approach to justice was not aimed at taking revenge against the perpetrators of heinous apartheid crimes, but recommended reparation for the victims and granted reparations to some perpetrators—described by Richard Bell (2002: 34) as a kind of justice that is compassion-based, embracing human self-esteem and mercy, and grounded in a communal responsibility towards all human beings as equal in their humanity. Thus, *ubuntu* justice through the recognition of equality, compassion and forgiveness is a way of enacting a moral concern for human beings, compassion and healing that could contribute to a culture of respect for human rights and dignity for all citizens as equals in the country.

When one considers that ethnic conflict is very prevalent in many African societies, *ubuntu* justice with its emphasis on moral equality, compassionate action and restoration could contribute towards addressing such a form of human antagonism. Any other form of justice runs the risk of facilitating more violence and antagonism and, most importantly, will not offer the understanding and language embedded within *ubuntu* justice. First, when humans are considered equal in their humanity, the chances of one ethnic group exercising its will over another would not be possible. What would be at stake is that different ethnic groups would not see the need to exert their influence over another because their inherent equality would allow them to exercise their will equally without having to anticipate any form of reprisal and exclusion. Humans are equal on account of their humanity and morality and thus do not see the need to antagonise one another. Second, different ethnicities would see things differently, and difference would invariably come to the fore. Sometimes such differences are interconnected with people's vulnerabilities and would require some form of acknowledgement on the part of the other. We are reminded that, at times, different ethnic groups on the African continent seem to be vulnerable on account of their differences and less authoritative political situations. In such a case, more authoritative ethnic groups should recognise the vulnerabilities of such groups and actually do something about remedying their unfavourable situation. In this way, compassionate justice as an instance of *ubuntu* justice would be enacted. Third, restorative justice has the potential to bring opposing ethnic factions to engage with one another for the purpose of building a shared community. On the basis of reconciliation and forgiveness, a community thus cultivated would be one where the advancement of the shared interests of the community would be prioritised. In this way, *ubuntu* justice could invoke moral autonomy, compassionate action and restoration among different ethnic groups and the potential for ensuing conflict might be thwarted.

3.5 Summary: Teaching for Change and the Cultivation of *Ubuntu* Justice

From our interactions via the discussion posts of Teaching for Change, our understanding of *ubuntu* justice can be elucidated as an interrelationship between the cultivation of education and the achievement of *ubuntu* living. We link the importance of *ubuntu* justice to an exercise of fairness, eradication of inequality and exercising respect towards one another. In the quest of attaining *ubuntu* justice, the healing of scars, prevention of violence, mediation of crises, and enactment of equality, freedom, inclusion and responsibility become necessary. What is evident from such an understanding of *ubuntu* justice is that the concept can be considered a morally worthwhile action towards which we ought to aspire. It is not that *ubuntu* justice will suddenly emerge as a panacea to societal problems. However, it offers African philosophy of education a distinctive feature in that such an understanding of education has non-violent, moral and restorative purposes that could be attained if Africans (and others) practise equality, compassion and reconciliation. In this way, *ubuntu* justice could be regarded as always in potentiality and not yet actualised. It is with such an understanding of *ubuntu* justice that the reason for African philosophy of education to manifest in human actions becomes increasingly desirable. Another example of *ubuntu* justice would be associated with the pursuit of equality through eradicating or lessening poverty. In the words of McLaren and Jaramillo (2007: 8), "eradicating poverty means providing people with full access to health, education, and other social provisions"—that is, performing acts of *ubuntu* justice.

Ubuntu justice ought to be an important and necessary outcome of education and such a form of justice ought to remain in potentiality. The point we are making is that *ubuntu* justice is always in-becoming as no form of justice should be considered conclusive and exhaustive. Once the latter occurs, both education and justice would have run their course. Rather, human co-existence and cooperation constituted by respect for the dignity of all and the acknowledgement of one another's humaneness, should always be a morally just action worth pursuing. The point about *ubuntu* justice is its interconnectedness with moral, compassionate and restorative justice. In addition, *ubuntu* justice is not just instantaneous, as if someone else is treated justly momentarily and then the need for justice is no longer required. On the contrary, *ubuntu* justice is relentless, and there cannot be a moment where justice is forgotten and by implication not enacted. Rather, *ubuntu* justice is a sustainable act of righteous human living whereby humans should always remain conscious of the possibility of doing wrong against other humans. It is not that justice is used only when people are treated inhumanely and when they would be in need of just treatment, such as the case currently in the Darfur region of Sudan where hungry and oppressed peoples are subjected to humiliation and shame, or in Mogadishu, the capital of Somalia, where more than 300 civilians had been killed through a terrorist car bombing in October 2017. *Ubuntu* justice should be everywhere, in the sense that even when someone knows about the evil intentions and actions of another, such a person should not only distance him- or herself from such acts but must also be committed to avoid at all costs the unfolding of such atrocious events. Only then can we speak more justifiably of an *ubuntu* justice in potentiality—that is, it has no end as the possibility is always there for unjust human actions to occur. It is such a notion of *ubuntu* justice that underscores an African philosophy of education. Consequently, doing African philosophy of education implies striving to enact *ubuntu* justice in all our encounters with humans and non-humans. One cannot begin to talk about an African philosophy of education as some sort of pedagogical action that does not go along with the cultivation of *ubuntu* justice. *Ubuntu* justice is, hence, a necessary condition of doing African philosophy of education.

In the next chapter, we show how pedagogic justice and its concomitant link with deliberative, responsible and risk-oriented action unfolds in pedagogic encounters as a manifestation of *ubuntu* justice.

References

Bell, R. (2002). Understanding African Philosophy: A Cross-Cultural Approach to Classical and Contemporary Issues. New York/London: Routledge.

Maathai, W. M. (2009). *The Challenge for Africa*. Croydon: Arrow Books.

Mandela, N. (1994). *Long Walk to Freedom: The Autobiography of Nelson Mandela*. London: Abacus.

McLaren, P., & Jaramillo, N. (2007). *Pedagogy and Praxis in the Age of Empire: Towards a New Humanism*. Rotterdam/Tapei: Sense Publishers.

Munyaka, M., & Motlhabi, M. (2009). Ubuntu and Its Social-Moral Significance. In M. F. Murove (Ed.), *African Ethics: An Anthology of Comparative and Applied Ethics* (pp. 63–84). Pietermaritzburg: University of Kwazulu-Natal Press.

Tutu, D. (1994). *No Future Without Forgiveness*. London: Ebury Digital.

4

Cultivating Pedagogic Justice Through Deliberation, Responsibility and Risk-Oriented Action Commensurate with an African Philosophy of Education

4.1 Introduction

In the previous chapter, we made an argument for the cultivation of *ubuntu* justice as the rationale for an African philosophy of education. As an extension of this view, we contend that an African philosophy of education is aimed at developing a conception of democratic African education that might contribute towards deliberative, responsible and risk-oriented action—actions that could contribute towards enhancing pedagogic justice as an instance of *ubuntu* justice. In other words, pedagogic justice is one way in which *ubuntu* justice manifests itself in pedagogic encounters.

In this chapter, we argue that, by provoking students towards deliberation, by encouraging responsibility, and through risk-oriented action in disrupting social injustices, students will hopefully learn to be attentive to those on the margins of transforming the existing societal and economic inequalities prevalent in Africa. Thus, in our attempt to offer a defence for a plausible conception of an African philosophy of education constituted by deliberative, responsible and risk-oriented action, we draw on MacIntyre's (1981) account of virtues, namely conversational justice,

© The Author(s) 2018
Y. Waghid et al., *Rupturing African Philosophy on Teaching and Learning*,
https://doi.org/10.1007/978-3-319-77950-8_4

51

truthfulness and courage commensurate with African communitarianism and *ubuntu* in order to justify an African philosophy of education towards enhancing pedagogic justice.

Alasdair MacIntyre's (1981) claim concerning certain virtues as universal, in the sense that they are necessary constituents for good social practices, is premised on the notion that without virtues, the goods internal to individuals and groups in a society, which include social bonding, human fulfilment and human gratification among others, are essentially excluded. This is what MacIntyre (1981: 32) avers when he claims that a virtue is "an acquired human quality the possession and exercise of which tends to enable us to achieve those goods which are internal to [social] practices and the lack of which effectively prevents us from achieving any such goods". Social practices are what MacIntyre (1981: 30) refers to as any coherent and complex form of socially established, cooperative human activity through which internal goods are realised in the course of trying to achieve standards of excellence, which are considered appropriate to and partially definitive of the social practices. Virtues in a MacIntyre (1994: 352) sense belong to the social practices in which one finds one's self and in which the desire for internal goods can be achieved only when one subordinates oneself to the most appropriate standards so far achieved, which entails subordinating oneself to social practices in communion with other practitioners. MacIntyre (1981: 32) posits that, as individuals in our social practices, we have to listen carefully to what we are told about our own inadequacies and to reply with the same carefulness through conversational justice. That is, we have to learn to recognise what is due to whom (responsibility/accountability through truthfulness); and we have to be prepared to take whatever endangering risks are demanded along the way (risk-oriented action through courage) (MacIntyre 1981: 32).

In the light of MacIntyre's account of virtues, we contend that the African concept *ubuntu*, or humaneness and human interdependence, is a virtue necessary for the enactment of good social practices in contemporary African society. Mbiti's (1970: 108) elucidation of *ubuntu* within a communitarian understanding of the individual in African society is that "[w]hatever happens to the individual happens to the whole group and [that] whatever happens to the whole group happens to the individual".

Mbiti (1970) avers that individuals exist as a constituent of a community and are influenced by the ideologies, needs and risks of the community while concomitantly being influenced by an individual's own self-understandings as well. The individual does not exist in isolation as an "atomistic" being, as Gyekye (1997: 41) argues, but the individual is rather embedded in a context of social relationships and interdependence. Accordingly, Gyekye (1997: 41–42) reasons:

> [A] community is not [seen] as a mere association of individual persons whose interests and ends are contingently congruent, but as a group of persons linked by interpersonal bonds, biological and/or non-biological, who consider themselves primarily as members of the group and who have common interests, goals and values.

The point is, atomistic beings are self-centred, narcissistic persons, whereas communal beings are autonomously engaged with one another (Gyekye 1997).

Furthermore, communitarianism is a necessary constituent of an African philosophy of education. Our contention is that an African philosophy of education cultivates a sense of community characterised by a concern for the other, sharing of values, and emotional and ideological attachment and synergy—that is, virtues necessary for attaining internal goods. Communitarianism embedded within an African philosophy of education, therefore, helps to establish synergies in which Africans are oriented towards working together—a situation that produces a greater effect than the sum of their individual parts. In other words, human beings are not merely aggregated together, but in community they are in association. A community premised on the notion of *ubuntu* would invariably contribute to the amelioration of the prevailing inhumane conditions in Africa caused by poverty, famine, unemployment, political oppression, civil wars, colonialism and economic exploitation (Oladipo 1992: 24). The point about acting in community in a spirit of *ubuntu* invokes an understanding that people ought to cooperate and co-exist in the quest of attaining internal goods—a matter of advancing the cause of justice, more specifically, *ubuntu* justice. It is in this regard that *ubuntu* justice can be linked to the enactment of defensible pedagogic encounters as shown through Teaching for Change. Hence, pedagogic justice is possible through encounters among educators and students. Our view is that deliberative encounters could engender more plausible forms of pedagogic justice and, by implication, *ubuntu* justice. The point about pedagogic justice is that it manifests in encounters among students and educators on the basis of their deliberative engagement and articulation of reasons. We shall now attend in more detail to this notion of deliberative engagement in the quest to cultivate pedagogic justice.

4.2 Deliberation Through the Virtue of Conversational Justice: Cultivating Pedagogic Justice

MacIntyre (1999: 110–111) claims that as a practical reasoner one would have to engage in conversation with others, that is, a conversation about what would be best for one or the other or "us" as a group "to do here and now, or next week, or next year" through the virtue of conversational justice. Conversational justice as a virtue, according to MacIntyre (1999: 111), requires, among other things, first that each individual "speaks with candor, to not pretend or deceive or [engage in] striking attitudes" and second that "each individual takes up no more time than is justified by the importance of the point that she or he has to make and the arguments necessary to make it". Within an African philosophy of education, as Hountondji (2002: 73) avers, one finds progressive "structures of dialogue and argument without which no science is possible". Hountondji (2002) depicts an African philosophy of education constituted by deliberation in relation with elements of conversation and open engagement. The significance of deliberation is that one values the narratives, stories or points of view of others as a means of what Hountondji (2002: 81) considers to be "facilitating dialogue", while "moderating, on occasion, the excessive passion of the most aggressive opponents". Hountondji (2002: 139) contends that deliberation happens through an acknowledgement of the importance of criticism on the basis of detailed analysis and assessment of the viewpoints of others. One is not willing to engage in a conversation but through only "conscious rationality" (Hountondji 2002), which he associates with being critically aware of and evaluative of the viewpoints of others. Such a practice of deliberation within a MacIntyre (1994) sense connected to the virtue of conversational justice implies that students are critically inclined to accept and re-evaluate the viewpoints and narratives of others, which may assist them (students) as a community in developing plausible solutions to practical problems and concerns permeating African society. In other words, deliberation lends itself implicitly to the achievement of pedagogic justice. If there is no deliberative engagement among students and educators, there cannot be pedagogic justice as the latter depends on deepening human conversations through listening, scrutiny and seeing the viewpoints of others. When students and educators do not see the points of view of others, it seems highly unlikely that engagement would be deepened and, by implication, pedagogic justice forthcoming. Pedagogic justice is inextricably linked to seeing the points of view of others in relation to which participants can make evaluative judgements or even repudiate others' truth claims.

In addition, Gyekye (1997: 29) recognises the importance of rationality and logic. Gyekye (1997: 29) posits that rationality is equated with a form of culture dependence in which less formal rules are required if people want to engage deliberatively in dialogue. Gyekye's (1997: 29) notion of culture-dependent rationality can be linked to a critical re-evaluation of the ideas of students and an intellectual pursuit related to the practical problems and concerns of African society by suggesting innovative and creative ways of thought and action. The idea of less formal rules of rationality has some connection with the recognition that human articulations are not always persuasive and that people's views can be considered as truncated in the sense that they (people) did not draw upon more convincing arguments in defence of their articulations. It is not that articulations are not acceptable or do not meet the demands of reasoning. Rather, the plausibility of the arguments is perhaps too unconvincing. In other words, the application of less formal rules of argumentation does not have to do with a misrecognition of argumentation, but rather means that argumentation seems to be less rigorous on account of a lack of justification. The point is that drawing on less formal rules can be considered as allowing even less developed points of view to be expressed and not that argumentation should be subjected to something lesser vis-à-vis rational articulations. According to such an idea of rationality, namely through the notion of communitarianism and, by implication, the deliberative proffering of reasons, Letseka (2000: 182) posits an interesting account of an African philosophy of education in that "it should provide rational tools for critical reflections on personal wellbeing or human flourishing, on communal ethics and how these [reasons] ought to impact on human conduct". Letseka (2000) avers that an African philosophy of education should provide students with rational tools—being able to reason persuasively and sensibly as a means of contesting one's own personal well-being as an atomistic being through welfare, security and comfort and, instead, as part of a community in disrupting the major socio-economic problems influencing the community at large. Simply put, practical reasoners should not act as atomistic individuals because of the emphasis of atomism on self-centred and narcissistic autonomy.

By inculcating in students the criticality and desire to disrupt and by implication to think differently about socio-economic problems beyond classroom practices, students are initiated into a discourse of pedagogic justice. Pedagogic justice can be realised through encouraging students and educators to engage in deliberative action because, by doing so, opportunities could be created to see things differently through questioning and debate, and to disrupt the socio-economic and political problems that affect a particular community. In this regard, deliberative action, as espoused throughout Teaching for Change, potentially offers students and educators opportunities to think anew about their societal concerns. Deliberative encounters connect with openness and reflexivity. In turn, such encounters could advance more humane, caring and just human relations. Without asking one another to proffer justifications for their points of view and without looking again and again at certain articulations, deliberative engagement would be absent. Unless deliberative engagement is present, the possibility of acting humanely and caringly would simply not be there. By implication, pedagogic justice would not be possible.

Furthermore, the question regarding how deliberation could be cultivated through an African philosophy of education premised on MacIntyre's

(1999) virtue of conversational justice may further resonate with the notion of inclusion. Biesta (2009: 107) claims that, as individuals, if "we can become even more attentive to otherness and difference we will eventually reach a situation of total democratic inclusion"—a situation in which democracy has become "normal". By implication, the need to respect and value each individual's contributions to society, where democracy would ensure that those who could make meaningful contributions to contemporary African society are included, is premised on the notion of inclusion. We refer to the term "inclusion" as it can be closely linked with deliberation, as both are integral components of a democratic African philosophy of education. Biesta (2009: 105) avers that the question regarding inclusion in deliberation is not so much about who should be included—although the latter concern is important as well—but rather about who is capable of participating efficaciously in conversation through deliberation. Young (2002, cited in Biesta 2009: 105) suggests other modes of political communication that should be added to the process of deliberation through the promotion of "respect" and "trust", that is, through conversational justice, and such understanding should be made possible across structural and cultural differences. Young (2002, cited in Biesta 2009: 105) goes on to mention that "greeting or public acknowledgement" is important for those who have difficulty in recognising others included in the discussion, especially where there are conflicting interests, opinions and social perspectives that influence the parties involved.

In the light of the aforementioned, Letseka (2000: 189) contends that the development and inculcation of deliberative skills in young individuals will certainly play a significant role in promoting and supporting this type of communal interdependence and concern with the welfare of others. Letseka (2000: 189) deems that this is the type of interdependence that accentuates the fundamental principle governing traditional African life. In this regard, there is an affinity for a mutual interdependence between an individual and the community. In such a relationship, the individual depends on others within a community just as much as others in the community depend on him or her. Letseka (2000: 191) further claims that the purpose of an African philosophy of education should be to promote *ubuntu*, cooperative skills, interpersonal skills and human flourishing. Letseka (2000: 191) proposes that such a pragmatic, experiential approach to education, during which students learn by example, by living in communities of people who are endowed with such capacities and by interacting with them regularly through deliberation, may cultivate transformative and conscientised students. If we describe Letseka's (2000) thoughts of an African philosophy of education through deliberation underpinned by conversational justice, it seems that deliberation ought to cultivate spaces for critically questioning one another's perspectives, allowing for a reflexive re-evaluation of the position one holds in a spirit of openness and for re-evaluating one's earlier position in the light of new information in quite a creative and innovative way. The latter understanding of deliberative action underscored by openness, reflexivity and constant re-evaluation, is invariably connected to the practice of moving towards some sense of pedagogic justice specifically and *ubuntu* justice generally.

Within the notion of communitarianism in relation to MacIntyre's (1999) idea of conversational justice, we contend that an African philosophy of education aims to signify the willingness and ability to evaluate the reasons or ideas of others, without dismissing their subjective views as being unworthy of consideration. The argument that an African philosophy of education invokes and advocates is that deliberation through conversational justice encourages others to develop the capacities of re-evaluation and adjustment of what others consider to be adequately good reasons for acting, and for imagining alternative possibilities that will enable them to (re)educate themselves rationally (MacIntyre 1999: 83). In this regard, an African philosophy of education cannot be detached from rational thinking because rational thinking involves what Habermas (1996: 107) purports as socially embedded human activities, which nurture some form of "rational action" and in which individuals engage. Such rational discourse, as Habermas (1996: 10) maintains, occurs under democratic conditions of communication that should include an "attempt to reach an understanding over problematic claims that enable the free processing of topics and contributions, information and reasons in the public space constituted by illocutionary obligation" (Habermas 1996: 10).

Habermas (1984) posits that the practice of deliberation can be linked to emancipation and a criticism of texts that involve signifying the culmination of inconsistent arguments as well as rejecting the dismissal of others' arguments. For Habermas (1984), emancipatory action involves listening to others' arguments, and identifying inconsistent arguments in texts, that is, acts of deliberation. In other words, individuals become liberated on the basis of offering free, equal and uncoerced speech, to which Habermas (1984) refers as ideal speech that could contribute to the emancipation of social action. Such emancipatory action would be critical and transformative—that is, action that could engender inclusive and deliberative exchanges among individuals in contemporary African society (Habermas 1984). What follows from the aforementioned views of democracy, inclusion and emancipation is that an African philosophy of education constituted by communitarianism cannot materialise without invoking deliberation through the virtue of conversational justice in the social, economic and cultural spheres of African society. Hence, if individuals show respect and become polite in their interactions, in other words, in their acts of deliberation, through an African of philosophy of education, the quest towards reconciliation would be more attainable than under acts in which dismissiveness of others' points of view hold sway. The point is that deliberative action connects strongly with a MacIntyrean notion of conversational justice on the basis that openness, reflexivity and a reconsideration of the views of others constitute what it means to act deliberatively. In doing the latter, educators and students would be well on the path of cultivating a sense of pedagogic justice because through deliberative engagement, acts such a seeing the points of others, looking at things differently and allowing for an acknowledgement that others have something worthwhile to say, would invariably enhance the opportunities to bring about societal change. It is the cultivation of societal change that connects the enactment of deliberative action among educators and students to the idea of *ubuntu* justice. However, without learning to be responsive to pedagogic justice, as advocated through Teaching for Change, it is difficult to think how the possibility that *ubuntu* justice will be realised.

4.3 Responsibility Through the Virtue of Truthfulness: Pursuing Pedagogic Justice

According to MacIntyre (1999: 149), a practical reasoner is a person who uses explanation and justification to advance the cause of an individual in relation to other members of society. MacIntyre (1999: 150) advocates for dialogue among different people premised on the virtue of truthfulness in which, as an individual, one is accountable or responsible to others. Likewise, MacIntyre (1999: 150) claims that for individuals to engage in dialogue one individual has to understand the other's point of view, so that the concerns of the other to which the individual responds in giving an account of his or her actions are in fact genuinely the concerns of the other. If one is successful in so doing, one then becomes "able to speak with the other's voice and, if the conversation between [the group] is sufficiently extended through time and is wide-ranging enough in its subject matter", then, as MacIntyre (1999:150) claims, people as a group will be "able to speak with the voice of the other systematically". In other words, people will be "able to assert, question and [be able] to prescribe in the light of the other's conception of our common good", that is, people have to perform acts of responsibility (MacIntyre 1999: 150). In this sense, through responsibility of one's actions premised on the virtue of truthfulness, individuals will have learned not only "how to speak to others [acts of deliberation] but also how to speak for others [acts of representing the voiceless]" (MacIntyre 1999: 150). As part of a community, in the home or in the workplace or in other shared activity, the individual and others will, in the words of MacIntyre (1999: 150), have become "friends".

In the light of MacIntyre's (1999) notion towards "becoming friends" within contemporary African society, we draw on a communitarian understanding of "friendship". At the heart of communitarianism, as Ogunbanjo and Van Bogaert (2005: 51) aver, is the "individual [being] embedded in a context of social relationship and interdependence". As "friend", one displays acts of generosity, compassion, solidarity and social well-being, which are considered the ethical values embedded within a communitarianism conception of friendship (Ogunbanjo and van Bogaert

2005: 51) in much the same way that *ubuntu* justice advocates for caring, compassion, autonomy and restoration. In fact, it is an individual's moral obligation to behave in a manner befitting the values, beliefs and ideologies of the group that make the individual morally aware of his or her actions. In this sense, the individual can be said to be conscientised through the virtue of truthfulness of his or her thoughts and actions in contemporary African society. Through this conscientisation, as Freire (1970) claims, empowerment of the individual and group in African society is certainly important for transformative change. More specifically, conscientisation becomes more than "learning to perceive social, political, and economic contradictions" but instead requires of one to "take action against the oppressive elements of reality" (Freire 2006: 35). Through an African philosophy of education premised on truthfulness, calls for a re-examining of oneself within a community to increase solidarity among the oppressed are enhanced. This is because an African philosophy of education accentuates responsibility in which members of a community, as Gyekye (1997: 42) expounds, "are expected to show concern for the well-being of one another, to do what they can to advance the common good, and generally to participate in the community life". More specifically, members "have intellectual and ideological as well as emotional attachments to their shared values and goals, as long as they cherish them, they are ever ready to pursue and defend them" (Gyekye 1995: 42).

Within the notion of responsibility for end goals, Rawls (1980: 545) claims that individuals as rational beings are responsible for forming "their aims and ambitions in the light of what they can reasonably expect". In this regard, people recognise that the "weight of their claims is not given by the strength or intensity of their wants and desires" (Rawls 1980: 545). Within the Rawlsian idea of (social) justice, this would infer that it is the responsibility of social structures in societies to provide a fair share of opportunities and resources for individuals to function efficaciously in the economy. The Rawlsian assumption that societal justice can best be achieved if individuals are afforded equal opportunities on the basis of giving preference to the least advantaged is certainly a misconception, which may undermine the very idea of (social) justice in African society in some instances. For instance, one might be appointed in a position that requires cognitive and critical capacities; however, when the position is offered to someone who is considered least advantaged but who might not have the capacity to perform the work functionally, such a person would not ably contribute to, but rather, exacerbate (under)development. The Rawlsian notion that societal justice is determined by the act of allocating resources to the least advantaged in society in fact heightens inequality because the acceptance of such resources makes the recipients reliant on welfare institutions in society and therefore less committed to self-sustainability. If equality is difficult to attain through the provision of resources, then it implies that equality should be seen as a practice that does not rely on receiving, but rather, by what one does—that is, acts of responsibility through truthfulness.

While Letseka (2000: 183) posits that traditional African life encourages altruism, it does not condone "laziness, idleness, or encouraging people to rest on their laurels and do nothing to improve their welfare and opportunities in life, secure in the knowledge that their family and the community at large would be there to take care of their individual problems". Instead, communitarianism commensurate with truthfulness requires of one to display a great deal of moral sensitivity and expenditure of moral effort for the benefit of the community in society (Gyekye 1997: 66). In turn, society will thrive through a high sense of morality of the individual (Gyekye 1997: 66). This is because communitarian moral theory, as Gyekye (1997: 66) claims, considers responsibility through truthfulness as an important principle of morality. Moreover, responsibility requires interdependence in which the individual acts in unison with society by making sacrifices in the accomplishment of his or her deeds. Through communitarianism, equity in society may further be achieved when certain minimum standards for treatment are adhered to and when individuals' sacrifices are taken into account to secure equitable treatment (Le Grand 1991: 42). A person is treated equitably if his or her needs are attended to minimally—that is, if he or she does not make unreasonable demands in terms of his or her needs, and if he or she has attended to his or her own needs. By implication, individuals in African society should not just be given everything they want in the name of welfare through the social structures in society, but should also contribute to attending to their own needs. If this happens, they are treated equitably and they would experience equity too. Hence, the communitarian attitude towards responsibility is mandated by one's willingness to seek alternative means to improve on one's existential societal conditions, rather than seeking others to resolve such conditions. The point is that responsibility comes with individual effort in harmony with that of the community.

Although responsibility signifies that one displays a caring attitude or conduct towards the well-being of another person or other persons, helping others in distress and not harming others, there are some limits to such a moderate communitarianism (Gyekye 1997: 66). Gyekye (1997: 69) argues that the individual as "an autonomous, self-assertive being, should, within his/her limits, care for his/her own well-being or needs just as s(he) cares for the needs of others". Gyekye (1997: 69) posits that through moderate communitarianism, the individual's rationality, moral consciousness of (and truthfulness about) the needs of others (the group) are invoked, and he or she acknowledges that the "intrinsic worth of the individual" should not be dismissed as the altruistic nature of the individual "cannot obliterate the responsibilities to the self". In other words, through moderate communitarianism, the group should also seek to improve its existing societal conditions provided that the group's minimum needs are met. Communitarianism premised on interdependence does not justify dependence on an individual to dismiss the individual's responsibilities in uplifting him- or herself in society, neither does the group expect of an individual to ameliorate solely the socio-economic problems facing the group in contemporary African society. As Hountondji (2002: 258) argues, responsibility rather means:

> [C]ontributing together [through social cohesion], in a thoughtful [or rational] manner, in a spirit of solidarity and sharing [through social cohesion], to the building of the common edifice, so that the germs of irrationality and progressively ignorance and poverty will be eliminated forever from planet earth.

What follows from the aforementioned views on responsibility is that an African philosophy of education constituted by moderate communitarianism commensurate with truthfulness implies that one is rational and truthful in one's decisions so as not to disregard one's potential. Neither does such a notion expect of groups to depend on one's unique qualities. Rather, the group and the individual succeed through a spirit of sharing their roles and responsibilities in society in which the minimum needs of both parties are met to cultivate a spirit of equity. By implication, exercising one's responsibility in harmony with the group to which one belongs is considered a way of practising moderate communitarianism. One does not ignore one's caring for and, by implication, responsibility to others in the same way as others recognise and enact their responsibilities in the service of one. In other words, responsibility is an act of mutuality whereby both the individual and the group could assume responsibility for one another. The upshot of such a view of responsibility is that *ubuntu* justice is not just dependent on the act of an individual but equally and collectively on the acts of others in the respective community as well. An individual does not merely act truthfully towards herself or himself but also in the interest of the wider community. When *ubuntu* justice manifests in people's practices, the concerns of the individual and the community are procured and advanced collectively. It is not only the case that others respond to one in the pursuit of one's needs, but also that one is responsive to others in the quest of attending to others' collective interests. This is the kind of moderate communitarian view of an individual in relation to the community where it is espoused throughout Teaching for Change. In a similar manner, the concept of *ubuntu* justice and, by implication, pedagogic justice, is articulated without accentuating the misconception that African philosophy of education prejudices a sense of community. Rather, the autonomy of an individual is exercised in a community without simply abandoning the autonomous actions of the individual.

In sum, by presenting ourselves to one another, both individuals and members of a group and/or community are engaged in mutual action. When we present ourselves to one another in mutuality, we envisage solving our problems collectively in the interest of both ourselves and others. Such a form of *ubuntu* justice has implications for pedagogic justice in the sense that both educators and students would be attentive to one another both in mutuality and in the recognition that they (educators and students) could be engaged in difference towards possibility. This brings us to an examination of risk-oriented action as an instance of pedagogic justice.

4.4 Risk-Oriented Action Through the Virtue of Courage: Towards Pedagogic Justice

MacIntyre (2007: 122) posits that courage, as a quality of individuals, is necessary to sustain a household and a community. This is because courage is equated with someone on whom reliance can be placed (MacIntyre 2007: 123). In this regard, courage is an important constituent of friendship (MacIntyre 2007: 123). We argue that Jacques Derrida's (1997) notion of friendship in which human relationships could be nurtured through acts of risk taking, is commensurate with MacIntyre's (1981) virtue of courage. More specifically, our argument in defence of risk-oriented action premised on a MacIntyrian virtue of courage resonates with the Derrida (1997) idea of friendship, which may hopefully lead to deliberative actions involving challenging, undermining and disagreeing with one's friends. MacIntyre's (1981) virtue of courage may further be linked to Burbules's (1995: 93) defence of fallibilism whereby a person is "not to be afraid of making mistakes, because it is only through the discovery of error, through some processes of falsification that we are driven by change". This is because a person who acts with courage is one who shows concern for him- or herself and others if he or she recognises when he or she is wrong and, more importantly being able to admit it to others. Erring is a fallibility of all human beings. However, humans ought to be courageous enough to concede their mistakes with the possibility that they can learn from their errors.

In the light of the aforementioned, when individuals engage in risk-oriented action they are not dismissive of the other's point of view, but rather appreciative of the intellectual engagement that may ensue. In fact, through risk-oriented action, the possibility exists for individuals to act with concern and to care for the other (friends) with the hope that such forms of democratic interactions would evoke both students' potentialities. We therefore infer that when individuals produce arguments, they are not afraid of being corrected by their friends. They take risks without the possibility of ridicule or castigation. When individuals' points of view are modified, it is not to say that they are obligated to do so; rather, they are oriented to explore alternative points of view on the basis of their inclinations towards taking risks. Such an idea of risk taking is connected to a Derridan conception of friendship through love or *philia*. For Derrida (1997: 8), "friendship consists in loving". Moreover, for Derrida (1997: 8), friendship entails the "act of loving, before being in the state of being loved". In this regard, friendship constitutes both an act and an activity, or as Derrida (1997: 8) pertinently states, "someone must love in order to know what loving means; then, and only then can one know [or experience] what being loved means". As individuals, we feel ourselves loving others when we care for them in a way that evokes their potentialities in order that they come up with possibilities of which we might not even have thought. Friendship expects of individuals in society that they possess feelings of love for others through acts of trust, empathy, honesty, mutual understanding and altruism without the expectation that they we ought to be loved in return. In this way, the friendship and love (for that matter) we exhibit are unconditional because there is no expectation that one's giving of love (friendship) ought to be reciprocated, at least coercively.

The interpersonal bonds established as a result of friendship are commensurate with the virtue of courage or *pistis*, as Derrida (1997: 15) posits. By implication, Derrida (1997: 15) asserts that one may have the inherent confidence in those being led towards taking risks in society without knowing in advance what the outcomes might be. In light of Derrida's (1997) notion of friendship through courage, the latter is important in MacIntyre's (2007: 122) view, not simply as a virtue of individuals, but rather as a virtue necessary to sustain a community. For MacIntyre (2007: 123), whereas the courage of one's friend assures one of that friend's power necessary to aid oneself in the community, it is one's friend's fidelity that assures one of his or her will (Macintyre 2007: 123). Therefore, as MacIntyre (2007: 123) contends, fidelity is "the basic guarantee of its unity". Whereas friendship exemplifies one's power through one's capability and capacity, it is one's will, through acts of desire or decree, that assists others in society. Such acts of friendship may further be expounded in the Nguni proverb *Umuntu ngumuntu ngabantu* signifying "I am because we are". This is because *ubuntu* "inspires us to expose ourselves to others, to encounter the difference of their humanness so as to inform and enrich our own" (Sindane 1994: 8–9). For Sindane (1994), while being clear on our own views and positions, courage requires of us also to possess the will and power to listen and share in the views of others, and at times alter our points of view and positions if reasonably persuaded. In this regard, risk-oriented action in relation to *ubuntu* implies that one may foresee opportunities for knowledge sharing and knowledge co-construction with others. As *ubuntu* perceives human need, dignity and interest as of fundamental importance and concern to society (Letseka 2000: 188), risk-oriented action premised on courage may evoke one's potentiality towards disrupting acts of dishonesty, corruption and other forms of wrongdoing by voicing one's dissatisfaction with such forms of human injustice in society.

Considering the above, an African philosophy of education ought to produce individuals in communities who embrace and value *ubuntu*, and who would hopefully be more inclined towards disrupting the social injustices in society, more specifically inequity and inequality. Bearing in mind that human co-existence requires of individuals to perform certain social and moral roles, duties, obligations and commitments (Gyekye 2004: 364), communitarian engagement would be possible. Through acts of solidarity, interdependence, cooperation, compassion and reciprocity, which we aver should be linked to acts of friendship, are what Gyekye (2004: 364) refers to as considerations that "elevate the notions of duties [responsibilities] to a priority status in the whole enterprise of communitarian life". For Gyekye (1997: 118), rights to equal treatment in society, to land or property, to socialise and associate freely with others and to have freedom of speech are equated to communitarian acts of humanity. Letseka (2000: 185) holds that individuals living a fulfilled life are those persons who are reasonably well fed, clothed, housed, in good health, loved and secure. Such persons are able to make a conscious effort to treat others with fairness or equity and humanness—more specifically with *ubuntu* justice—because they in turn are expected to be treated in the same manner. In this regard, an African philosophy of education is primarily aimed at achieving *ubuntu* justice to enable Africans to make socially conscious decisions for the betterment of African society on the basis of acts of friendship, that is, love and fidelity.

Through an African philosophy of education, individuals are not primarily involved in acts of deliberation and acts of responsibility but also through risk-oriented action, which may establish possibilities where others through the virtue of courage can come up with ideas and understandings not thought of previously. In other words, through risk-oriented action, the possibility exists for people to develop plausible meanings irrespective of what others may want from the encounter. In this regard, individuals in contemporary African society ought to be encouraged towards adopting a risk-oriented action approach through acts of friendship and *ubuntu* in attending to the interests of themselves and others in the community. People inclined towards *ubuntu* would be "caring, humble, thoughtful, considerate, understanding, wise, generous, hospitable, socially mature, socially sensitive, virtuous and blessed [that is, all acts of friendship]" (Le Roux 2000: 43). In this regard, *ubuntu* in relation to the virtue of courage may contribute towards the cultivation of human relationships aimed at enhancing human dignity, reciprocity and human value necessary for social cohesion and unity in Africa. Considering that *ubuntu* justice ought to be associated with the virtues of courage, human dignity, reciprocally deliberative engagement and social interconnectedness, it follows that pedagogic justice would alter relationships among educators and students in a positive way. It is to such a discussion that we now turn to.

4.5 Pedagogic Justice Through Deliberation, Responsibility and Risk-Oriented Action

Our pedagogic activities through Teaching for Change are linked to the cultivation of pedagogic justice that can be associated with deliberative, responsible and risk-oriented action. Doing the unexpected and going against the grain are forms of human engagement that connect with the potential of pedagogic justice to be realised. To go against the grain implies that people have to do things they are not inclined to do. It could be that rival ethnic groups might not want to engage with one another and the perpetuation of violent action against one another would be relentless. However, being drawn to *ubuntu* justice implies that even rival ethnic groups would deliberatively engage because they want to do something different or unexpected for the sake of curbing violence in their society. They do the unexpected by acting responsibly and taking the risk of listening to one another irrespective of how challenging the situation might be. It is a risk to listen to another person if one's life is at stake. One might not be aware of the other's intention and, hence, the willingness one shows towards listening is a risk. Such a notion of *ubuntu* justice also affects pedagogic justice where students and educators are prepared to take risks, and through deliberative engagement they endeavour to act responsibly in association with one another. It is not that listening to and articulating views in the presence of one another can be conceived of as risk-free, especially in the light of ongoing ridicule and resentment among people. It is a risk, however, that people are willing to take on the grounds that the possibility that violence will subside or be eradicated might just ensue. Furthermore, it is worthwhile to take the human risk to engage with one another irrespective of how irreconcilable situations might seem to be. For society, the advantage is that a human predicament might just be resolved, which would be a risk worth taking.

In the main, an African philosophy of education constitutes three practices in a MacIntyrian sense: deliberation through conversational justice; responsibility (accountability) through truthfulness; and risk-oriented action through courage. This brings us to the question in terms of how an African philosophy of education could contribute towards pedagogic justice in contemporary African society. A socially just education system advocates human agency and enables the self-development and self-determination of all its citizens (Pendlebury and Enslin 2004: 40). Such a socially just education system provides opportunities and support for all students to exercise the range of functions necessary for developing their mature adult capabilities (Pendlebury and Enslin 2004: 40). A socially just education system reduces or, better, abolishes structural forms of oppression that restrict people's access to resources and opportunities for developing and exercising their capacities or capabilities for living a decent human life (Pendlebury and Enslin 2004: 40). Furthermore, a socially just education system excludes no children from access to schooling (that is, it respects the equal right to education for all); and excludes no children from access to learning within schools (thus guarding against internal exclusion) (Pendlebury and Enslin 2004: 40). In this regard, pedagogic justice within a socially just education system is a means of disrupting acts of oppression in multiple forms with the aim of taking corrective action in the classroom as a means of preparing students for the social, cultural and economic spheres of society. The latter potentially offers ways to transform the cycles of oppression permeating the African context.

In the light of the above, an African philosophy of education as a pragmatic approach towards cultivating pedagogic justice is threefold. First, through deliberation premised on conversational justice, an African philosophy of education has the capacity to cultivate within students the ability to understand and share their experiences of the societal or structural roots and causes of inequitable societal conditions and problems that they may have encountered. These include but are not limited to instances of xenophobia, racism, sexism, homophobia and their social, cultural and economic status within contemporary African society through acts of deliberation. More specifically, an African philosophy of education has the capacity to develop in students the ability to listen to what others (students) have to say no matter how ill-informed their points of view might seem to be. This is because an African philosophy of education encourages deliberatively democratic engagements in social practices and institutions such as schools, universities and colleges, premised on developing human agency, self-development and self-determination. In essence, deliberation framed within an African philosophy of education allows for critical and reflexive reasoning. Through such forms of reasoning, the possibility is there for students to be more appreciative while listening attentively in conversations with others (students), conversations that hold much promise for mediating equitable learning in a pedagogic encounter. Moreover, teaching within contemporary African society along the lines of an African philosophy of education has a better chance of cultivating pedagogic justice if enacted along the lines of deliberation through conversational justice.

Second, one common understanding of pedagogic justice is that it explicitly recognises the disparities in societal opportunities, resources and long-term outcomes among marginalised groups in society (Shakman et al. 2007). In order to ascertain the relationship between the aims of an African philosophy of education and pedagogic justice, we turn our attention to the seminal thoughts of Paulo Freire (2006). Freire (2006:

47) purports that pedagogic justice creates opportunities for students to achieve freedom that is considered both intellectual and physical. Freire (2006: 77) refers to these intellectual and physical freedoms as the "indispensable condition for the quest for human completion". For Freire (2006), every student has a specific identity, and the educator needs to develop experiences with, and not for, students, thus integrating their experiences and voices into the educational experience itself. This is why we are attracted to pedagogic justice through an African philosophy of education to take into account the identities and situations within which students find themselves. In this way, students would hopefully be better oriented towards autonomous learning where critical reflection and authentic thinking are attainable (Freire 2006: 77). Hence, students can be empowered as responsible students in their own learning in contemporary African society.

Third, the importance of establishing conditions for the empowerment of students has some connection with what it means to cultivate pedagogic justice through an African philosophy of education. Schools, universities and colleges must be organised along the notion of an African philosophy of education, taking into account that pedagogic justice is most appropriately learned in a democratic setting in which deliberation is encouraged, responsibility is enacted, and risk-oriented action manifests itself. Such practices framed within an African philosophy of education would hopefully nurture qualities within students, such as democratic engagement, respectful cooperation, and the enactment of people's social and moral consciousness. Schools, universities and colleges as the social institutions of civic virtue have an important role to embark on in cultivating acts of virtue, namely conversational justice, truthfulness and courage, particularly in the light of escalating levels of xenophobia, prejudice, crime and insecurity, which seem to permeate and threaten the fabric of African society. Therefore, it is necessary for students to practise skills in pedagogic encounters pertaining to the virtues that we have linked to three practices, namely deliberation, responsibility and risk-oriented action commensurate with an African philosophy of education. By implication, students will be able to learn these skills, which will become instilled in their minds as part of their everyday lives in contemporary African society. In this regard, our schools, universities and colleges need to nurture students who can act socially and justly and assume responsibility to make choices along with others. We contend that exercising a communitarian notion of an African philosophy of education further unlocks the capacity of an African culture in which students are able to contribute towards deliberation, responsibility and risk-oriented action. Hence, the responsibility of educators to provide education that can transform students into democratic citizens might hopefully lead to deep transformation and, by implication, social change in African society.

4.6 Summary

The social institutions, namely, universities, schools and colleges, should teach and engage students in what it means to engender deliberation through conversational justice, responsibility through truthfulness, and risk-oriented action through courage, that is, virtues connected with the achievement of social change in contemporary African society. More specifically, we have to listen carefully to what we are told about our own inadequacies and to reply with the same carefulness through the virtue of conversational justice; we have to learn to recognise what is due to whom through the virtue of truthfulness; and we have to be prepared to take whatever self-endangering risks are demanded along the way through the virtue of courage. Without these virtues, pedagogic justice cannot resist the corrupting power of some educational institutions whereby students, and educators for that matter, could possibly succumb to doctrinaire thinking and uncritical attitudes on account of the prevalence of complacency. Furthermore, an African philosophy of education aims at contributing to the cultivation of pedagogic justice, in particular at empowering students to participate in their own development and in contributing towards the economic, political and social uplifting of communities as a means of eliminating the various socio-economic challenges permeating the African continent. Our contention is that students and university educators ought to be, or become, deliberative, responsible and risk-oriented if they are to appropriate the values of an African philosophy of education, and hence respond to the needs and often challenging circumstances of students within contemporary African society. Considering that an African philosophy of education constituted by deliberative engagement, responsible and risk-oriented action is inextricably connected to the notion of pedagogic justice, next we examine why and how pedagogic encounters seem to be more responsive to forms of human and non-human injustice if enacted along the lines of assemblages of learning. Next, we show how assemblages of learning, through Teaching for Change, can engender more plausible pedagogic encounters that connect with the pursuit of *ubuntu* justice.

References

Biesta, G. (2009). Sporadic Democracy: Education, Democracy, and the Question of Inclusion. In G. Biesta, M. Katz, & S. Verducci (Eds.), *Education, Democracy, and the Moral Life* (pp. 101–112). Dordrecht: Springer.

Burbules, N. C. (1995). Reasonable Doubt: Toward a Postmodern Defense of Reason as an Educational Aim. In W. Kohli (Ed.), *Critical Conversations in Philosophy of Education* (pp. 82–102). New York: Routledge.

Derrida, J. (1997). *Politics of Friendship* (G. Collins, Trans.). London/ New York: Verso.

Freire, P. (1970). *Pedagogy of the Oppressed*. London: Continuum.

Freire, P. (2006). *Pedagogy of the Oppressed, 30th Anniversary Edition*. New York: Teachers College Press.

Gyekye, K. (1995). Indeterminacy, Ethnophilosophy, Linguistic Philosophy, African Philosophy. *Philosophy, 70*(273), 377–393.

Gyekye, K. (1997). *Tradition and Modernity: Philosophical Reflections on the African Experience*. Oxford: Oxford University Press.

Gyekye, K. (2004). *Beyond Cultures: Perceiving a Common Humanity*. Washington, DC: Council for Research in Values and Philosophy.

Habermas, J. (1984). *The Theory of Communicative Action, Volume. I: Reason and the Rationalization of Society*. London: Heinemann.

Habermas, J. (1996). *Between Facts and Norms: Contributions to a Discourse Theory of Law and Democracy*. Cambridge, MA: MIT Press.

Hountondji, P. (2002). *The Struggle for Meaning: Reflections on Philosophy, Culture, and Democracy in Africa*. Athens: Ohio University Center for International Studies.

Le Grand, J. (1991). Tales from the British National Health Service: Competition, Cooperation or Control? *Health Affairs, 18*(1), 27–37.

Le Roux, J. (2000). The Concept of *ubuntu*: Africa's Most Important Contribution to Multicultural Education. *Multicultural Teaching, 18*(2), 43–46.

Letseka, M. (2000). African Philosophy and Educational Discourse. In P. Higgs, N. A. G. Vokalisa, T. V. Mda, & N. T. Assié-Lumumba (Eds.), *African Voices in Education* (pp. 179–193). Cape Town: Juta.

MacIntyre, A. (1981). The Nature of the Virtues. *Hastings Center Report, 11*(2), 27–34.

MacIntyre, A. (1994). *After Virtue: A Study in Moral Theory*. London: Duckworth.

MacIntyre, A. (1999). *Dependent Rational Animals: Why Human Beings Need the Virtues*. Peru: Open Court.

MacIntyre, A. (2007). *After Virtue: A Study in Moral Theory*. Notre Dame: University of Notre Dame Press.

Mbiti, J. S. (1970). *African Religions and Philosophy*. London: Heinemann.

Ogunbanjo, G. A., & van Bogaert, D. K. (2005). Communitarianism and Communitarian Bioethics. *South African Family Practice, 47*(10), 51–53.

Oladipo, O. (1992). *The Idea of African Philosophy: A Critical Study of the Major Orientations in Contemporary African Philosophy*. Ibadan: Molecular Publishers.

Pendlebury, S., & Enslin, P. (2004). Social Justice and Inclusion in Education and Politics: The South African Case. *Journal of Education, 34*(1), 31–50.

Rawls, J. (1980). Kantian Constructivism in Moral Theory. *The Journal of Philosophy, 77*(9), 515–572.

Shakman, K., Cochran-Smith, M., Jong, C., Terrell, D., Barnatt, J., & McQuillan, P. (2007). *Reclaiming Teacher Quality: The Case for Social Justice*. Paper presented at the Annual Meeting of the American Educational Research Association, Chicago.

Sindane, J. (1994). *ubuntu and Nation Building*. Pretoria: ubuntu School of Philosophy.

5

Cultivating Assemblages of Learning: From Teaching to Learning and Back to Teaching

5.1 Introduction

In much the same way that Gilles Deleuze and Felix Guattari (1987: 3) describe the concept of a book, we conceive of Teaching for Change as "lines of flight, movements of deterritorialisation and destratification". Like Deleuze and Guattari (1987: 4), the lines of flight rupture in all directions with measurable speeds constituting an "assemblage". We shall now expound on the pedagogic notions espoused through Teaching for Change as assemblages of learning. In order to explain what Teaching for Change comprises, we need to show: first, how it functions; second, with which connection it intensifies; and third, which metamorphosis it undergoes. In this way, we examine Teaching for Change as an assemblage of learning whereby we accentuate some of the pedagogical actions as embedded in Teaching for Change.

5.2 Mapping an Assemblage

Teaching for Change functions like a map that "is open and connectable in all of its dimensions: it is detachable, reversible, susceptible to constant modification" (Deleuze and Guattari 1987: 12). Comprising four

© The Author(s) 2018
Y. Waghid et al., *Rupturing African Philosophy on Teaching and Learning*,
https://doi.org/10.1007/978-3-319-77950-8_5

interrelated themes, Teaching for Change is open and connectable in all dimensions—that is, themes one to four, dealing with African ways of knowing, doing and being, are connected with the enactment of just human action and, more specifically, *ubuntu* justice. All four themes can be detached from one another, yet offer ways towards understanding African thinking and doing. Teaching for Change is reversible in the sense that one does not have to begin with the first theme dealing with enunciations of African ways of thinking in order to complete the fourth theme on working towards human justice later. In other words, Teaching for Change is an open initiation into its fourth theme and then even to venture into themes two and three afterwards. What remains crucial about one's learning through Teaching for Change is that Teaching for Change itself is disposed to constant adjustments. It is not that Teaching for Change has been authored and designed in a particular way and thereby closed to ensuing amendments and adjustments. In this way, as with an assemblage, Teaching for Change has multiple entryways (Deleuze and Guattari 1987: 12). Teaching for Change has been authored with a specific design. However, after the first stage of implementation, our pedagogic engagements with students and ourselves resulted in particular adjustments and amendments being made to Teaching for Change, especially considering the comments we received (as educators). In addition, in the light of the positive ways in which students respond to the comments, we thought it apposite to make various curriculum changes. Even the comments of students and our responses could now be considered another entryway in terms of which students could pursue their learning. This idea of learning is ongoing and there are no limits to what is being learned relative to Teaching for Change and beyond the pedagogic encounters espoused in it.

5.3 Pedagogic Intensification

Teaching for Change surged into higher education discourse in collaboration with FutureLearn—our academic partner—in the same manner as online courses are offered through edX (the Harvard–MIT project, Coursera), the Yale University initiative, and Udacity (the Stanford model). Teaching for Change comprises course content in and about African philosophy of education with a distinct orientation towards the cultivation of *ubuntu* justice. Apart from introducing participants to a course overview, it categorises ways of doing African philosophy of education according to a particular framework of analysis with intended and unintended goals vis-à-vis the discussion of case studies. Every theme—four themes are examined over a period of a month—concludes with a summary, and engaging questions to which students can respond. In addition, the course content is delivered through short introductory videos, whereby the educator articulates some of the poignant meanings related to the following themes:

- Giving thought to African philosophy of education;
- Exploring different approaches to an African philosophy of education;
- Towards a communitarian understanding of an African philosophy of education; and
- African philosophy of education and the cultivation of *ubuntu* justice.

Unlike other MOOCs that use computer-scored assignments/essays and multiple-choice quizzes, Teaching for Change uses self-supporting discussion forums to engage and formally evaluate students' knowledge contributions. Teaching for Change is further intensified by offering a weekly podcast in response to students' comments and (mis)understandings. In a way, Teaching for Change is in itself a pedagogic invitation to engage students deliberatively, responsibly and riskfully in pedagogic encounters.

Teaching for Change comprises themes and topics of engagement that require some form of autonomous or self-directed learning. Autonomous learning is not just related to the voluntary registration of the course. Rather, autonomous learning relates to the willingness of participants to engage with concepts and meanings and, in turn, to offer forms of critical scrutiny in a deliberative way, whereby both students and educators can articulate responsible and riskful meanings. This in itself is a form of learning that is commensurate with self-directed learning. We now examine in more detail the practice of self-directed learning.

Learning through online materials, videos, writing and supporting comments of other learners and educators seems to reify the practice of self-directed learning. Teaching for Change undoubtedly offers students an opportunity to learn from its self-education platform. Of course, through the online FutureLearn platform, students pursue Teaching for Change on their own, often supported by other online students whom they hardly know and ourselves as online educators. The point about pedagogic encounters within Teaching for Change is related to experiencing what others present as they proceed through the course. It is not that students have to know exactly who other students are, for that is most likely not possible. What is possible is to get to experience one another in pedagogic ways of representation. This results in students and educators getting to encounter one another pedagogically.

The question is, What makes students' learning self-directed? In the main, self-directed learning consists of at least three aspects. First, when students post comments on a discussion forum after they have read texts and listened to videos, they can be said to have constructed their own personal learning contexts. From our reading of students' posts, we infer that students interpreted and contextualised information posted on the platform, and through their comments actually created brief thought pieces on the matter under discussion. These thought pieces eventually extended to more protracted pieces, thus accentuating what they had learned and how they made sense of what they had learned. What is quite evident from these personal learning contexts is that some students showed a maturity of mind—that is autonomy—to engage with the learning material and also responded intelligently to others' comments about their articulations. This in itself is a crucial pedagogic activity—having the capacity to learn autonomously without being restrained in doing so.

Second, most of the students' comments involve expressions of justifications. That is, students offer reasons for their claims and do not hold back in proffering their reasons. What is evident from students' justifications is that they interpret and reinterpret the sources at their disposal and come up with their own justifications even though at times, some of their justifications are ill-conceived reasons put together and then shared with others. Often these justifications elicit responses from which students and others could learn. Quite clearly, many students exercise utmost patience in responding to the reasons of others and rarely are they insulting. Yet, there are moments of provocation that do not minimise the justifications of others. In many ways, online students exercise an autonomous respect in the sense that they are prepared to engage with one another's justifications irrespective of how ill-conceived some students' justifications are at times.

Third, when online students exercise their autonomy they remain open to one another's perspectives even to the extent whereby they are provoked by one another to reach their own justifiable conclusions on what has been argued for. Curinga (2016: 372) avers that self-learning with MOOCs involves a community of learners intent on creating useful knowledge that is open to rethinking, revitalisation and radicalisation. In much the same way, we have found that students pursuing Teaching for Change constructed knowledge on the discussion forums aimed at thinking differently about their situations and resolving to improve on their situational contexts. Small wonder that Curinga (2016: 369) reminds us that MOOC supporters laud online courses for opening up education autonomously. By this, he means that MOOCs open up students to act autonomously by taking risks and by pursuing creative thinking, collaboration and sharing (Curinga 2016: 374).

5.4 Summary: Towards a Metamorphic Pedagogy

By now, as has been alluded to, it is evident that Teaching for Change is not just another online course, a collection of videos, textual enunciations and discussion posts. Teaching for Change is a course because it is bounded in terms of time and content (as has been mentioned). It is massive—over 4500 students followed two four-week courses of study over a period of two years, which involved textual readings, watching videos, posting discussion posts and responding to podcasts. Teaching for Change is open because –

- the course materials are published under an open licenced agreement between FutureLearn and Stellenbosch University;
- course activities are engaged with openly;
- the course is open to multiple contributions;
- enrolments are open; and
- the course is free of charge.

Next, we examine how metamorphic Teaching for Change actually is.

First, after we had authored, designed, developed and implemented Teaching for Change for the first time and based on the feedback and comments of students after the first run, we endeavoured to use some ideas and suggestions to adjust Teaching for Change. What was particularly rewarding for us were some of the suggestions related to our podcasts and comments. Some students felt that our feedback to students' probing questions was less rigorous in comparison with the theoretical demands of the course itself. Feedback like this during the first running of the course was used to revise and adjust the second version of Teaching for Change. Furthermore, we adhered to the same procedure in preparation for the third run of Teaching for Change in January 2018. By theoretically expanding the course, we tweaked it in such a way that more substantiated claims have been used to justify particular claims. Through a process of reflective practice, we amended our feedback posted on discussion forms and also adapted our podcasts to be theoretically more responsive to students' queries. In line with Morwenna Griffiths's (2009: 12) explication of reflective practice, we continually checked and adjusted Teaching for Change, recognising participants' constructive contributions to improving Teaching for Change.

Second, the alteration we envisaged with Teaching for Change can only be inferred from the comments that students offered. This would give us some understanding of how students internalised concepts espoused, and how they began to think differently about their own contextual issues. Of course, it would be rather premature to claim that alteration has occurred among students. However, by examining discussion posts, one can ascertain that alteration among students, even though just in articulation, is in the making. We are by no means claiming that Teaching for Change is not without its critics. However, by drawing on selected comments, we learn that students have been opened up to thoughts in reflexive ways. That is, they could ponder over issues and even enter into controversy about some issues. By implication, students learn from one another's perspectives in ways that are pedagogically enriching. Some students are specifically intrigued by a defence of *ubuntu* justice as the *raison d'être* of pedagogic encounters of a deliberative, responsible and risky kind as espoused in the previous chapter.

Third, metamorphosis is not just concerned about pushing the boundaries towards change but also with what Derrida (1978: 125) refers to as the alterity of the other. Here, alterity refers to what one or the other could be on account of his or her freedom (Derrida 1978: 138). For instance, students do not merely try to understand our course content and what is different in the course material; they are also prepared to be moved from their own assumptions, presuppositions and certitudes about the course. Similarly, we as educators are prepared to listen to students' comments on and about our work to the extent that they (students) share things that we might not have thought of before. In other words, our alterity has been moved towards an appreciation of that which we might not have considered before. That is, we have been enriched through an ongoing transformation, especially having been open to both one another and an unexpected, incalculable alterity. By gleaning from some of the comments of students, it is evident that their alterity is accentuated through an appreciation of the improbable, which at the same time has infinitely moved them.

In sum, mapping, intensifying and metamorphosing Teaching for Change are practices that interconnect with one another to produce assemblages of learning. These assemblages have mostly opened up students and educators to act autonomously yet riskfully, and also reflectively with the possibility that we (students and educators alike) might experience an alterity—and rupturing our course materials in relation to what is still to come. Following Deleuze and Guattari (1987: 23),

[An] assemblage establishes connections between certain multiplicities drawn from each of these orders, so that a book [on Teaching for Change] has no sequel nor the world as its object nor one of several authors as its subject.

Teaching for Change comprises assemblages of learning on the basis of which students engaged with meanings to the extent that they endeavoured to extend and by implication co-construct meanings of concepts. Students exercised their autonomy as they embarked on taking risks and as they reflected on concepts and explications with the possibility to understand and see things differently. Even if their previously held understandings were criticised, they showed a willingness to engage with ideas anew in recognition that things could, of course, be altered. In addition, it did not surprise them when they encountered new meanings as a consequence of their expectation to be prepared for the unimaginable, the unexpected. What is quite pertinent to this discussion is that their pedagogic assumptions about particular concepts have been ruptured—that is, their understandings and reflections on meanings gave rise to new meanings, which they could relate to their own socio-economic and politico-pedagogic situations and encounters. In a way, Teaching for Change stirred them up to find alternative ways of looking at and remedying real-life experiences known to them. In a way, their affinity to *ubuntu* justice should not be underestimated, as the lines of flight they pursued opened up new assemblages of learning, which we as educators could not have known in advance.

References

Curinga, M. X. (2016). The MOOC and the Multitude. *Educational Theory, 66*(3), 369–387.

Deleuze, G., & Guattari, F. (1987). *A Thousand Plateau: Capitalism and Schizophrenia* (B. Massumi, Trans.). Minneapolis/London: University of Minnesota Press.

Derrida, J. (1978). *Writing and Difference* (A. Bass Trans.). Chicago: University of Chicago Press.

Griffiths, M. (2009). Action Research for/as/Mindful of Social Justice. In S. E. Noffke & B. Somekh (Eds.), *The SAGE Handbook of Educational Action Research* (pp. 85–98). Washington, DC: SAGE.

6

Designing and Implementing a Course on African Philosophy of Education: Cultivating Cosmopolitan Justice

6.1 Introduction

We were asked to initiate our institution's first ever massive open online course (MOOC). After several discussions, we agreed that African philosophy of education, more specifically, 'Teaching for Change: An African Philosophical Perspective' would be an appropriate MOOC to begin with, considering that Teaching for Change would be the first of its kind on African philosophy of education. Already, the idea of an African philosophy of education is considered problematic as it is erroneously and unjustifiably assumed that African traditions and cultures cannot be associated with a discourse as demanding and rigorous as philosophy of education. On the contrary, this is not our view, as every community or all communities for that matter have a philosophy and educational experience to share. African philosophy of education is thus a term we consider significant for relating a story on Africans' ways of thinking, being and doing. In other words, an African philosophy of education accentuates the traditions, ideologies, cultures and narratives associated with diverse peoples on the African continent, and a philosophy of education from Africa would not be unrealistic at all.

© The Author(s) 2018
Y. Waghid et al., *Rupturing African Philosophy on Teaching and Learning*,
https://doi.org/10.1007/978-3-319-77950-8_6

Together we contrived, designed and authored Teaching for Change with a focus on what constitutes African philosophy of education, and how its rationale points towards the cultivation of *ubuntu* justice. Subsequently, we endeavoured to connect the notion of *ubuntu* justice to democratic justice and, as shown in the previous chapter, to pedagogic justice. In this chapter, we connect the idea of *ubuntu* justice to current understandings of cosmopolitan justice on the grounds (as we shall show) that autonomous, reflexive and responsible actions are relevant to both forms of justice. In what follows, we offer an account of Teaching for Change and why and how cosmopolitan justice, as an instance of *ubuntu* justice, can be considered a desirable outcome of such a course.

6.2 Reconstituting African Philosophy of Education

African philosophy of education is constituted by at least two notions: African philosophy and education. First, African philosophy is considered an activity of the mind that focuses on forms of inquiry specifically related to the African condition. To talk about African philosophy as an activity of the mind is not new. Paulin J. Hountondji (1993: 63, 65), an African scholar, posits that African philosophy involves promoting and sustaining unconstrained discussion about Africa's problems on the part of those geographically situated and related to the continent in relation to literature about Africa and the Western world. The aforementioned view of African philosophy seems to underscore Teaching for Change in the sense that problems are identified on the continent, and deliberations about these problems in relation to literature produced by both African scholars and those attuned to the Anglo-Saxon and European traditions of philosophic thought. Consequently, it is not unusual for us to rely on the seminal thoughts of Kwase Wiredu, Kwame Gyekye and N'Dri Assié-Lumumba, together with expositions by Amy Gutmann, Alasdair MacIntyre and Jacques Rancière. In other words, an examination of literature in the contexts of African and Western thought was considered apposite to examine problems on the African continent. The unconstrained discussion that African scholars are encouraged to pursue relates to a particular understanding of African philosophy, which is attuned to ongoing criticism and free articulation of 'truth' claims in much the same way that post-structuralism advocates free and rigorous discussions among those intent on keeping philosophic inquiry in potentiality. In other words, African philosophy is constantly developing in the form of literary texts that may have particular (indigenous or local) concerns and universal (global) significance. As a corollary of such a view of African philosophy, Hountondji (1996: 67) avers that "[b]y reorienting their [African philosophers] discourse in this way, they will easily overcome the permanent temptation of 'folklorism' that limits their research to so-called African subjects ...". We have aligned our thoughts to a view of an African philosophy that breaks with a distinctive focus on folklore and cultural particularities. However, we have not been oblivious to the significance of folklore, cultural peculiarities and ethno-belief systems. Rather, we have argued for a conception of African philosophy that engages with ethno-beliefs and cultural values in an attempt to contrive a new imaginary of the discourse—that is, an imaginary that draws on a deluge of African and Western literature to be responsive to real problems on the African continent. In the latter regard, it is apposite to refer to Hountondji (1996: 65) at length because his articulation of African philosophy seems most poignantly to have manifested in Teaching for Change:

> African philosophical literature ... include all the research into Western philosophy carried out by Africans. This broadening of the horizon implies no contradiction: just as the writings of Western anthropologists on African societies belong to Western scientific literature, so the philosophical writings of Africans on the history of Western thought are an integral part of African philosophical literature. So, obviously, African philosophical works concerning problems that are specifically related to African experience should also be included. In this sense, the articles of the Ghanaian J.E. Wiredu on Kant, on material and the concept of truth, are an integral part of African philosophy, as are analyses of the concept of freedom or the notion of free will by the Kenyan Henry Odera or the Nigerian D.E. Indoniboye.

As scholars, reading on and working in African philosophy of education, we used Western philosophical lenses and analyses to examine problems on the African human experience. For instance, deliberative encounters as enunciated in Western literature have often been adapted and contextualised by ourselves in relation to pedagogic encounters espoused within a paradigm of African philosophy of education.

Second, more specifically about education in Africa, Catherine A. Odora Hoppers (2000: 1) espouses such an understanding of education as "a point of convergence with numerous others" on how to be, exist, advance and live without coercion. Education as convergence among different and diverse African people intent on moving away from oppression and exclusion involves humans participating in courses of change and "fulfilling the vision of learning to know, learning to do, learning to be, and learning to live together as equals with others" (Odora Hoppers 2000: 6). Thus, education for Africans is at once concerned with:

- a deepening of knowledge relevant to the continent;
- living together on the basis of mutual recognition and understanding; and
- being African in particular advancing "indigenous forms of knowledge as part of a universal heritage and universal resource" (Odora Hoppers 2000: 7).

Our interest is in the concern of African education to give prominence to both knowledge advancement in relation to indigenous and universalist understandings, and, its advocacy in defence of humans living together in mutuality and understanding without abandoning their own identities. What can be inferred from such a view of education in Africa, is that the latter emphasises the significance of constructing and reconstructing African identities that are autonomous, self-sustaining, and empowering in the sense that communities ought to be emancipated from "inhumanity, despotism, [and] superstition" (Odora Hoppers 2000: 8).

Considering that African philosophy of education aims to examine and resolve problems on the continent on the basis of an unconstrained deliberation among a community of thinkers, such a philosophy of education envisages to identify and respond to problems on the continent with the aim of liberating societies from inhumanity, autocracy and irrational belief systems. In this regard, Odora Hoppers (2000: 8) poignantly associates an African philosophy of education with a process of deliberate scrutiny (analysis) through which hegemonic forms of power and knowledge are reinterpreted and reimagined to move away from Africa's domesticated past, in particular, the colonial, capitalist, irrational, non-literate and undemocratic past (Odora Hoppers 2000: 8). In consonance with the latter view of African philosophy of education, Teaching for Change can be considered an attempt to scrutinise major problems on the African continent critically with the aim of examining its implications for education. Before we examine the notion of African philosophy of education that underscores Teaching for Change, we first analyse why and how the aforementioned understanding of African philosophy of education connects with cosmopolitan justice.

6.3 African Philosophy of Education and Cosmopolitan Justice

Drawing on the seminal work of Kwame Anthony Appiah (2007: 157), cosmopolitan justice "requires us to feel about everyone in the world what we feel about our literal neighbors (a strength of feeling that is perhaps exaggerated by the suggestion that for them, at least, we would risk our lives)". In this sense, cosmopolitan justice, first, enunciates an obligation humans have to all other humans, even if the latter were to be strangers to us (Appiah 2007: 158). Second, cosmopolitan justice is intent on inculcating in all humans a responsiveness based on reason and conscience to those who suffer vulnerabilities, in this instance, on the African continent (Appiah 2007: 174). Thus, cosmopolitan justice emphasises two dimensions: a responsibility to all other human beings, and a responsiveness to those who suffer vulnerabilities, whether starvation, poverty, hunger, oppression, exclusion or violence. Considering that *ubuntu* justice focuses on the cultivation of moral autonomy, compassion and restorative action, being responsive to all humanity (even strangers) and recognising the importance of changing the unfavourable and, at times, grotesque conditions of vulnerable people, seems to be commensurable with *ubuntu* justice. By implication, cosmopolitan justice, like pedagogic justice and democratic justice, can be considered an instance of *ubuntu* justice. By making a claim for cosmopolitan justice, we inherently enunciate a defence of *ubuntu* justice. In other words, raising the claims of cosmopolitan justice is another way of invoking the claims of *ubuntu* justice.

Bearing in mind that an African philosophy of education is oriented towards an analysis of problems on the African continent and towards examining the implications of such problems for education, one can infer its connection with cosmopolitan justice. African philosophy of education is concerned with major problems suffered by human beings whereas cosmopolitan justice, as an instance of *ubuntu* justice, is intent on alleviating such problems. The point is that it is not sufficient to identify problems; we should actually do something about eradicating or minimising such problems. In addition, once such problems have been identified, African philosophy of education offers an opportunity for people to determine the effects that such problems might or might not have on education. In turn, cosmopolitan justice involves finding ways to respond to human problems, such as poverty, hunger and starvation on the African continent. When the implications of the aforementioned problems are considered for education, then we would be doing African philosophy of education.

In sum, African philosophy of education is not just about identifying and analysing major problems faced by humans on the African continent. Neither is such a philosophy only concerned with examining the implications of such problems for education. Rather, an analysis and examination of the implications of the problems for education are considered, as those practices make an African philosophy of education what it is. Following on from our discussion of cosmopolitan justice, it is evident that the implications of problems are not our only concern, but that the problems must also be resolved according to meanings of cosmopolitan justice. In doing so, we would be advancing the cause of *ubuntu* justice on the grounds that the latter is constitutive of an African philosophy of education. This brings us to a discussion of the major problems we have identified as significant to Teaching for Change and why these problems are inextricably connected to the cultivation of cosmopolitan justice (as an instance of *ubuntu* justice). We shall now look at these problems as they unfolded in Teaching for Change and offer some thoughts about why they could be connected to the cultivation of cosmopolitan justice.

6.4 Cosmopolitan Justice and Teaching for Change

Teaching for Change introduces five case studies that highlight major problems on the African continent: student protests, terrorism, food insecurity, nation building and reconciliation, and military dictatorships. We analyse these problems and justify, first, why they are problems. Second, we consider some of the implications of these problems for education; and third, we examine how addressing these problems is inextricably linked to the cultivation of cosmopolitan justice (an instance of *ubuntu* justice). Thereafter, in the following chapter, we examine how Teaching for Change specifically relates to enhancing equal pedagogic encounters.

First, student protests at several of the 26 public universities in South Africa have been instigated mostly by the desire of many students to hold back on the payment of tuition fees. The #FeesMustFall campaign started at the end of the 2015 academic year and continued throughout 2016 with some sporadic protests erupting during the early part of 2017. As a consequence of the predicament of South African higher education in dealing with student inequality—especially the majority of black students who cannot come up with fees—its academic programmes have been under constant threat for some time. This is a major problem because in a neoliberal context, which frames the route that higher education takes, especially along the lines of knowledge commodification—that is, knowledge and learning are two things for which students have to pay—universities cannot function optimally because student fees largely contribute towards the academic success of these institutions. Although more than a third of the institutional budget of universities is generated from the state-subsidy income, at least a third comes from student fees and another third and more from private donations and/or investments. It is thus inconceivable that universities would function without the student fee component. Hence, when students assume the right not to pay their fees, then universities in South Africa become prone to dysfunctionality. Yet, paradoxically, tuition fees are quite expensive and especially challenging for the majority of disadvantaged students who cannot gain equal access to higher education. That is, student fees have become a major constraint for university education. Of course, a university's teaching/learning, research and community engagement—nowadays, described as "social impact"—cannot be unfunded initiatives, and when the financial viability of an institution is threatened, irrespective of the availability of grants and bursaries, the academic functioning of such an institution would be seriously undermined. It is here that the notion of cosmopolitan justice comes into play. Cosmopolitan justice requires that all students be treated justly and that equal access to education should not exclusively privilege those students who can afford to pay for their tuition fees. Alternatively, it becomes an institutional responsibility in conjunction with perhaps the private sector to be attentive to fee constraints that potentially deny underprivileged students access to education. An African philosophy of education is concerned with an analysis of the problems that underprivileged students encounter in settling their tuition fees and with an examination of what the implications would be for such students to be deprived of education. In this way, an African philosophy of education and cosmopolitan justice seem to work together. The upshot of the latter claim is that if education on the African continent cannot be responsive to the creation of equal opportunities for many students to pursue their studies, then ways have to be found to counteract such a predicament. Cosmopolitan and, by implication, *ubuntu* justice requires that compassionate action be taken whereby more underprivileged students be granted tuition fee reductions—perhaps on a sliding scale—that would not necessarily put the universities at risk. If not, it does seem unlikely that the restoration of African societies would be forthcoming. That is, it might be that resolutions to address the tuition dilemma at South African universities might not be forthcoming because it seems that the willingness of those involved to move towards a shared compromise does not seem to be imminent, at least at this stage.

Secondly, the Boko Haram (anti-Western education) terrorist group situated in the north-western part of Nigeria is intent on violating people's rights to an education of their choice. Instead, the group is renowned for having captured young girls and enforced their medieval religious views on them, in particular having coerced them to embrace a misguided conception of Islam. Many of the terrorist tactics of the group are aimed at inculcating fear in people who not only become victims of terror but who are also indoctrinated with a skewed understanding of Islam, in particular to undermine any form of Western education they are expected to acquire. An African philosophical-educational analysis of the problem related to Boko Haram's understanding of education reveals that, in the first place, is associated with doctrinaire thinking in the sense that people are not allowed to question and scrutinise the assumptions of a Boko Haram type of Islam. In turn, traditional sources of Islamic knowledge—mostly the Quran and Sunnah of the Prophet Muhammad—are considered uncritical sources of knowledge that cannot be subjected to human interpretation as if knowledge is objectively neutral and devoid of any form of human subjectivity. Our understanding is that the primary sources of Islamic knowledge should not be accepted blindly as if knowledge from an Islamic perspective is indifferent to critical scrutiny. The point is that knowledge in Islam is open to analysis and critical reflection, and interpretations are not merely monolithic elucidations of human actions. Nothing is absolute and inflexible. Interpretations are always subjected to difference and contexts and ways of meaning-making. In any case, a Boko Haram interpretation of knowledge provokes the group to deny people holding varying understandings of the revealed sources of Islam. Such interpretations seem twisted towards some dogmatic and often archaic understanding of the Islamic faith that prompts in people a desire to resolve disputes through violence. The implication is that the education of Boko Haram-affiliated people is prejudiced towards an uncritical acceptance of and conformance to dogmatic views of Islam that do not always resonate with Islamic concepts of *ijtihad* (intellectual exertion of a critical kind) and *shura* (critical engagement of a deliberative kind). Such dogmatic views instigate the group to oppose any form of plurality and difference violently. The result of the latter is that educational discourses in Boko Haram-controlled institutions are biased towards uncriticality and indoctrination that invariably engender in people a desire to act with contempt to difference and change. In any case, through such educational endeavours of an uncritical kind, it seems rather unlikely that cosmopolitan justice would ever be perpetuated on the basis that the latter recognises an openness to difference and rationality as important pedagogic concerns. Cosmopolitan justice seems to be far remote from the practices of Boko Haram-indoctrinated persons on the grounds that non-dogmatic views and reasonable justifications do not seem to be part of the pedagogy of the group. Instead, Boko Haram only seems to respond violently to difference, and its educational agenda is also seemingly remotely distanced from any form of human enlightenment.

Third, food security for the growing African population is one of the most daunting challenges that face the agricultural sector on the continent (Garrity et al. 2010: 197). Of the more than 1 billion undernourished people in the world, the most severe deprivation occurs in sub-Saharan Africa where 218 million people are subjected to poverty and hunger—that is, 30% of Africa's population (Garrity et al. 2010: 198). Considering that agriculture contributes around 25% of the gross domestic product (GDP) and employs 70% of the workforce in Africa, the uncertainty about crop output—worsened by erratic weather conditions caused by climate change—results in continuous land degradation, low crop yields, persistent poverty and malnutrition (Garrity et al. 2010: 198). It is estimated that in the next decade, food insecurity will increase by 43% due to drought and declining agricultural capacity, a situation that is further exacerbated by a lack of African governments' support for agriculture, and many farmers' incapacity to organise farming resources (Garrity et al. 2010: 200). The inability of African governments and many farming communities to unlock Africa's potential to respond to the agricultural predicament is a major problem for the continent. In turn, if food security is at risk due to alarming decreases in food, land degradation, climate change and an unorganised agricultural sector, the lack of food production would invariably enhance poverty and hunger that could prompt indigenous farming communities to act more swiftly in relation to building healthy soil and environments to enhance food crop production. This would imply that agricultural education by which farming communities are taught to care better for the land and to increase food production, would have to be prioritised (Garrity et al. 2010: 2010)—a point of view that resonates with the cultivation of cosmopolitan justice. Our concern is that an African philosophy of education should not be oblivious to a major problem such as a lack of food production on the African continent. Failing to be responsive to the food predicament on the continent is tantamount to ignoring a dire call for cosmopolitan justice.

Fourth, the colonial and post-colonial periods on the African continent had been characterised by several genocidal incidents and child wars. Sudan (demarcated as North and South Sudan since 2011) had been ravaged by civil war since the 1950s in which in excess of half a million mostly civilians had been killed as a result of indiscriminate violence. During the 1970s, Uganda's Acholi and Lango tribes were subjected to genocide under the terror reign of Idi Amin. Between 300,000 and 500,000 people were killed, especially former prime ministers, judges, members of the clergy, cabinet ministers, journalists, students, intellectuals and artists who protested against the government. In the early 1990s, Rwandan ethic conflict between rival Hutu and Tutsi tribes resulted in an estimated 1.2 million brutal massacres out of a population of 7.3 million people, mostly perpetrated by Hutu militia. Again, in the early 2000s, the Sudanese government enlisted Arab Janjaweed militia together with the Sudanese military to quell the uprising of non-Arab ethnic groups in the Darfur region. Since then, more than 400,000 people (mostly civilians) have been massacred with more than 3 million people having been displaced and living in camps, with more than 350,000 people being deprived of humanitarian support. More recently, after the demise of Muammar al-Gaddafi, the entire population of the Libyan town of Tawergha was either killed or forced to flee, resulting in deaths, abductions and the rape of women and children (IPAHGP 2016).

The aforementioned are examples of how acts of genocide had been committed on the African continent even after the United Nations Convention on the Prevention and Punishment of the Crime of Genocide was held in 1951. Moreover, several African countries, in particular, Sudan, Somalia, Libya, Mali, Chad, Uganda and Central Africa use child soldiers (under the age of 18) to fight wars and perpetrate atrocities even among their own relatives. Currently, there are between 200,000 and 300,000 child soldiers often involved in brutal wars on the African continent (Chikoze 2017). The problem with genocide and child wars is that humans are mostly recruited forcefully into militia to perpetrate acts of genocide against other humans, thus disrespecting the lives of human beings in the first place. Such heinous crimes put human co-existence at risk as peace and reconciliation would be difficult to achieve in the face of humans violating one another's rights to peaceful living. At once, perpetuating violence through genocide and child wars does not augur well for education as the latter, in the first place, demands that people engage with one another. Of course, nation building and reconciliation could ensue through education as has been the case in post-apartheid South Africa, but then societal conditions ought to be in place to cultivate human co-existence and interdependence. Genocidal wars work against the cultivation of human co-existence which further makes education a seemingly impossible task, and the cultivation of *ubuntu* justice invariably remains at large.

Fifth, it seems that military dictatorships coupled with a sentimentality for autocratic rule are very much preferred by almost half the African states despite a general inclination of many states towards democracy. Although in the wake of the Arab Spring, North Africa should be more inclined to democratic rule, countries in North Africa seem to have the lowest demand for democratic rule on the continent: Tunisia is at 27%, Algeria at 18% and Egypt at 16%. Only in Morocco—a constitutional monarchy—is demand for democracy at 40% (Mungai 2014). On the African continent, three types of countries emerge:

- 16 out of 34 countries have a high demand for democracy yet the latter is not forthcoming, for example in Cote d'Ivoire, Nigeria, Zimbabwe, Togo and Uganda;
- countries where the supply of democracy exceeds its demand, that is, countries where demand is surpassed by an excessive supply of political elites that control the countries, for example in Algeria, Niger, Namibia and Tanzania; and
- 7 countries have high levels of democracy, for example Ghana, Senegal and Benin (Mungai 2014).

Those countries that are very vulnerable to political control by elites often succumb to military rule—a situation, which undeniably constrains democratic rule although the demand for democracy might be very high. The problem with military dictatorships is that the political voice of the population is not always adhered to and a type of political coercion that favours the elite is enforced on people without them having the freedom and choice to decide upon the form of rule. As is invariably the case, military dictatorships result in the exclusion of the masses, which enhances violence and, at times, ethnic conflict, wars and even genocide as government forces and their opposition set out to destroy one another. Any form of political dictatorship causes people to be silenced, which increases the chances of alienation, intimidation, threats and even political expulsions and deaths. When political coercion and control hold sway, democratic rule is invariably sidelined and political elites have to invest in clandestine ways to subvert any legitimate opposition.

Now that we have emphasised why student protests, terrorism, food insecurity, a lack of nation building and reconciliation, and military dictatorships are problems on the African continent, we shall examine what the implications of the aforementioned problems are for education on the continent. First, for Gert Biesta (2014), on the one hand, education only works through the connections of communication and interpretation, interruption and response while, on the other hand, to educate means to have a concern for those subjects who should be held responsible for their own actions, as well as being responsible for what their actions bring about. Thus, following Biesta (2014), to be educated implies that people are interconnected within encounters where they (people) act responsibly towards themselves and others. According to Biesta (2014), the latter understanding of education manifests in three domains: qualification, socialisation and subjectification. About qualification, Biesta (2014: 2) avers that education involves the quest for knowledge, values, skills and dispositions. In terms of socialisation, education is enunciated according to the ways in which people become part of the existing traditions and ways of doing and being. The third dimension of education has to do with the subjectivity in which people become free, emancipated and responsible. Together, the aforementioned three domains of education are ways in which new beginnings and new beginners can come into the world (Biesta 2014: 4). If one considers the aforementioned problems identified on the African continent, Biesta's (2014) theory on education helps us to contextualise such problems as being political. The political dimensions of the problems are corroborated by an insistence that problems ought to be addressed in relation to emancipation. As he posits, "the intimate connection between education and democratic politics" ought to be recognised (Biesta 2014: 8). The latter implies that problems on the African continent cannot be delinked from Africa's political existence. Addressing the political dimension of problems on the continent is a way of situating such problems as educationally related. It is Biesta's (2014) emphasis on education as being political that immediately challenges the "strong" emphasis that African educational institutions place on preparing students for society through the acquisition of knowledge, skills, values and dispositions, and socialisation into existing traditions of doing and being. Yet, not always do institutions (through their curricula) emphasise the significance of invoking students' subjectivities, orienting them to think about their freedom and emancipation within educational settings. Only when problems are looked at as real challenges to the political situatedness within which people find themselves, would Africans for that matter adequately address the educational concerns of people on the continent.

For example, nowadays, much is being made of the decolonisation and decoloniality agendas of education in Africa. Unless the decolonisation and decoloniality initiatives, following Biesta, are going to be addressed in relation to the political, it would be unlikely that any educational pursuit to be freed of the remnants of colonialism and coloniality would succeed. Biesta's (date) theory on education helps us to think more politically about the problems with which people are confronted on the African continent. A poignant example is the introduction of pre-packaged learning outcomes and graduate attributes into the realm of the African university. The political motivation behind such efforts is linked to the production of a working clientele that could serve the economic interests of the competitive labour market. However, such efforts seemed to have eroded students' capacity to think for themselves as they have merely been inducted into a situation where critical questioning has been absent and an emphasis on skills development for the world of work seemed to have been prioritised. The latter situation, in turn, has resulted in an uncritical attitude on the part of students that merely serves the interest of capitalist production at the expense of their legitimate freedom and emancipation. When students are not free, their subjectivities have not been evoked and their emancipation might have been dealt a heavy blow. A lack of political education, therefore, further exacerbates the problems Africans encounter on the continent as it makes education oblivious of the risks it offers people to act more freely and responsibly.

Second, building on the seminal thoughts of Jane Roland-Martin (2013) education ought to be connected to the culture In other words, education should be attentive to the cultural realm of people—that is, an education that does not invoke people's cultural stock (Roland-Martin 2013), more specifically their traditions, customs, values, artefacts and language, cannot justly respond to the debilitating human experiences such as poverty, hunger, violence or other forms of injustice they might experience. The point is that an identification of human problems on the continent requires that we respond in such a way that people's cultural experiences are attended to. In addition, failure to address people's cultural concerns would not do justice to their education at all. It is an invocation of cultural realties that envelop people's lived experiences that would enable one to address their educational encounters, as aptly stated by Roland-Martin (2013). To this end, becoming responsive to human problems on the African continent requires of one not to be oblivious to people's cultural contexts, which invariably envelop and guide their educational encounters. Roland-Martin (2013: 17) posits:

> Our theory holds that education only occurs if there is an encounter between an individual and a culture in which one or more of the individual's capacities and one or more items of a culture's stock become yoked together; or if they do not in fact become yoked together, it is intended that they do.

Roland-Martin's (2013: 45) elucidation of a cultural educational encounter is framed along three dimensions:

- cultural knowledge and understanding constitute people's ways of being and living;
- cultural knowledge undergirds people's ways of being, such as those reflected in their beliefs, values, traditions and languages and guides their educational encounters; and
- cultural knowledge allows people to act in community on the basis of their understandings and knowledge becoming yoked together (Roland-Martin 2013: 76).

98   Y. Waghid et al.

The result of the latter argument is that failing to respond to people's cultural education constrains their educational aspirations to become better communities in which they learn and act together to address their collective concerns.

Third, Seyla Benhabib (2005) assigns a profoundly moral dimension to education. In other words, all humans are equally entitled to moral rights, which requires of the individual to others them hospitably. In her words (Benhabib 2005: 25):

> [T]he right to universal hospitality, for example, if it means anything at all, imposes an obligation on the political sovereign, by prohibiting states from denying refuge and asylum to those whose intentions are peaceful and if refusing them sojourn would result in their demise.

The latter implies that, first, all humans ought to respect one another on the grounds of their humanity; second, all human beings ought to be protected as citizens who co-belong; and third, all humans should be protected from crimes against humanity (Benhabib 2005: 25, 29). For the latter to happen, humans ought to engage in democratic iterations in which they give account of their cultural and political selves through an exchange and justification of reasons. By giving reasonable accounts of their actions, humans engage iteratively in democratic action whereby they accentuate their sense of moral agency in the pursuit of just human action. By implication, when human problems are identified on the African continent, people ought to respond morally, that is, reasonably in deliberatively iterative ways as they seek to combat their undesirable human condition.

In sum, doing African philosophy of education is inextricably connected to identifying human problems that constrain justifiable human co-existence and interdependence. This implies that in order to be responsive to such problems, people have to act in ways where they treat human experiences as political, cultural and moral issues that require educational responses. People would not only be obliged to act riskfully, but also collectively and iteratively on the basis of giving an account of their reasons that are politically, culturally and morally situated. When people act in such a manner, they would be able to transcend their own political, cultural and moral prejudices on the grounds that their risk taking would occur in democratically iterative ways. People would be prepared to engage with one another with their diverse and often incommensurable understandings with the intent to make political, cultural and moral sense of their proffering in an atmosphere where risk taking would not be constrained. By enacting their political, cultural and moral biases iteratively, the chances of dismissiveness and exclusion would be unlikely. The result is that human problems would be considered more intensely, that is, reasonably without the possibility that incommensurable views and articulations would drive people apart. They would resist such unengaging ways on the grounds that they always want to take risks as they extend themselves collectively and iteratively in deliberative fashion. In this way, cosmopolitan justice and, by implication, *ubuntu* justice would not be out of reach after all.

Cosmopolitan justice demands that people act responsibly and with conviction to address the human dilemmas with which they are confronted. When they act riskfully, collectively and iteratively—that is, deliberatively—there is always the possibility that the human predicament will be counteracted. The rationale of Teaching for Change has the latter in mind. First, students have to engage with one another without being constrained to take risks. Second, their engagement ought to be collective but not at the expense of undermining their individual autonomy. Third, in iterative ways, they come up with ideas and solutions to human dilemmas on the African continent in ways that we as educators have not thought of before. These students take the risk to engage in deliberative educational encounters where nothing is conceived in advance and where the possibility of coming to equal speech is never constrained. Through Teaching for Change, we are intent on provoking students to express their equal intelligence in a positively disruptive way (Rancière 1991).

6.5 Towards Equal and Disruptive Pedagogic Encounters

The main thrust of this section is to show that pedagogic encounters ought to be cultivated within democratic spaces where counter-speech (disruptive speech) undermines hate speech. If hate speech is not avoided, authoritarianism, oppression, discrimination and closeness to the unfamiliar and strange could possibly continue to dominate teaching and learning in many educational institutions. A lack of cultivating counter-speech or disruptive speech might even shut the doors to the unexpected and incalculable moments of democratic education that have found some (dis)comfort in human experiences of a transformative kind. Hence, democratic pedagogic encounters envisage to set people free, to leave them unbounded in their encounters with one another and without acting with injustice towards one another. In this way, it is argued that pedagogic encounters on the basis of disruptive speech could become provocative—leaving much room for dissent—yet become more inclusive.

In a previous work, *Pedagogy out of bounds: Untamed variations of democratic education* (Waghid 2014), one of us expounded on a liberal conception of democratic education that is intertwined with actions such as self-reflexive iterations, belligerent and distressful engagements, narrative pronouncements, compassionate imagining, just expressive freedoms, and caring (Waghid 2014). In all such actions, the potentialities of students and educators are evoked to the extent that conditions have been established for them (the students and educators) to encounter one another through reasonable speech, compassionate imagining, caring and justice. Although democratic education is not blind to the practice of disruptive action, such as belligerent, distressful and rhetorical speech, it is its emphasis on reasonable, caring and compassionate speech that seems to counteract the possibility of legitimate disruptive action—that is, action that could possibly open up democratic forms of engagement to unforeseen and unpredictable encounters (Waghid 2014). The concern being raised here is that liberal conceptions of democratic education might not be disruptive enough to evoke and maximise student participation and the enactment of their moral imaginations. That is, liberal forms of democratic education might be too restrictive in advancing a more disruptive kind of democratic education that could ensure that both students and educators take risks to work towards the improbable, the unexpected, or even the unheard of. For this reason, this section is an attempt to move beyond the limitations imposed by liberal forms of democratic education.

Moreover, if doing justice to the other is important to democratic education, then just democratic education, following Gutmann (2003: 26), respects the ethical agency of individuals, where ethical agency includes the capacities of individuals to live their lives as they see fit, yet consistent with respecting the equal freedoms of others and their capacities to do justice to their societies and the world. At the heart of doing justice to others in democratic relationships is to respect the liberty of all individuals "to live a decent life with a fair chance to choose among their preferred ways of life" (Gutmann 2003: 27). In other words, democratic relationships should not have in mind coercing individuals into accepting the dominant views, but rather enhancing their "civic equality, equal freedom, or opportunity" to speak their minds (Gutmann 2003: 200). In fact, excluding individuals on the grounds that they cannot express themselves freely, and discriminating against them on the basis of gender, race, sexual orientation, ethnicity or religion, are unwarranted sources of civic inequality that would deem democratic education unjust (Gutmann 2003: 200). In the words of Gutmann (2003: 200):

> Many voluntary groups do no injustice by excluding various people; they support the ability of free individuals to live their own lives as they see fit. Free individuals must be able to associate as they see fit within the limits of doing no injustice to others. Problems arise, however, when exclusions are unjust, and especially when the excluded individuals are among the most vulnerable in society and lack the same expressive freedom as those who are excluding them.

Expressive freedom that leads to preventing invidious discrimination is constitutive of democratic education. Yet, as cautioned by Gutmann (2003: 200), an advocacy for a particular point of view that cannot be separated from excluding others is tantamount to doing them an injustice As aptly stated, "[f]ree expression must not become an unconstrained licence to discriminate" (Gutmann 2003: 200). We concur with Gutmann that unconstrained expressive freedom could limit what democratic education has in mind—that is, doing justice to all individuals, irrespective of such individuals' association. In her words, "the morally relevant feature of justice-friendly associations is that they similarly recognize all people, regardless of ascriptive identities, as entitled to be treated as civic equals with equal freedom and opportunity" (Gutmann 2003: 204). Because democratic education is aimed at securing justice based on respect for persons and protection of their freedoms, the practice itself cannot permit unconstrained freedoms that discriminate against others. In fact, democratic education that is bound to give rise to just relations cannot be intolerant towards non-discrimination. The promise of democratic education premised on the idea of justice "is to grant individuals equal freedom and opportunity to live their lives as they see fit rather than to see their identities writ large in their very own society" (Gutmann 2003: 210). Hence, democratic education involves people connecting with one another without individuals discriminating against others on the basis of over-exuberant expressive freedoms. Expressive freedoms cannot be such as to discriminate against others on the basis of their ways of being. This in itself would undermine the just orientation of democratic education. Thus, it is apposite to consider the following non-discriminatory ways in which individuals in association could continue to engage one another democratically. Such individuals as agents of a just democratic education should publicly express what they consider an important aspect of their identity; conserve their culture, which they identify with the group; and fight against discrimination and other injustices (Gutmann 2003: 201). However, the counter-argument can be used that excessive expression—often considered hate speech—is commensurate with the liberty of some individuals. Furthermore, limiting their speech—even if such speech is considered doing an injustice to others—would not necessarily be an appropriate means to enact democratic education. Hence, even though Gutmann's position sounds plausible, it does make democratic education liable to exclusion, because others' views are considered undesirable for human engagement. Unless the addressor of hate speech, for instance, does not consider the addressee as not assaultive or offensive, it does not give democratic education in its current liberal form the edge to deal adequately with such speech acts. Therefore, something else has to be thought of in relation to countering offensive speech, more specifically, where the issue of counter-speech (disruptive speech) as in opposition to hate speech is dealt with. But first, we make an argument for the cultivation of untamed pedagogic encounters.

Liberal approaches to pedagogic encounters abound. Challenges to such pedagogic encounters (more specifically, teaching and learning) remain at large, and include racial and gender stereotyping, harassment, hatred, bigotry, greed and an obsession with consumerism. Of course, to contest the very notion of liberalism that affords individuals the freedom to venture autonomously on some kind of democratic pedagogic path seems to be paradoxical for an untamed pedagogy. An untamed pedagogy is in itself dependent on the autonomy of individuals and groups, in terms of which they can express their freedoms without unreasonable curtailment. However, liberal forms of democratic engagement, if left untouched, potentially constrain pedagogy, which should be left untamed if (post)modern societies envisage to throw off the shackles of those forms of education practised in the name of democracy, which inhibit imaginative pedagogic encounters—that is, encounters that could enhance human relations towards taking an ethical and political stand in relation to the challenges mentioned earlier.

Consequently, we have attempted to modify liberal forms of democratic education with the purpose of effecting pedagogic encounters more sceptically along the lines of disruptive speech (counter-speech). If this happens, and it has the potential to do so, pedagogic encounters would be more responsible and free and therefore might have a more positive influence on teaching and learning. Articulating the argument for untamed pedagogic encounters convincingly has some connection with what it means to think and act differently—that is, in the words of Alain Touraine (2009: 92), "open[ing] the doors that give us access to ways of understanding new behaviours and the new ways in which societies are being transformed". Thus, we argue that pedagogic encounters, which might assist educators and students to respond to the use of assaultive (hate-) speech or offensive speech (Lloyd 2007: 107), could go some way to broaden the efficacy of such encounters. If pedagogic encounters between educators and students cannot engender opportunities to deal with assaultive or hate speech, then both parties would be remiss in an important aspect of human relations that has become the subject of intense scrutiny over the past decade. In relation to pedagogy and democratic politics, learning to contest hate speech in novel and unforeseeable ways would be "a fitting tactic for dealing with wounding words" (Lloyd 2007: 126).

We shall now expound on pedagogic encounters that bring into contestation hate speech. In this way, pedagogic encounters could perform the task of responding to hate speech—a form of language use that often causes harm to others. We are thinking specifically of ongoing hate speech that announces all fair-skinned people as racists, all Jews as Zionists, or all Muslims as religious bigots and terrorists. For example, with the tenth anniversary of 9/11, a trailer of an obscure US-made film, *The Innocence of Muslims*, was posted on YouTube. The scenes in the trailer of the film depict Islam as cancerous and the Prophet Muhammad as a buffoon, lascivious and condoning of paedophilia. Considering the outrage generated by previous incidents, such as the publication of Salman Rushdie's (2008) *Satanic verses*, the controversy surrounding the Danish cartoons, and the public burning of the Quran, the release of the trailer provoked protestations all over the world because the film enraged many people, especially Muslims. Although it can be argued that the release of the film is a manifestation of freedom of expression, it is filled with hate speech, which incited (violent) protestations much in the same way that some radio broadcasts in Rwanda in 1993 incited genocide against the Tutsis.

We continue to show how educators and students could respond to hate speech in pedagogic encounters by considering such encounters as sites of resistance, "where (disruptive) counter-speech becomes possible" (Lloyd 2007: 120). Our contention is that if pedagogic encounters can deal with words that wound, it would give such encounters "a radical and empowering direction" (Lloyd 2007: 133) that would make relations between educators and students perhaps more inclusive. It is for this reason that we refer to Judith Butler's *Excitable speech* (1997), in which she argues that hate speech can best be dealt with through "talking back" (Lloyd 2007: 133).

Assaultive or hate speech is very much evident in the trailer of *The Innocence of Muslims*, for the reason that words are used to humiliate and denigrate people, often resulting in such people being further stigmatised. In other words, uttering hate speech can be conceived of as either having an "illocutionary" or a "perlocutionary" purpose (Butler 1997: 3). Whereas illocutionary speech acts are acts that "in saying do what they say, and do it in the moment of that saying", perlocutionary speech acts are acts that "produce certain effects as their consequence; by saying something, a certain effect follows" (Butler 1997: 3). Simply put, for Butler (1997: 3), "[t]he illocutionary speech act is itself the deed that it effects; the perlocutionary merely leads to certain effects that are not the same as the speech act itself". On the one hand, uttering speech that refers to a religion as a "cancer" and its prophet as a "buffoon" already signifies, following the distinction between illocutionary and perlocutionary speech acts, an injurious act of causing harm to certain people (that is, Muslims). On the other hand, such speech acts have the effect of people being stigmatised and marginalised further. What follows from the aforementioned distinction of speech acts is that hate speech has a certain injurious force caused by the performance of language, and each time such speech is reiterated, the harmful and demeaning effects have the potential to be felt by people. Simply put, people will be hurt through hate speech and will often want to respond in a retaliatory fashion, as if the potency of hate speech can and will be wished away, or as if hate speech can be hated away by equally repugnant speech, or worse. We hold a different view for which we shall now argue in relation to the thoughts of Butler (1997).

Butler proposes a political response to hate speech by arguing that, inasmuch as hate speech has the potential to cause harm and humiliation of others, if it is re-signified, it has the potential not to cause harmful injury. That is, Butler (1997) offers an alternative linguistic contestation of hate speech that has the capacity to defuse the power of such speech acts. In Butler's (1997: 163) words:

> [B]eing called a name can be the site of injury [illocutionary speech], and conclude by noting that this name-calling may be the initiating moment of a counter-mobilization ... The word that wounds becomes an instrument of resistance in the redeployment that destroys the prior territory of its operation. Such a redeployment means speaking words without prior authorization and putting into risk the security of language life, the sense of one's place in language, that one's words do as one says ... Insurrectionary speech becomes the necessary response to injurious speech, a risk taken in response to be being put at risk, a repetition in language that forces change.

Following Butler (1997), referring to a religion as a cancer and its prophet as a buffoon, one who condones paedophilia and who has unusual sexual desires, is both a manifestation of illocutionary speech that puts the adherents of such a religion at risk—that is, it has also a perlocutionary effect that could cause harm to people being injured by such speech acts. How does one counter-mobilise hate speech or re-signify speech? Instead of accepting the speech as hate speech, Butler proposes that such speech should be received, reclaimed positively, and then returned to the person who utters such speech in a re-signified manner. According to Butler (1997: 39), "the possibility of defusing the force of that speech through counter-speech" should be applied. Islamophobia, racism and anti-Semitism are poignant examples. When Islam, for example, is announced as being "cancerous", the pernicious potential of such speech can be defused by re-signifying the linguistic use of "cancer". For instance, "cancerous" can be linguistically recycled as being malignant to proponents of those who deny the submission to the existence of an Omnipotent God. The idea that the producers of the film *The Innocence of Muslims* originally had in mind to cause injury to adherents of the Islamic faith through unrestrained, injurious speech could potentially be refuted "through a language that counters the injuries of speech ... [t]he resignification of speech [that] requires opening new contexts, speaking in ways that have never [been] legitimated" (Butler 1997: 41).

All that remains to be done in this section is to consider how counter-speech could make pedagogic encounters more inclusive. In the first instance, leaving hate speech uncontested would rule out the possibility that educators and students engage in some form of iteration—that is, the possibility of being internally excluded in pedagogic relations is enhanced when hate speech is not re-signified—redirected and reconstructed into a language that defuses the power of hate speech (Butler 1997: 99). This act of counter-speech, however, is conditional on an adjudication of hate speech itself. Educators and students ought to deliberate first what counts as hate speech, for example in relation to racial and sexual slurring as a perlocutionary scene, that is "one in which the effects of such speech must be shown" (Butler 1997: 101). We are thinking specifically of how to learn to counter or re-signify hate speech in relation to the film under discussion. If words such as "buffoon", "lascivious" and "paedophilia" are used to injure a religion's prophet illocutionarily, then students and educators should deliberate on how such wounding words could be inverted positively without necessarily encouraging censorship. For Butler (1997: 102), "hate-speech is repeatable speech, and it will continue to repeat itself as long as it is hateful. Its hate is a function of its repeatability". In other words, hate speech is always there, even if one wants to wish it away. In South Africa, unwarranted references to people have been established linguistically and the harmful effects are in its persistent and undesirable linguistic reiterations. The use of wounding words—that we do not wish to repeat here—although injurious to many South Africans, has in any case not been censored in its entirety, and it might never be possible to censor these words from the minds and tongues of those who choose to use them, although their censorship would be desirable for a community. So, learning to give new meanings to wounding words and to throw them back at their users would create the possibility to minimise the trauma caused by the use of such words, thus enhancing "[their] constitutive possibility of being [considered] otherwise" (Butler 1997: 102). If the post-apartheid university hopes to find ways to deal with the use of offensive speech in society, it has to cultivate pedagogic encounters in which learning to talk back to counter hate speech should become a priority for educators and students. That is, pedagogic encounters should re-signify injurious speech in order to ensure more openness between students and teachers—a matter of making classroom and online activities an "optimum site for democratic struggle" (Lloyd 2007: 150). This means that if instances of hate speech should arise, educators should use this as an opportunity for students to learn how to re-signify hate speech because, while hate speech might not be obviously evident in the university, it is an unwelcome part of society.

What emanates from a discussion of re-signifying hate speech through pedagogic encounters is the notion that not only would such encounters create the possibility for more inclusiveness and openness between educators and students, but they would also situate encounters in terms of "the human and the possibility of its survival" (Lloyd 2007: 156). In other words, as Butler's (1997) *Excitable speech* illustrates, the interest in making pedagogic encounters more inclusive cannot just be about becoming more responsive to hate speech, but also about securing human survival and its liveability—a clear indication of Butler's (1997) concern to link human liveability to a politics of radical democracy (Lloyd 2007: 135). For Butler (2004: 3–4), liveability, or "a politics of human life" (in our view, her approach to radical democracy), is:

> [The] capacity, invariably collective, to articulate an alternative, minority version of sustaining norms or ideals that enable me to act ... [and] not to celebrate difference as such but to establish more inclusive conditions for sheltering and maintaining life that resist models of assimilation.

Just as counter-speech is an alternative that allows people to act—to take up a position—resisting being assimilated into hegemonic discourse is an act of radical democracy. When people can resist being assimilated into a dominant view—a form of hegemony that might undermine their cultural positions—then they have maximised the possibilities of a liveable life—"what minimizes the possibility of unbearable life or, indeed, social or literal death" (Butler 2004: 8). How can the possibilities of a liveable life then be cultivated and maximised through pedagogic encounters? Drawing on Butler (2004), we offer three ways that the possibility of learning how to maximise a liveable life could be cultivated in pedagogic encounters.

First, Butler (2004) accentuates the importance of the disruptive rather than the rational intent of democratic action. Much like learning to respond through re-signifying hate speech, students should engage in incessant contestation—meaning that they should be vigilant about the radicalisation of important terms in liberal democratic education, such as equality, freedom, justice and humanity, in order to make them "more inclusive, more dynamic, and more concrete" (Butler 2004, cited in Lloyd 2007: 148). Contestation and disagreement are acts of radicalisation that suggest that democratic education is always in-becoming and that it "can never actually be attained ... that [it] is always in some sense out of reach" (Lloyd 2007: 148).

Second, students must be taught that a language of vengeance is not a counter-speech to hate speech. A language of counter-speech ought to be developed along Butler's (2004) account of grief and mourning. These states of human experience expose humans' precariousness of life and their vulnerability to the other, for they are symptomatic of one's sense of dependence on others (Lloyd 2007: 141). As noted by Butler (2004), grief and mourning reveal something about ourselves in relation to others. When death occurs and one grieves and mourns, one expresses a moment of "dispossession" from the other—a vulnerability towards the other and a recognition that death is a loss experienced by one. One's feelings of grief and mourning are expressive of one's identification with the other. The point about grief and mourning as a resource to support inclusive of pedagogic encounters is that students should be taught what it means, how the precariousness of human life so evident after 9/11 can be attended to through a recognition of human interdependence and a sense of community (Butler 2004, cited in Lloyd 2007: 141). If one recognises how interdependent humans are, one would restrain oneself in using a language of vengeance in a context of contestation and agonism where democratic education thrives. While we were writing this chapter, a student who was registered for a postgraduate certificate in education at our institution was tragically killed in a road accident. She was just 21 years old—on the brink of her life as a young adult and as a new and enthusiastic high-school teacher. Her death naturally evoked immense sadness in the students and the faculty, leading to a call for a posthumous awarding of her certificate. The point being made here is that her death drew the entire faculty together—even those who had never encountered her—on the basis that humanity is most present in the face of death.

Third, should hate speech be censored? In the first place, "[c]ensorship is most often referred to as that which is directed against persons or against the content of their speech ... constraining in advance what will and will not become acceptable speech" (Butler 1997: 128). If the film *The Innocence of Muslims* is censored because certain kinds of speech are uttered that offend a particular religious community, and some would argue is intent on provoking hatred and acts of violent response, it would imply that the person "addressed by such speech is effectively deprived of the power to respond, deauthorised by the derogatory speech act by which that citizen is ostensibly addressed" (Butler 1997: 137). In other words, people who are seemingly harmed by hate speech would themselves be censored by a pre-emptive "foreclosure" to respond to such speech acts (Butler 1997: 138). We share

Butler's position that censoring hate speech without responding to it is a form of dogmatism at the cost of "both life and thought" (Butler 1997: 162). That is, any effort to limit speech that potentially injures, threatens and offends is to assume an anti-intellectual stand that could in fact prevent the destabilisation of hate speech and the possibility of re-signifying wounding words—that is, dislodging them from their prejudicial contexts. Hence, pedagogic encounters ought to remain open to responding—talking back—to any kind of speech. It is worthwhile taking the risk of responding to speech acts that in any case make people vulnerable to unexpected and incalculable risks that could inflict injury. For the reason that "language is the site and vehicle of injury ... it is also the site and vehicle of resistance" (Lloyd 2007: 123). Thus, what has been argued for in this chapter is the articulation of counter-speech in order to quell the harmful intentions and effects of injurious speech. The possibility that pedagogic encounters will become enduring and inclusive is always there if hate speech is not censored and if the possibility remains for participants to respond to speech acts that are in themselves assaultive and therefore unbecoming.

6.6 Summary

This far, we have argued that equal and disruptive pedagogic encounters intertwined with a re-signification of unacceptable or hate speech have the potential to engage students and educators more deliberatively, iteratively, responsibly and riskfully. In the main, when students and educators begin to see the point, of one another on the grounds that they hope to respond justly towards one another in recognition of one another, they would have succumbed to the cultivation of cosmopolitan justice. Also, considering that cosmopolitan justice is an instance of *ubuntu* justice, their claims to African philosophy of education would not be unreasonable. They would have embraced such a form of education and its inextricable pursuit of cultivating *ubuntu* justice. Next, we examine our own narratives as co-authors and co-participants on this book and Teaching for Change, as an attempt to reimagine the notion of democratic education.

References

Appiah, K. A. (2007). *Cosmopolitanism: Ethics in a World of Strangers*. London: Penguin Books.

Benhabib, S. (2005). *Another Cosmopolitanism*. Oxford: Oxford University Press.

Biesta, G. J. J. (2014). *The Beautiful Risk of Education*. Boulder: Paradigm Publishers.

Butler, J. (1997). *Excitable Speech: A Politics of the Performative*. New York: Routledge.

Chikoze, E. (2017). *Ten Shocking Facts About Child Soldiers in Africa*. http://answersafrica.com/child-soldiers-in-africa.html. Accessed 14 Dec 2017.

Garrity, D. P., Akinnifesi, F. K., Ajayi, O. C., Weldesemat, S. G., Mowo, J. G., Kalingnire, A., Larwanou, M., & Bayala, J. (2010). Evergreen Agriculture: A Robust Approach to Sustainable Food Security in Africa. *Food Security, the Science, Sociology and Economics of Food Production and Access to Food, 2*(3), 197–214.

Gutmann, A. (2003). *Identity in Democracy*. Princeton/Oxford: Princeton University Press.

Hountondji, P. (1993). *African Philosophy: Myth and Reality*. Indianapolis: Indiana University Press.

Hountondji, P. J. (1996). *African Philosophy: Myth and Reality* (2nd ed.). Bloomington/Indianapolis: Indiana University Press.

IPAHGP (Inter-Parliamentary Alliance for Human Right and Global Peace). (2016). *Acts of Genocide Since World War II*. http://www.ipahp.org/index.php?en_acts-of-genocide. Accessed 14 Dec 2017.

Lloyd, M. (2007). *Key Contemporary Thinkers: Judith Butler*. Cambridge: Polity.

Mungai, C. (2014). *Africa Loves Democracy, but Also Likes Its Military Dictators, One-Party Rule, and Big Men—Study*. http://mgafrica.com/article/2014-10-20-what-the-concept-of-democracy-means-in-africa. Accessed 14 Dec 2017.

Odora Hoppers, C. A. (2000). African Voice in Education: Retrieving the Past, Engaging the Present and Shaping the Future. In P. Higgs, N. C. G. Vakalisa, T. V. Mda, & N. T. Assie-Lumumba (Eds.), *African Voices in Education* (pp. 1–11). Lansdowne: Juta.

Rancière, J. (1991). *The Ignorant School Master: Five Lessons in Intellectual Emancipation* (K. Ross, Trans.). Stanford: Stanford University Press.

Roland-Martin, J. (2013). *Education Reconfigured: Culture, Encounter, and Change*. London/New York: Routledge.

Rushdi, S. (2008). *Satanic Verses*. London: Penguin.

Touraine, A. (2009). *Thinking Differently* (D. Macey, Trans.). Cambridge: Polity Press.

Waghid, Y. (2014). *Pedagogy Out of Bounds: Untamed Variations of Democratic Education*. Rotterdam/Boston/Tapei: Sense Publishers.

7

Reflexive Thoughts on Teaching for Change: Democratic Education Reimagined

7.1 Introduction

In this chapter, we offer an account of three narratives (our stories) about how Teaching for Change, more specifically its emphasis on *ubuntu* justice, affected pedagogical actions. We show why and how we began to think differently in and about democratic education; that is, our interest in reimagining democratic education. As we show through our narratives, our argument in defence of a reimagined notion of democratic education draws on the practices of cosmopolitan reflexivity, democratic equality and disruption, which we contend should be extended to the idea of decoloniality. Put differently, our argument is for an expansive view of democratic education that connects cosmopolitan reflexivity, democratic equality and disruption to the emancipatory discourse of decoloniality in Africa, more specifically, philosophy of education in Africa.

© The Author(s) 2018
Y. Waghid et al., *Rupturing African Philosophy on Teaching and Learning*,
https://doi.org/10.1007/978-3-319-77950-8_7

113

7.2 Yusef Waghid on Cosmopolitan Reflexivity

On engaging in Teaching for Change, Yusef considered himself a cosmopolitan who co-constructed a place of learning with the aim to engage in meaning-making, interpretation and critical reflectiveness as aptly stated by Hansen (2011: 113). Yusef considered himself not only as one of the lead educators but, most importantly, as a person who belongs to "a community of human beings aspiring to dwell together" (Hansen 2011: 113)—that is, a global citizen intent on conducting himself in deliberation with students whereby we could talk together, listen to one another and interact with one another (Hansen 2011: 86). Thus, central to Yusef's deliberative engagement with students is the notion of reflectiveness, through which students and educators always remain in the process of becoming (Hansen 2011: 86). Yusef became inspired by a notion of cosmopolitanism whereby, in association with students, he wanted to "experience … [a] reflective openness to the new fused with loyalty to the known" (Hansen 2011: 86). In other words, through deliberative engagement with students, educators do not merely reject others' cultural differences, but rather, "[find] way[s] of establishing deeper recognition and respect for fundamental differences" (Hansen 2011: 74). Following on from this, in Hansen's terms, deliberative engagement through Teaching for Change allowed students and educators to engage deliberatively with the aim of learning from one another, through which students and educators could cultivate their humanness—a matter of advocating *ubuntu*/pedagogic/cosmopolitan justice.

Yusef considered himself an educator who is not a stranger to the world, but rather "an individual uniquely adapted to difference and who appreciates the plurality of cultures made inevitable by globalization [and through others]" (Papastephanou 2015: 88). In his engagement with students, Yusef acted "for a time yet to come" (Papastephanou 2015: 100). Such a view of education in-becoming does not take for granted that cosmopolitanism already exists or that it has been actualised. Actuality would mean that the concept of a cosmopolitan education has already come to fruition and by implication exhausted, which would render its cosmopolitan and educational causes superfluous. Consequently, there would be nothing more to learn, as finality would already have been attained.

Of importance to Yusef's attraction to cosmopolitan reflexivity is that through Teaching for Change an African philosophy of education was espoused with an *ubuntu* justice focus. That is, African philosophy of education cannot be education unless the principle aim of the discourse is the cultivation of *ubuntu* justice in all spheres of human living. Yusef offers here some account of how three main aspects of Hansen's (2011) and Papastephanou's (2015) views on cosmopolitanism could contribute towards an enhancement of an expansive view of democratic education espoused through Teaching for Change.

First, to be open reflectively to the new and to remain loyal to the known, where to be loyal to the known implies that one honours one's understandings of matters. When confronted with different understandings, such as proffered by participants in Teaching for Change, that could disrupt one's understandings in a pedagogic encounter with others, one would at least deliberate with others. That is, one would be open to adjust one's understandings (although established and local) in the light of what is new and convincing. One does not deliberate with others and adhere uncritically to one's points of view. Rather, one engages deliberatively with others and honours one's established views by bringing such views into controversy with others with the aim of abandoning or modifying previously held views that might be unconvincing.

Second, to be a stranger nowhere in the world is to be welcome everywhere. Deliberative encounters informed by such a view of cosmopolitanism (as Papastephanou [2015] purports) is to encounter hospitality, whatever the level of argumentation. This implies that one cannot just dismiss a person's views on account that one deems such views inappropriate and unconvincing. Rather, to be encountered by strangeness is to remain hospitable in the encounter irrespective of how ill-conceived another's views are. How else would views be welcome everywhere, if even the most ill-conceived and repugnant views are not given some consideration?

Third, to be just and humane is to be free, peaceful and good in relation to all. Cosmopolitan education cannot reify the views of one person or a group as immutable. Freedom is undermined if people do not have the right to exercise their own cultural orientations (that is, to be loyal to the known). Merely to expect others to be assimilated into the dominant cultural orientation is to deny their legitimate right to be different and indifferent. To consider one's own perspectives as good for all others is to dismiss others' ways of being as too arbitrary and inconsequential. One cannot assume that one has the absolute monopoly to goodness, as such a view would be remiss of the multifarious differences that exist in the world today. To treat others as if their views are unbecoming and irrelevant to humanity is to deny the other their very existence—that is, to treat them inhumanely. Cosmopolitan education that advocates good for all would not deprive people of one another's legitimate right to be what and who they are and/or want to be. A view that prevents others from yet coming to be, is tantamount to misrecognising that what is and can still come, which might just be more apposite for human living and co-existence. As experienced through Teaching for Change, sometimes being reflectively open to the new can also result in modifying or abandoning the known, while at other times restraining the collective self can also work against undermining the self as being part of the collective. This brings us to Faiq's narrative about engaging with students in Teaching for Change.

7.3   Faiq Waghid on Democratic Equality

Faiq realised his attachment to and cultivation of democratic inclusion in three instances, the first through his engagement with Teaching for Change. Equal democratic relationships (following Rancière [1992]) were made possible through the contributions of participants who had no power in the social order, but who could disrupt modes of action to make things happen. The students' contributions to the understanding of African philosophy of education, as vindicated by their insightful comments posted on the FutureLearn site, corroborated their capacity to speak their minds. They showed that they possessed an equal ability to speak, think and act in their efforts to create a learning environment in which they could adjust their views about African ways of thinking, being and acting, and even related in many instances an African account of education in regard to their own contexts. Through their comments and interventions, they verified their "intellectual equality" (Rancière 1992: 59) to speak, understand, share and construct their opinions in collaboration with other participants.

Second, what emanated from our readings of participants' discussions and comments on the Teaching for Change platform is that some students seem to have become agents of rhizomatic thinking. In a Deleuzo–Guattarian fashion, explains Le Grange (2011: 745), rhizomatic thinking "not only enables students to understand how phenomena/constructs become stabilized or normalised in society but also enables them to ascertain … what the vectors of escape are … [where] best can become worst and worst has the potential to become best through a process called deterritorialisation". Vectors of escape, or lines of flight (a Deleuzo–Guattarian (1987) metaphor), refer to the multiple possibilities in which students constructed knowledge about African philosophy of education. Like the offshoots of a rhizome that forge links with other rhizomes, the students' thoughts were scattered and then scrambled together to form new assemblages of knowledge. When offering justifications for their views on education, the students happened to find themselves in "deterritorialised" knowledge spaces, where they departed from fixed ideas to produce new "reterritorialized" knowledge through the rupturing of their "old" thoughts (Le Grange 2011: 747). In other words, their understandings of education had been subjected constantly to what Le Grange (2011: 747) refers to as "rupturing or exploding into lines of flight", shifting the way in which they previously thought about education in Africa. Hence, their learning was influenced rhizomatically. In a way, Teaching for Change offers participants an opportunity to go on a voyage where they are challenged to bring into controversy their previous understandings of education and never be quite sure what they will come up with. That is, the participants' views on education emerge as deterritorialised lines of flight that do not cease, "but [branch] out and [produce] multiple series and rhizomatic connections" in-becoming reterritorialised vectors of escape

(Deleuze and Guattari 1987: 15). Simply put, students made rhizomatic connections with other understandings throughout the course.

Faiq's approach to teaching has shifted significantly towards encouraging collaboration and deliberation in pedagogic activities. He is now more willing to listen to the views of students as an "ignorant master", rather than just offering advice. Through Teaching for Change, pedagogic encounters can engender in students a desire for learning, where "desire" refers to an autonomous and affirmative force that influences students' deliberative encounters with other students and educators (Zembylas 2007: 334). For Deleuze and Guattari (1987: 28), desire is not restricted to a feeling or emotion such as pleasure or fantasy in dreams, but is a force that radicalises students in-becoming deeply connected to other students in an assemblage that constitutes them. As aptly put by Deleuze (1994: 192), cultivating in students a productive desire to learn (through Teaching for Change) means "composing the singular points of one's own body or one's own language with those of another share or element, which tears us apart but also propels us in a hitherto unknown and unheard-of world of problems".

Teaching for Change became a "site of the symbolic visibility of equality and its actual negotiation" (Rancière 1991: 55). Consequently, our roles as educators became that of "ignorant masters" and "amateurs". Rancière, Masschelein and Simons (2011: 162) point out that an amateur educator does not only inform students about education, but can also inspire them to be "present". The educator thus assumes that students are equal in the sense that they are able to make sense of what the educator puts on the table (Masschelein and Simons 2011: 163). In other words, an educator as "ignorant master" and "amateur" does not consider him- or herself the only authority who understands education, but believes that students are equally able to do so and also generate ideas that confirm both their understanding and knowledge of education. Put differently, Teaching for Change could be a place where there is a possibility for movement within the restricted confines of a prescribed curriculum—that is, "it is a place where knowledge and practices can be released and set free … a sphere in which something [learning and teaching] is in play" (Masschelein and Simons 2011: 158).

7.4 Zayd Waghid on Education as Disruption

According to some students' views of their critical understandings and awareness of African philosophy of education, their comments corroborate that they had developed an awareness and understanding of social injustices that need to be eradicated on the continent of Africa and elsewhere. They knew that they needed to disrupt the social inequalities, inequities, exclusion and oppressions that undermine the quest towards more equitable and sustainable societies. Students can be said to have acquired a sense of disruptiveness. In other words, they learned to disrupt social injustices as a means to bring about societal change in and through their pedagogic encounters. In a way, the students presented themselves in opposition to privilege, oppression, exclusion and inequity. They became disruptive agents of change.

When Zayd became initiated into Teaching for Change, he played a far lesser instructional role as an educator in comparison with what he thought would be necessary. In many ways, this pedagogic initiative through Teaching for Change also enhanced his own enthusiasm for teaching. He was excited to know what students would comment on and how they would understand and develop a critical awareness of an African philosophy of education in relation to *ubuntu* justice. In a way, he summoned participants to use their intelligence and to come to reason about education. However, in summoning them to use their own intelligence, he actually took a slightly different approach to teaching. That is, he also became less of a master educator who had to tell students things of which they were not aware. Rather, he also adopted the role of "ignorant" educator (Rancière 1991), who invited students to use their "intellectual equality" to produce their own understandings of education for *ubuntu* justice. The students did not just rely on his explanations and comments, but rather came up with their own independent, and at times collaborative, understandings of education for change. He also became more of an ignorant (Rancière 1991: 12) educator who did not claim to know the answers to everything or believe that only his explanations were authentic.

Unlike the major study of Enterline et al. (2008: 267), which focuses on teaching teacher educators how to teach for social justice, Teaching for

120 Y. Waghid et al.

Change offers a way in which educators in universities could initiate themselves into a discourse on education for *ubuntu* justice. In other words, learning to teach for *ubuntu* justice can be done with educators if they hold themselves accountable for the quality of students they prepare for society. Of course, learning to teach is a complex matter and ought to be constructed as a legitimate outcome of formal teacher education (Enterline et al. 2008: 267). However, educators in service ought to orient themselves—especially in post-colonial Africa, where inequities and social injustices are still rife—towards learning to teach for *ubuntu* justice if their students are to challenge the inequities of school and society (Zeichner 2005). Learning about *ubuntu* justice does not happen on its own. Educators in conjunction with students ought to take the initiative in this regard, and Teaching for Change can be considered as one such initiative. This brings us to an exposition of an expanded view of democratic education.

7.5   Democratic Education Expanded

Thus far, we have reflected on our pedagogic encounters with students who engaged in Teaching for Change and who have shown us how cosmopolitan reflexivity, democratic equality and disruption could enhance our deliberative engagements with them. Considering that *ubuntu* justice has been enunciated as the *raison d'être* of democratic citizenship education on the African continent, we now offer an expanded view of democratic education that invokes *ubuntu* justice in the forms of cosmopolitan reflexivity, democratic equality and disruption with reference to the seminal thoughts of Du Bois, Fanon, and Wa Thiongo.

First, in the *Souls of black folk,* Du Bois (1994) posits that freedom of thought and an openness to a multiplicity of perspectives should be the educational pursuit towards humanisation. In much the same way, cosmopolitan reflexivity foregrounds a reflective openness about humans' socio-cultural conditions together with a reflective openness to the cultivation of a democratic society that is receptive to the new (Du Bois 1994, cited in Anderson 2007: 53). The point is that Du Bois's (1994: 51) cosmopolitan reflexivity involves delving truthfully into reflecting on both the good of living—that which is known to one—and to be openly reflexive to the hidden beauties of life—that is, what is still in-becoming. Searching for the hidden beauties of life invariably involves humans striving to emancipate themselves from mental stasis and to delve reflexively deeper into the unknown meanings of life (Du Bois 1994: 51). What makes a Du Boisian practice of cosmopolitan reflexivity even more promising is its commensurability with seeing through things in the world, and to unveil racial prejudice, segregation and oppression. In this way, cosmopolitan reflexivity has a connection with dignifying the humaneness of marginalised and oppressed peoples, thus stretching the notion of democratic citizenship towards embracing the plurality of human cultures.

After having graduated with a PhD from Harvard in 1895 under the mentorship of William James, the renowned pragmatist, Du Bois continued with his anti-racist agenda to couch a position of democratic citizenship education that could be responsive to a truly diverse, cosmopolitan culture where people (especially in the United States at the time) could pursue democratic ways of living high enough to overlook life (Du Bois 1994: 5)—a clear indication of the expansive democratic citizenship education agenda that Du Bois vehemently advanced. To go "high enough" in the quest to "overlook life" in a Du Boisian way is tantamount to striving towards that which might not be attained—a matter of reaching out towards the unimaginable, the unattainable, the improbable. This in itself intimates that democratic citizenship education is without limitations, as there is always more to understand, and even more to experience. The point about searching for the unreachable is like the quest to go after that which cannot be reached—a matter of reaching out to what one might not be destined to achieve. In this way, democratic citizenship education remains unrestricted, that is, it remains in potentiality as an expansive practice.

Second, Frantz Fanon (1963: 254), the French psychiatrist, in his book, *The Wretched of the Earth*, put forward a view of human equality where he claims that humanity's advancement to a different and more humanised level is dependent on people's inventiveness and find out equally about human living as Africans, Europeans and Americans. Quite importantly, Fanon (1963: 254–255) avers that humanity's exertion of its equality is corroborated by its capacity to "advance a step farther ... turn over a new leaf ... and try to set afoot a new [wo]man". According to Fanon, Africans in particular should not merely imitate Europeans, but rather exercise their intellectual equality without replicating "racial hatreds, slavery, exploitation and above all the bloodless genocide" (Fanon 1963: 254) that have dehumanised African peoples. In a different way, exercising one's equality is tantamount to subverting all forms of domination and to "equally ... pay attention to the liquidation of all untruths in his [man and woman] being by oppression" (Fanon 1963: 250). For Fanon (1963: 250), enacting one's equality is an act of the imagination whereby humans oppose and subvert the violence of colonialism on the basis of exercising their intellectual and political equality in the pursuit of total liberation.

It is such a Fanonian notion of equality that resonates with democratic equality whereby students and educators come to speech in the pursuit of liberating themselves from the possibility of indoctrination and the uncritical acceptance of others' thoughts. Fanon's preoccupation with decoloniality—like our affinity to the exercise of democratic equality—is about rehumanising the human condition. As aptly put by Fanon (1963: 252):

> When I search for Man [Woman] in the technique and the style of Europe, I see only a succession of negations of man, and an avalanche of murders. The human condition, plans for mankind and collaboration between men in those tasks which increase the sum total of humanity are new problems, which demand true inventions. Let us decide not to imitate Europe; let us combine our muscles and our brains in a new direction. Let us try to create the whole man, whom Europe has been incapable of bringing to triumphant birth. Two centuries ago, a former European colony decided to catch up with Europe so well that the United States of America became a monster, in which the taints, the sickness and the inhumanity of Europe have grown to appalling dimensions. Comrades, have we not other work to do than to create a third Europe.

Based on the aforementioned understanding of Fanonian politics, democratic education would invariably be expanded if enacted in relation to the decolonial liberation of Africa's peoples. It is not enough to have democratic equality, for that in itself would give voice to the voiceless. However, what is also significant for the emancipatory struggle against colonialism and coloniality is that humans ought to become responsive through both equal speech and opportunities to live their lives as equals unhindered by the ghosts of an imperialist past. When this happens, their enactment of a democratic citizenship education would have become more expanded.

Third, Wa Thiongo's (1979) *Decolonising the mind* and his later work, *Globalectics: Theory and the politics of knowing* (Wa Thiongo 2012) accentuate the importance of disrupting coloniality in Africa. For Wa Thiongo (1979), decoloniality implies doing things against the grain to disrupt patterns of coloniality that have kept the human mind captivated. It is his insistence on procuring indigenous languages—a return to the mother tongue—through which African peoples can articulate their real-life aspirations and, in particular, their cultural concerns in relation to others in the world—a perspective that has given his understanding of decoloniality a significant impetus (Wa Thiongo 2012). His argument that people's dignity and self-determination would be procured through a disruption of coloniality that has taken over and undervalued African people's culture, art, dances, religions, history, geography, education, orature and literature, is indeed a powerful argument in defence of decoloniality (Wa Thiongo 1979). Put differently, through disrupting coloniality, which enslaves people politically, economically and culturally, Africans might have a real and legitimate chance to reimagine their subjectivities, knowledge patterns and humaneness. Thus, for Wa Thiongo (2012), as for us, Teaching for Change, disruptive pedagogic encounters would not only be highly deliberative but would also remain open to a search for a more humane society. Simply put, disruptive action within and through pedagogic encounters has a liberatory and, by implication, rehumanising agenda. It is in this context that Teaching for Change could be considered a critically post-humanist approach to teaching and learning and a preoccupation with multiple forms of decoloniality.

This brings us to the question: What is an expansive view of democratic education? Of course, as has been internalised and articulated by us, democratic education draws on aspects such as autonomous action, deliberative engagement and expressions of reflexivity, equality and disruption. Yet, what makes our understanding of democratic education more expansive is that it has both a pedagogic and political preoccupation, more specifically towards the cultivation of forms of decoloniality. Just as much as we are concerned with enhanced and disruptive pedagogic encounters, we are equally oriented towards the cultivation of decoloniality in and through education. In this way, we are concerned with a reimagined form of democratic education. Such a view of democratic education does not only align itself with autonomous, equal and disruptive encounters, but also with those that have a real decolonial or emancipatory post-humanist orientation.

7.6   Summary

Our argument in defence of a reimagined notion of democratic education through Teaching for Change is constituted by at least three premises: cosmopolitan reflexivity, democratic equality and disruptive encounters vis-à-vis the enactment of decoloniality. As has been argued, decoloniality as an expansion of democratic education gives cosmopolitan reflexivity, democratic equality and disruption a real emancipatory impetus to counteract and change the debilitating effects of coloniality. Without the latter three notions, democratic education would not have been reimagined. However, an expansive view of democratic education should be intertwined with the cultivation of decoloniality on the grounds that the latter undermines forms of cultural, political and economic hegemony. Next, we elucidate why and how a reimagined understanding of democratic education could help us to think more imaginatively about the idea of a university.

References

Anderson, R. F. (2007). W.E.B. Du Bois and an Education for Democracy and Creativity. In D. T. Hansen (Ed.), *Ethical Visions of Education: Philosophies in Practice* (pp. 46–61). New York/London: Teachers College Press.

Reflexive Thoughts on Teaching for Change: Democratic...   125

Deleuze, G. (1994). *Difference and Repetition* (P. Patton, Trans.). New York: Columbia University Press.

Deleuze, G., & Guattari, F. (1987). *A Thousand Plateaus: Capitalism and Schizophrenia* (B. Massumi, Trans.). Minneapolis: University of Minnesota Press.

Du Bois, W. E. B. (1994). *The Souls of Black Folk.* Toronto: Dover Publications.

Enterline, S., Cohran-Smith, M., Ludlow, L. H., & Mitescu, E. (2008). Learning to Teach for Social Justice: Measuring Change in the Beliefs of Teacher Candidates. *The New Educator, 4,* 267–290.

Fanon, F. (1963). *The Wretched of the Earth.* London: Penguin Books.

Hansen, D. T. (2011). *The Teacher and the World: A Study of Cosmopolitanism as Education.* New York/London: Routledge.

Le Grange, L. (2011). Sustainability and Higher Education: From Arborescent to Rhizomatic Thinking. *Educational Philosophy and Theory, 43*(7), 742–754.

Masschelein, J., & Simons, M. (2011). The Hatred of Public Schooling. In J. Masschelein & M. Simons (Eds.), *Rancière, Public Schooling and the Taming of Democracy* (pp. 150–165). London: Wiley-Blackwell.

Papastephanou, M. (2015). *Thinking Differently about Cosmopolitanism: Theory, Eccentricity, and the Globalized World.* New York/London: Routledge.

Rancière, J. (1991). *The Ignorant Schoolmaster: Five Lessons in Intellectual Emancipation.* Stanford: Stanford University Press.

Rancière, J. (1992). Politics, Identification and Subjectivization. *October, 61*(1), 58–64.

Wa Thiongo, N. (1979). *Decolonising the Mind: The Politics of Language in African Literature.* Oxford: James Currey.

Wa Thiongo, N. (2012). *Globalectics: Theory and the Politics of Knowing.* New York: Columbia University Press.

Zeichner, K. (2005). A Research Agenda for Teacher Education. In M. Cohran-Smith & K. Zeichner (Eds.), *Studying Teacher Education: The Report of the AERA Panel on Research and Teacher Education* (pp. 737–760). Mahwah: Lawrence Erlbaum.

Zembylas, M. (2007). Risks and Pleasures: A Deleuzo-Guattarian Pedagogy of Desire in Education. *British Educational Research Journal, 33*(3), 331–347.

8

A Democratic University Without Ruins: Some Reflections on the Possibilities and Particularities of an African University

8.1 Introduction: Departing from Bill Readings's *University in Ruins*

Now that we have reflected on Teaching for Change, we want to examine how the rationale of such a form of online learning, namely to cultivate educational encounters and *ubuntu* justice, could assist us in thinking differently about an African university vis-à-vis the notion of a democratic imaginary. Although Bill Readings's (1996) pessimism that the contemporary university is "in ruins" is a monumental idea that held sway for more than two decades since its publication, it might neither be plausible nor helpful to think of a university in that way. This is so because one cannot assume that global capitalism, enmeshed in a consumerist ideology, accentuates the importance of graduate throughput and success for national and international markets and, hence, undermines a university's status as a free, open and responsible institution of higher learning. Furthermore, one would not expect a university to remain in the vanguard of national culture and therefore be perceived to be in peril if it undergoes cultural change. Such an idea of the university rests in any case on an erroneous assumption that culture and society remain the same

© The Author(s) 2018
Y. Waghid et al., *Rupturing African Philosophy on Teaching and Learning*,
https://doi.org/10.1007/978-3-319-77950-8_8

over time. Ron Barnett's (2016) *Understanding the university* announces, "the university is a task *without end* … [and] since the university is always on the move, always moving in its spaces – economic, social, political, cultural, institutional and so on – its possibilities will always be moving on" (Barnett 2016: 9). We concur with Barnett's cogent analytical take on the contemporary university, and draw on his three-pronged analysis, namely that a university is an institution and an idea; it is an institution in the present with future possibilities; and it embodies a set of particulars and universals. The particulars and universals want to offer: first, a defence of a university as a democratic educational institution; and second, in line with Jacques Derrida's (2004) novel thoughts on a contemporary university, we make a case for a university as a responsible institution-in-becoming within an African context, thereby bringing into contestation the notion that a university could ever be "in ruins".

8.2 Barnett's "Three Planes" of Understanding a University

Barnett's (2016: 9) take on a contemporary university can be construed as an attempt "to open a space for imagining the university anew". No longer can a university strictly be conceived of in the liberal sense as solely a "space for free inquiry" (Barnett 2016: 17). In the first place, a contemporary university has to respond to the predicaments of our time, and this implies that inquiry ought to be responsive to debased and violent narratives of terror, war, racial injustice, ecological abuse, state violence and so on (Giroux 2007: 10). Stated differently, a university has to be responsive to the perceived "ruins" within which it finds itself. This, however, does not mean that a university itself is "in ruins". By implication, inquiry ought to be responsive to the university, and exercised freely "in concert with larger concerns over social justice" (Giroux 2007: 5).

What follows from the aforementioned is that the exercise of free inquiry ought to be looked at concomitantly with a particular understanding of a contemporary university. In doing so, we find Barnett's (2016) three planes of understanding of a contemporary university quite appealing to ascertain why and how a university ought to position and present itself in relation to the contemporary era. The latter idea puts a different spin on how one construes a contemporary university, say, on the African continent. First, to look at a university in terms of being an institution and an idea has to be tied to universal concepts of openness, service to society and a commitment towards global communities (Barnett 2016: 49). We consider Teaching for Change an example of an online programme that is commensurate with openness, societal engagement and responsiveness to a globalised learning community. A university that is at once not open to diverse and contending (dissensus) or contentious ideas, for that matter, would undermine academic freedom and subvert its independent thought processes and institutional autonomy. Such a university, argues Giroux (2007: 10), not only undercuts critical thinking, speaking and acting, but also "positions the university as a site that is losing its claim as a democratic public sphere". Unless a university is considered to be moving in a configuration of openness in which ideas are openly traded and openness with society and the world for that matter is widened (Barnett 2016: 47), one would not remain hopeful of new educational paths for such a university. For example, we cannot imagine a university in the contemporary era not enhancing the possibility of increasing its use of multimedia, or constructing Teaching for Change as new pedagogic spaces for openness and open engagement among university staff and students. Further, considering that we were committed to the implementation of Teaching for Change, we have become oriented towards the cultivation of a democratic imaginary—one that foregrounds an advocacy for openness, engagement and responsibility to a global learning community—that is, our Teaching for Change participants.

Second, a university that comes to be in the present, and which is concerned about future possibilities is one that is attached to the real world but simultaneously sees its way to be detached from it. The idea of a university remaining attached to its presence is one that can be responsive to challenges faced by it, whereas a university that is detached from the real world is one that discerns imaginative possibilities for itself (Barnett 2016: 49). In turn, a university with an imaginary ethos is one that commits itself to taking risks—that is, "to help open regions that were not present before" (Barnett 2016: 97), especially in combining innovative explorations in medicine and the humanities, biology and archaeology, genetics and sociology, and computing and philosophy. Likewise, taking risks under the guise of pursuing imaginative possibilities implies that a university should be "sensitive to the potential callings of the wider world" (Barnett 2013: 154). In other words, such a university reaches out into communities and makes available the institution's course texts, research data and publications in order to contribute more imaginatively to an ever-evolving public understanding of a university's intellectual resources. By implication, a university intent on seeking new imaginings, new possibilities for itself, opens new lines of flight that may even lead to a re-territorialisation of itself (Barnett 2013: 155). Invariably such an imagining university becomes both an engaging and listening university, one that is willing to be self-critical—aspects of a university's openness to new democratic visions. Teaching for Change is an attempt to open up new lines of light and possibilities that invariably enhance its allegiance to a democratic imaginary.

Third, a university that embodies a set of particulars and universals, focuses, organises and applies its research in terms of the interests of the nationalised structures within specific countries, and simultaneously leaves open the possibility that research will also serve universal aims. For instance, particular research that is technically profitable for a specific nation could also be considered advantageous for humanity. The point is that the benefits that might ensue from research on preventing terrorism and war, particularly of interest to a specific nation or continent for that matter, might be considered universally relevant, perhaps for curbing such violence occurring elsewhere. We consider Teaching for Change to be a democratic imaginary that has the potential to evoke the potentialities of participants wherever they might be. From our gleanings of discussion posts on the Teaching for Change platform, we encountered many claims about *ubuntu* justice, in particular its relevance to non-African societies.

In summary, a university that is oriented towards exercising thinking (whether in the form of ideas, institutional structures, possibilities, particularities or universals) in an autonomous way, acts with sufficient risk tantamount to enacting its goals with a renewed responsibility (Derrida 2004: 151). It is to a discussion of such a responsibility of a university in Africa that we now turn.

8.3 An African University and the Enactment of Responsibility

Following the examination of the notion of a university in relation to Ron Barnett's (2016) compelling theoretical framework, which constitutes a university in relation to its ideas and being an institution, its possibilities, and its particularities and universals, we now consider how a university could present itself responsibly in the sense that responsibility is linked to all three aspects of its representation. Jacques Derrida (2004: 154) contends that a university reproduces society's "scenography, its views, conflicts, contradictions, its play and its differences, and also its desire for organic union in a total body". The latter implies that a university reflects society and through enacting its responsibility, responds to crises in society on the basis of renewal of what it does not have "and of what is not yet" (Derrida 2004: 155). In addition, being responsible for what a university "does not have, and is not yet" (Derrida 2004: 155) calls upon a university to risk its future, in such ways as its academics knowing how to shut their eyes "in order to be better listeners" (Derrida 2004: 131). Our interest in a university that acts responsibly, such as in taking risks for the future, is connected to adopting attitudes of improved listening, which invariably provokes more informed, nuanced thinking. If university academics were more intent on listening, they would have learned to give ground, to justify and to account for the practices of a university (Derrida 2004: 137). If academics do not seek to understand the norms and values that constitute their own institution, they will not be acting responsibly. Academics who merely construe a university on the basis of mediocrity and innuendo and "to say whatever comes into their heads" (Derrida 2004: 147) will not act with a "watchful vigilance of the principle of reason", which invariably has obscurantist and nihilist effects on the institution. Put differently, without a community of thinking, a

132   Y. Waghid et al.

university and its academics "lose all sense of proportion and control" (Derrida 2004: 147). In this way, a university loses its prestige and by implication its authority.

Some African universities are in chains because of the absence of thinking, making judgements and assuming responsibility. When a university (or faculty for that matter) lacks critical thought, judgement, dialogue and imagination itself, the "possibility and a culture of openness, debate, and engagement … are now at risk in the latest and most dangerous attack on higher education" (Giroux 2007: 182). For example, when a faculty does not publicly acknowledge its research interests and pioneers, or when a faculty fails to provide students with the skills and knowledge to expand their capacities "both to question deep-seated assumptions and myths that legitimate the most archaic and disempowering social practices that structure every aspect of society and to take responsibility for intervening in the world they inhabit" (Giroux 2007: 182), then such an institution has lost its soul. In addition, when such an institution's unconditional freedom to question and assert—through research and student throughput—is threatened, its commitment to a future democratic project will be curtailed. Democratic pedagogy should always represent a responsible commitment to the future, and it remains the task of academics to ensure that the future points the way to a socially more just world in which "the discourses of critique and possibility in conjunction with the values of reason, freedom, and equality function to alter, as part of the broader democratic project, the grounds upon which life is lived" (Giroux 2007: 181).

Recently, we have become concerned with the lack of research production and lack of students who have the critical human agency both to question freely and to assert themselves authoritatively, and also concerned about academics who do not enter the fray of critical engagement through awareness and listening. Maybe it is about time that academics seriously rethink their responsibility to higher education in relation to a university without ruins! Such a university would be one committed to the democratic project of always questioning itself and preventing itself from ever being conceived of as a finished product. It is in the latter regard that Teaching for Change could be considered a serious democratic imaginary within the realm of online higher education.

8.4 Disruptive Pedagogic Encounters

In this section, we argue that Teaching for Change has the potential to enhance disruptive pedagogic encounters in higher education, especially in relation to an African philosophy of education. First, we expound on Teaching for Change as an initiative in higher education that grew out of a concern to advance access to higher education. Paradoxically, we show that Teaching for Change might not strictly advance equal access and inclusion but have the potential to cultivate student capacities of a critically transformative kind, more specifically, rhizomatic thinking, criticism and recognition of others. Second, we show, with reference to Teaching for Change, how an African philosophy of education should be considered as apposite to advance disruptive pedagogic encounters in higher education.

It is widely acknowledged by pioneering MOOC educators in the world that this fast-growing trend "will change the [higher] education landscape" (Kim 2015: vii). It is further contended that MOOCs, as a manifestation of the use of technology in higher education, will "open up new educational possibilities" (Kim 2015: vii). We concur and contend that in South African higher education, MOOCs have emerged as innovative online curriculum and pedagogic initiatives to provide access to non-traditional university students to engage in higher education studies. Basically, MOOCs are "online courses mediated by information and communication technology" (Klobas et al. 2015: 10). As one of the leading universities in South Africa, Stellenbosch University, like the University of Cape Town and Witwatersrand University, has recently implemented its first MOOC entitled "Teaching for Change: An African Philosophical Approach" under discussion throughout this book. As has been alluded to previously, the rationale for this MOOC is aimed at engaging students in pedagogic activities that orientate them towards identifying major societal problems on the African continent and then proceeding with examining some of the implications of such problems for higher education in particular. This MOOC on an African philosophy of education is not only geared towards making people think differently in and about education on the African continent, but also towards showing that philosophy of education could be thought about differently in relation to African higher education. Through the link provided, you may get some idea of what our MOOC entails: https://www.futurelearn.com/courses/african-philosophy. Thus, this MOOC has been designed and developed within a conceptual framework of what it means to engage in pedagogic encounters if one were to be situated in an educational institution or to participate in an educational practice uniquely relevant to Africa. Put differently, for too long higher education on the African continent had been subjected to some of the prejudices of Africa's former colonial powers. One way of contributing towards a decolonisation agenda is to show how African higher education could be reconceptualised within a post-colonial paradigm that draws on ideas and concepts that could foreground African thinking and doing vis-à-vis decolonisation and, more specifically, decoloniality.

Moreover, generally, MOOC learners are mostly school learners, university students and life-long learners, many of whom already have some university qualification (Klobas et al. 2015: 17). Some of the reasons offered as to why students enrol for MOOCs range from pleasure and experience of MOOC participation, to those concerned with utilitarian motivations, that is, reasons mostly associated with instrumental returns gained from participation or, in some cases, completion of an academic programme (Klobas et al. 2015: 17). We infer from some of the comments from students that many of those who enrolled for Teaching for Change wanted to deepen their knowledge of an African philosophy of education and/or even to think differently about such a form of education, whereas other students considered the course an entry into a leading African university at which they could pursue a university course.

As has already been discussed in previous chapters, for this specific course, dystopias such as dictatorships, food insecurity, terrorism, student protestations against fee increases and mediatory processes of truth and reconciliation have been identified as major societal problems besetting contemporary societies. In an analytical and political way, students in Teaching for Change are expected to examine some of the implications of the aforementioned problems for higher education, more specifically teaching and learning in higher education institutions. In the main, the philosophical approach of identifying a problem and looking for its educational implications, underscores the pedagogic activities on which students and university educators embark collectively. The latter approach to analytic educational inquiry is linked to what has been couched as African philosophy of education (Waghid 2014). As has been argued for previously, such a philosophy of education is constituted by what is known as traditional ethno-philosophy (such as using artefacts, poems, literature and the cultural experiences of Africans to analyse education) on the one hand, and communitarian philosophy of education (that is, doing things in community without abandoning one's autonomy) on the other. Together, these two interrelated forms of philosophy of education have been articulated as an *ubuntu* philosophy of education, that is, a philosophy of education geared towards the cultivation of humaneness, human interdependence and cooperation, and justice. Small wonder we have articulated the rationale for Teaching for Change as *ubuntu* justice.

Interspersed with videos, summaries of texts, activities and podcasts (audio recordings of university educators' responses to student queries), the course is presented over a four-week period allowing for autonomous, open, reflexive and deliberative student engagement in and about understandings of an African philosophy of education and its implications for pedagogic change. Together with our collaborating partner, FutureLearn in the United Kingdom, students are exposed to online course material and activities that allow them to engage critically with one another and with the thoughts and responses of the lead educators. This approach to online teaching and learning is not uncommon—other MOOC platforms and university choices for partnerships include Coursera (United States), edX (United States), Blackboard Course sites (United States), and ALT (United Kingdom) (Haywood and Macleod 2015: 47). Among the most pertinent pedagogic decisions that have informed the design and development of Teaching for Change at our institution have been the following: course rationale, goals and themes; course timing and pacing; course structure and content, self-assessment activities; and assessment of the course in relation to course outline and content. Besides having followed established instructional and web design techniques, we want the students who participate in Teaching for Change to act autonomously and reflexively, yet deeply respectful of other students with whose thoughts and ideas they could engage critically. This implies that our self-assessment and open assessment activities invariably have to invoke students' potentialities as they endeavour to speak their minds—a view of learning commensurate with what it means to decolonise higher education in Africa. Speaking one's mind does not imply that one merely says what comes to mind. Rather, speaking one's mind means opening oneself up to criticism by others who might find one's views acceptable or not. In the same way, one is expected to offer responses to others' thoughts of one's views. In other words, students are not just told what to do, but are also motivated to reach their own justifiable conclusions. It is in the light of the aim of the course that students should come to speech that we shall now examine how three different and intertwined understandings of learning contribute towards the enhancement of what can be referred to as a pedagogy of decolonisation and decoloniality. Following that, we examine why a case can be made for rhizomatic, critical and recognisable pedagogy as a corollary of human actions (of both students and lead university educators) of a decolonised and decolonial kind.

Our course design and development, especially authoring, instructional design and video recordings, can be presented as a rhizomatic map that "is open and connectable in all of its dimensions: it is detachable, reversible, susceptible to constant modification … [with] multiple entryways and exits" (Deleuze and Guattari 1987: 12). Referring to the four themes, students were encouraged to (re)construct and deconstruct meanings of an African philosophy of education that could be detached from a linear understanding of knowing things. That is, students did not have to examine first what multiple notions of an African philosophy of education involve; rather, with some idea of the practice, they were required to embark on some pursuit of what the implications of this approach would be to higher education and concomitantly to an education for *ubuntu* justice. In much the same way as examining a rhizome, students could start off with a "shattered" or "broken" thought at any point in the course and then rupture their thoughts in such a way that these thoughts followed their own "lines of flight". This means that they could use their rudimentary understanding of the practice and then set out to examine its implications for education. Therefore, a thought is rhizomatic in the sense that "[i]t has neither beginning nor end, but always a middle (*milieu*) from which it grows and [from] which it overspills" (Deleuze and Guattari 1987: 21). When students embark on such an approach to learning, they pursue lines of segmentarity and stratification or lines of flight by which they come to enunciate assemblages of understanding, not in some arborescent or hierarchical way—such as moving from one point of understanding to another—but rather, in a way that signifies "coming and going rather than starting and finishing" (Deleuze and Guattari 1987: 25). Put differently, learning rhizomatically as encouraged through Teaching for Change means that students could connect any particular thought to any other thought—establishing different lines of flight—in their attempts to "make new connections" (Deleuze and Guattari 1987: 15). That is, they could connect understandings of doing an African philosophy of education with making a case for good living. As pointed out in some of the comments on the Teaching for Change site, students pursued different lines of flight to derive particular understandings of an African philosophy of education. For them, it seems as if their often diverse and contrasting understandings of African philosophy of education are connected with their own situational views on education, and then they try to make links with meanings of the concept as they are confronted by it. Their learning of the concept also brought them into conflict with ideas such as what makes the concept of African education uniquely African. This is to be understood, as working with a concept rhizomatically does not mean that one ever has a complete understanding of the concept. Instead, one's understanding of the concept evolves as one endeavours to be on the move constantly searching for new lines of flight and, by implication, understandings of an African philosophy of education. One thing of which students are aware is that the concept is constantly in the making, depending on the new understandings and perspectives they encounter in their pedagogic online moments.

Next, the question is, what makes such a way of learning critical? To practice criticism—a matter of learning to act critically—involves students being "grown up enough to make up their own minds" (Foucault 1988: 152). In their identification of problems on the African continent, the students who engage in the Teaching for Change pedagogic activities demonstrated the capacity "to grasp the reality of those problems and to react to them" (Foucault 1988: 152). As lead university educators, we encounter many students making up their minds about societal problems without always having to be told why the problems are so pernicious to education. Many students who offered views on the discussion posts show the inclination to resolve problems in a critical manner. This involves students "pointing out on what kinds of assumptions, what kinds of familiar, unchallenged, unconsidered modes of thought the practices that we accept rest" (Foucault 1988: 154). In a different way, it seems that students no longer think of problems on the African continent as they perhaps formerly thought of them in some linear and even causal ways. They raised concerns about the problems, in particular those that manifest in, for instance, genocide, famine and deforestation. This shows that their understanding of problems on the African continent was not only about the political but also about the moral and environmental. Their thinking had been transformed in a free atmosphere whereby they expressed their critical and reflexive views about the problems, constantly being agitated by "a permanent criticism" (Foucault 1988: 155). They were prepared to conjure up reasons and justifications as to why problems on the continent are untenable and, most poignantly, point out what some of the debilitating consequences of such problems are for education and pedagogic encounters specifically. The numerous discussions among students on the Teaching for Change platform corroborate their interest in learning to "speak up" as an instance of criticism.

What has been quite significant about the pedagogic exchanges that occurred among many students and ourselves was the willingness of all to speak their minds and to act within the present. That is, we were intent on listening to one another's views and criticisms, as was evident in our comments of engagement on the discussion forums. We were not affronted by one another's comments even if such comments appeared belligerent and distressing at times. In a way, our encounters were guided by the art of recognition. Following the seminal thoughts of Giorgio Agamben (2011: 46), it is only through recognition of others that a person constitutes him- or herself as a person. For once, students publicly exhibited their thoughts in "the absence of secrets [and] beyond all mystery and meaning" (Agamben 2011: 90). In other words, students were not afraid to denude their thoughts to the extent that they were willing to share with others what they were thinking and in this way wanted to be recognised as humans willing to disclose what they knew. Some of the comments and exchanges among students on the Teaching for Change site confirmed their insistence on being recognised as persons in pedagogic encounters. The point about recognition is that students are willing to make public their understandings of some of Africa's problems without feeling constrained to do so. It did not matter for students if their views were at times unconvincing or perhaps emotive instead of reasonable, but they were prepared to be known by others concerning their thoughts. In Agambanian fashion, they denuded their thoughts and by implication made their views accessible and vulnerable to scrutiny by others. It did not matter how ill-conceived their views were at times; they only wanted to be recognised for having a point of view to share with others. Furthermore, students desired the articulations of others even if others were in disagreement with them. It is quite an empowering moment in pedagogic encounters to be able to speak one's mind and, simultaneously, to expect the views of others on one's views without being offended by what one hears. To our mind, such pedagogic encounters—where views are denuded and criticised without the possibility of offending one another—are highly critical and reflexive.

This brings us to a discussion of how Teaching for Change engendered disruptive pedagogic encounters. Our reason for focusing on disruptive pedagogic encounters is corroborated by the argument that in any act of decolonisation and decoloniality in which thoughts and practices ought to be framed differently, one ought to rely on a pedagogic art of disruption in order to unsettle the taken-for-granted, established and often debilitating understandings of education. At least three salient benefits can be identified in the quest to cultivate disruptive pedagogic encounters in higher education through MOOCs. First, students' experiences with Teaching for Change enhanced their deliberative interaction with learning course material in association with online peers. Through this course, students learned together and from one another, especially "by real access to other students around the world" (Ranaghi et al. 2015: 97). In other words, the potential of students to rethink taken-for-granted assumptions in their lives through the power of the social web has been amplified (Ranaghi et al. 2015: 97). Second, the high level of student engagement in the absence of the traditional incentive of a university degree is inspiring. The opportunity that students' comments offered others and us to learn from their intellectual work is immense, especially considering how students uniquely create their own pathways to learning as confirmed in several discussion posts. Finally, to have become a learner outside the physical classroom brought to the fore another aspect of learning, namely a learning revolution that enabled these students to create connections and meanings that would invariably affect their own lives.

The high completion rate of students enrolled for Teaching for Change (about 30%) is a testimony of its pedagogic success, considering that many MOOCs have a below 10% completion and success rate. Likewise, success is not measured only in terms of completion rates for that in itself would not give a justifiable account of learning. Success is seen in relation to learning having been critical, reflexive and responsive—a matter of learning having some morally worthwhile ends that could affect societal advancement positively. In addition, the responsiveness about learning connects with the practice of bringing about transformative change in society. In addition, if pedagogic encounters have been instigated by learning of the latter kind, it would not be too presumptuous to equate learning with success. Similarly, learning also resulted in teaching to the extent that teaching was informed and by implication constituted by learning. It is not as if learning required only teaching. Instead, learning influenced teaching in the same way that teaching influenced learning. In this way, teaching and learning in relation to Teaching for Change have been mutually informed pedagogic encounters. Through Teaching for Change, teaching and learning were intertwined as if the two pedagogical actions were inseparable. Teaching influenced learning and learning in turn influenced teaching. In a way, Teaching for Change deepened an understanding of an African philosophy of education and *ubuntu* justice according to learn–teach and teach–learn approaches.

Moreover, for students to have created their own connections and meanings about the course content, which potentially affected their thoughts and practices, it can be argued that through Teaching for Change students came to express what Jacques Rancière refers to as their "equal intelligence"—that is, through course material students were summoned to use their intelligence (Rancière 1991: 39). In this way, the

A Democratic University Without Ruins: Some Reflections...   141

students demonstrated the capacity to learn for themselves without always having to be dependent on the university educators. In other words, the university educators did not assume that students lacked the capacity to speak and offer comments. Rather, in a subjectified or disruptive way, students autonomously appeared within the pedagogic activities and began to reconfigure their learning experiences (Rancière 1995: 35). That is, students were able to come to their own speech as they probed the course material. Our role as university educators was to remind these students that they can see and think for themselves and that they (students) are not dependent on others for their learning, more specifically that they (students) can see and think without our teaching. As Rancière (1991: 12) puts it, these students learned without a "master *explicator*"— that is, we (university educators) engaged in teaching without explanation "by summoning ... students to use their intelligence" (Biesta 2011: 34). Moreover, the fact that they could determine their own learning and teaching, for that matter, allowed them to immerse themselves in the pedagogic online encounters without any fear of being constrained. They did not bother too much about the outcome of their learning but focused on the process of learning as being critical and reflexive interactions with thoughts. Furthermore, students learned without explanation by (de) constructing meanings in the course, thus having created their own paths to learning and having amplified the possibility for societal change. Students and university educators were intellectually equal in the very act of disrupting the Teaching for Change pedagogic activities.

Teaching for Change can be associated with the cultivation of democratic education that remains in potentiality. Students and ourselves recognised that in the pedagogic activities of Teaching for Change there is always the potentiality on our part to see things anew, and to think differently about our pedagogic experiences in relation to societal matters. Of concern in our deliberative pedagogic encounters has always been the cultivation of just human relations. In a way, Teaching for Change offered us (students and university educators) an opportunity to engage in what Jacques Derrida refers to as a "democracy to come"—that is, a radical possibility of deciding and making come about (Derrida 2004: 27). Such a view of democratic engagement is different from liberal understandings that always have some action in mind. We think about Benhabib's (2011) view of deliberative iterations according to which students and educators have to look at things again and again—that is, reflexively; Callan's (1997) view of belligerent democratic occurrences that require participants to enact their encounters distressfully; and Habermas's (1995) view of democratic consensus such as to find ways to agree, even if disagreement seems inevitable. These liberal notions of democratic engagement have been reimagined according to democratic experiences that remain in-becoming. The point is that democratic engagements that remain in potentiality are not yet actualised (and should not be so), for that would mark the end of such a form of engagement. If democratic engagements are yet to come, they invariably remain in potentiality as students and educators engage deliberatively and reflexively without any conditions for reaching some sort of desirable outcome. The outcomes of democratic engagement lie in the ongoing pedagogic activities themselves and there would also be pedagogic spaces to look at things over and over again as they could be otherwise—a pedagogic promise that remains in the making. Teaching for Change has the structure of a promise and not of orienting students towards pedagogic certainty for bringing about change tomorrow. When the students engaged with societal problems in an analytical fashion, they came to the realisation that societal change has the potentiality to come about, thus linking their pedagogic encounters with (im)possible human experiences (Friedrich et al. 2011: 70). It is not that change would ensue instantly. Rather, through disruptive pedagogic encounters, societal change becomes imminent—that is, there is always the possibility that change will be realised.

At the moment, we remain optimistic about the pedagogic advantages of Teaching for Change in the sense that students are included in pedagogic activities and are recognised for their coming to speech. In this way, learning through Teaching for Change is potentially liberating in the sense that students can act autonomously with pedagogic content and even contribute towards (re)shaping and reimagining such content. Teaching for Change cannot be considered a critical pedagogic course, primarily because the potential is always there for students to act with an openness to others' points of view without necessarily withholding and/or abandoning their own critical judgements. Such a form of learning, then, is associated not only with reflexive criticism in a Foucauldian sense but also with the cultivation of democratic experiences that are yet to come for the reason that what is yet to come is contrived and deliberated on collectively or democratically. Such democratic encounters would invariably motivate students and curriculum developers towards considering their work as being always in potentiality, as there is always more to be known because one cannot completely know at everything a given point in time. Our experiences have been guided by what is still to come, as ongoing critical student feedback on new pedagogic courses invariably influences the authenticity of curriculum (re) design and development. Pedagogic encounters in-becoming invariably influence democratic action to such an extent that the latter cannot be exactly determined. Rather, like pedagogic encounters, democratic education is always subjected to ongoing change—a matter of always being inclined to reimagination.

8.5 Summary

Teaching for Change represents a pedagogic opportunity for students and educators to be deliberatively, openly and reflexively engaged in encounters that remain out of bounds. In a way, such pedagogic moments are reflective of untamed variations of democratic education (Waghid 2014) whereby participants are held accountable to one another according to free and unconstrained speech acts. Although pedagogic encounters remain unhindered, it does not mean that injustice to others should be condoned. Rather, speech acts ought to advocate and/or re-signify moments in which injustice would be dealt with meaningfully. Likewise, through Teaching for Change, students are guided by encounters where completeness and certainty are never at play. Instead, they are in pedagogic conversations where rupturing and the fostering of new re-beginnings are always ethical and political possibilities. Students and educators have much to learn as they deal with the unimaginable mysteries and strangeness that their pedagogic contributions incite in the encounters. In the next chapter, we examine why and how critical, reflexive and responsive pedagogic encounters guide decolonisation and decoloniality in education.

References

Agamben, G. (2011). *Nudities* (D. Kishik & S. Padatella, Trans.). Stanford: Stanford University Press.

Barnett, R. (2013). *Imagining the University.* New York: Routledge.

Barnett, R. (2016). *Understanding the University: Institution, Idea, Possibilities.* New York: Routledge.

Benhabib, S. (2011). *Dignity in Adversity: Human Rights in Troubled Times.* Cambridge: Polity Press.

Biesta, G. (2011). Learner, Student, Speaker: Why It Matters How We Call Those We Teach. In M. Simons & J. Masschelein (Eds.), *Rancierè, Public Education and the Taming of Democracy* (pp. 31–42). London: Wiley-Blackwell.

Callan, E. (1997). *Creating Citizens: Political Education and Liberal Democracy.* Oxford: Oxford University Press.

Deleuze, G., & Guattari, F. (1987). *A Thousand Plateaus: Capitalism and Schizophrenia* (B. Massumi, Trans.). Minneapolis: University of Minnesota Press.

Derrida, J. (2004). *Eyes of the University.* Stanford: Stanford University Press.

Foucault, M. (1988). *Politics, Philosophy, Culture: Interviews and Other Writings 1977–1984* (L. D. Kritzman, Ed.). London: Routledge.

Friedrich, D., Jaastad, B., & Popkewitz, T. S. (2011). Democratic Education: An (Im)possibility that Yet Remains to Come. In M. Simons & J. Masschelein (Eds.), *Rancierè, Public Education and the Taming of Democracy* (pp. 60–75). London: Wiley-Blackwell.

Giroux, H. A. (2007). *The University in Chains.* Boulder: Paradigm.

Habermas, J. (1995). *Justification and Application: Remarks on Discourse Ethics* (C. Cronon, Trans.). Cambridge: Polity Press.

Haywood, J., & Macleod, H. (2015). To MOOC or Not to MOOC? University Decision-Making and Agile Governance for Educational Innovation. In P. Kim (Ed.), *Massive Open Online Courses: The MOOC Revolution* (pp. 46–60). New York: Routledge.

Kim, P. (Ed.). (2015). *Massive Open Online Courses: The MOOC Revolution.* New York: Routledge.

Klobas, J. E., Mackintosh, B., & Murphy, J. (2015). In P. Kim (Ed.), *Massive Open Online Courses: The MOOC Revolution* (pp. 1–22). New York: Routledge.

Ranaghi, F., Saberi, A., & Trumbore, A. (2015). NovoEd, a Social Learning Environment. In P. Kim (Ed.), *Massive Open Online Courses: The MOOC Revolution* (pp. 96–105). New York: Routledge.

Rancière, J. (1991). *The Ignorant Schoolmaster: Five Lessons in Intellectual Emancipation*. Stanford: Stanford University Press.

Rancière, J. (1995/1999). *On the Shores of Politics*. London: Verso.

Readings, B. (1996). *The University in Ruins*. Cambridge, MA: Harvard University Press.

Waghid, Y. (2014). *Pedagogy Out of Bounds: Untamed Variations of Democratic Education*. Rotterdam/Boston/Tapei: Sense.

9

Decolonised Education: Cultivating Curriculum Renewal and Decoloniality

9.1 Introduction

At the time of implementing Teaching for Change for a second time via the FutureLearn platform, one of us had been invited to offer presentations at two institutional initiatives regarding university curriculum renewal. Considering that Stellenbosch University is celebrating 100 years of existence, the institutional management deemed it apposite to commemorate the occasion by making curriculum renewal one of its primary initiatives. The latter in itself is an acknowledgement that the rationale that undergirds teaching and learning ought to be reconceptualised in relation to a different university context. What is even more poignant about the renewal agenda of the institution is its focus on decolonisation and decoloniality in relation to curriculum change.

© The Author(s) 2018
Y. Waghid et al., *Rupturing African Philosophy on Teaching and Learning*,
https://doi.org/10.1007/978-3-319-77950-8_9

9.2 Towards an Understanding of Decolonisation

As the term implies, "decolonisation" is an attempt to move away from that which has previously been colonised. As has by now been universally established, colonisation accentuates a fractured approach to human living whereby some dominant group of people considers it appropriate and justifiable to impose their ways of living and being on others, which often results in a dismissal of the others' rights to decide things for themselves. In a way, colonisation implies assimilating some people into the dominant ways of being in a society that often results in excluding and marginalising people who might not necessarily have the capacity to resist such a form of control and alienation. For example, in its heyday, the apartheid curriculum in South Africa mostly reflected the dominant groups' interests at the expense of others' cultural, intellectual and political ways of being. Decolonising education implies that the dominant ways of being of a selected few should be ruptured in order for education to become reflective of the knowledge interests of all a society's people.

The upshot of rupturing a dominant curriculum is that people have to take the initiative to think and act for themselves rather than constantly being told what to do. Simply put, decolonisation implies an intent on the part of all people to look critically at the curriculum, and this would allow people to question the underlying assumptions of such a curriculum. In the first place, we use the concept "curriculum" as referring to a "complicated conversation" as espoused by the prominent curriculum scholar, Bill Pinar (2004: 9). In such a curriculum, "academic knowledge, subjectivity, and society are inextricably linked" (Pinar 2004: 11). The conversation about curriculum further requires "intellectual judgement, critical thinking, ethics, and self-reflexivity … [and] a common faith in the possibility of self-realization and democratization" (Pinar 2004: 8). Here, "self-reflexivity" and "democratisation" refer to a kind of questioning that brings into controversy what people encounter without just endorsing uncritically, say, a curriculum and its goals. When students and educators question a university curriculum, they rupture subjectively its knowledge interests, that is, they contest its reasonableness and legitimacy as a curriculum that can be responsive to a transformative societal context. In relation to Teaching for Change, our expectation has always been that students should rupture the assumptions of African ways of thinking, doing and acting. Most importantly, it was our expectation that students would think more openly and reflexively about what they have encountered in Teaching for Change and then look at changing some of the undesirable aspects of their own education and perhaps societal contexts, or even take issue with some of the concepts espoused through Teaching for Change as they endeavour to make better sense of their societal concerns—a matter of enacting curriculum inquiry. Hence, it is not surprising that some students reinterpreted the notion of an *ubuntu* justice as relevant to education in multiple educational spheres. By implication, decolonisation does not exclusively mean questioning the underlying assumptions of a curriculum, but actually coming up with ways as to how detrimental educational agendas can be rethought and reimagined in pedagogically more apt ways and then to imagine how societal concerns can be addressed. Some aspects of the post-apartheid university curriculum, for instance, still reflect a deep affiliation to prediction and control as if educational matters ought to succumb to manipulation. The latter has been compounded by the democratic state's insistence on embracing an outcomes-based approach to education. Although outcomes-based education has been contested in most policy contexts, the remnants of this untenable education approach seem to have manifested in subsequent curriculum policy statements, most notably the National Curriculum Statement (NCS) of 2006 (DoE 2006) and the Curriculum Assessment Policy Statement (CAPS) of 2012 (DoE 2012). Both these policy statements were inextricably connected to a form of outcomes-based education that focused on pre-packaged curriculum materials vis-à-vis the teaching of learning outcomes and aims of education, respectively.

Although the aforementioned curriculum statements were intended to break with the apartheid educational aims, in many ways they reinforced an education system that did not allow critical and autonomous thinking to flourish. The upshot is that such curricular statements seem to be related to producing a type of student who does not actually have the capacity to engage self-reflexively and democratically in societal issues of major concern. This is so despite curriculum policy makers arguing on the contrary that a post-apartheid curriculum aims to produce autonomous and critical-minded citizens. Not much can be made of aspirations such as the latter, if curriculum statements seem to be incommensurate with transformative change. Similarly, through their teaching and learning strategies, prominent universities on the African continent make the claim that university education should produce global citizens in order to ensure world competitiveness. This in itself seems to be a clear remission of the importance of students to be locally responsive to their societal contexts. Yet, quite ambiguously, such prominent HEIs are adamant that they should also be concerned with social justice, which in itself is possible only if students were to be initiated into understandings of local responsiveness. In fairness to such universities, the recognition of producing graduates with critical thinking capacities is important in relation to cultivating their disciplinary and professional knowledge vis-à-vis society at large. Of course, developing critical and reflexive capacities on the part of students is important to address concerns in their societies. However, the latter happens as a consequence of such students' local responsiveness first, and not through becoming a global citizenry. Thus, we contend that universities ought to produce global citizens, which would empower them to be locally responsive yet, simultaneously, global as well.

Moreover, for example, we think of how theoretical aspects of a curriculum are considered as ways to impose dominant thinking on students' learning without their potentialities being evoked. Unless students are not considered beings who have to be subjected to control and manipulation, their learning would not be transformative or, for that matter, educational at all. The advantage of a decolonised approach to students' learning is that their potentialities would be evoked to the extent where they subjectively think for themselves without being controlled and manipulated by university educators. In sum, decolonisation implies that, first, a curriculum should be looked at differently to such an extent that its probing reflects a deep desire to look at things anew. Second, decolonisation draws on the human subjectivities of people so that they become reflective beings intent on accentuating lasting change. Third, decolonisation aims to give critical voice to people on the grounds that they have something to offer in relation to societal and pedagogic

Decolonised Education: Cultivating Curriculum Renewal... **151**

change—that is, they can rupture what is sometimes considered to be inappropriate forms of living and learning.

We now want to show how decolonised education could enhance a more credible form of democratic citizenship education, considering that the latter ought to be one of the primary goals of a decolonised curriculum. A justification for a decolonised curriculum being linked to democratic citizenship education is based on the view that such a form of education considers the cultivation of responsible, critical and empowered individuals as important to their collective development.

9.3 Rethinking Democratic Citizenship Education

Thus far, we have argued that decolonised education involves the following aspects: critically thinking anew, reflexively bringing about change and evoking people's potentialities. Next, we examine how such an approach to education could engender a renewed understanding of democratic citizenship education. In a most recent work, *African democratic citizenship education revisited* (Waghid and Davids 2018) African democratic citizenship has been couched along the following dimensions: deliberative engagement, human co-belonging and attunement with African interests (Waghid and Davids 2018). Although African democratic citizenship education is contested in many academic circles (most notably by those who want to dissociate democratic citizenship education from anything African and quite prejudicially are prepared to assert that such a form of education—that is, democratic citizenship education—can be associated with Anglo-Saxon and European contexts only), we hold a different view. Unlike Kai Horsthemke and Penny Enslin (2005: 54) who pose the question of whether there is indeed a uniquely African philosophy of education and, by implication, a tenable form of African democratic citizenship education, we hold the view that democratic citizenship education cannot be distanced from African educational interests. In contrast to Horsthemke and Enslin (2005: 75) who assert that such a view of education is pedagogically and morally contentious and uneasy, we contend that African democratic citizenship education is not only distinctively African but also holds the promise of engaging humans in deliberation and of an attunement to co-belonging.

Considering the above, we now offer a reconceptualised notion of democratic citizenship education vis-à-vis decolonisation. First, a curriculum that does not cultivate deliberative engagement is oblivious of an understanding that education in itself is an encounter whereby people listen to one another and proffer articulations in defence of their points of view. When people engage, they bring to the encounter ways of seeing things differently without unjustifiably dismissing the "truth claims" of others. The very act of deliberation allows people to bring their contending views into consideration by one another without the possibility that such views would be unreasonably and unjustifiably dismissed. Here, the very act of decolonisation resonates with deliberative engagement in the sense that both practices are connected to listening to alternative perspectives and rupturing that which confronts people. Simply put, decolonisation implies taking issue with colonisation, which manipulates, controls and coerces humans to do things seemingly against their will. Decolonisation brings into disrepute the hegemony of those who dismiss others and puts forward a claim to a recognition of others and others' differences. In much the same way, deliberative engagement allows humans to engage with difference, and does not permit humans to dismiss otherness unduly. Deliberation requires that humans exercise their moral and pedagogic autonomy and stake their claims to that which is still in-becoming. Simply put, deliberating about this or that matter is not some mechanical and conclusive exercise. Rather, educators and students engage deliberatively when they take into critical controversy one another's articulations and justifications with the intention that something more plausible might ensue. In a way, there is no end to learning, as learning about this or that has no finality. One can always learn more and new perspectives might constantly challenge one's firmly held views. Thus, the spirit of deliberative inquiry is that there is always the possibility to learn more and to come up with more credible justifications. Failing to do so, would not only signal the end of learning, but also the end of education. Deliberation is an act of education that allows educators and students to take issue with that which dismisses, overpowers and excludes.

Deliberative inquiry is a necessary practice in the pursuit of decolonising the curriculum. Decolonisation of the curriculum is not a once-off pedagogic form of engineering. Instead, decolonisation is an act of taking issue with the debilitating consequences of colonisation. Furthermore, for decolonisation to take place, educators and students require deliberation. In a previous work (Waghid and Davids 2014: 177), it is argued that embarking on an ethics of responsibility, humanity and dignity, pedagogic encounters might turn out to be more deliberative. In extension of the latter view, we contend that inserting such a deliberative ethics of responsibility, humanity and dignity within pedagogic encounters holds the potential to decolonise such curricular activities.

Second, whereas citizenship insists that people co-belong unconditionally, decolonisation implies that people already co-belong in their effort to actuate changes in their lives. In a way, decolonisation takes further what citizenship initiates. The point is that people can experience a sense of co-belonging when they interdependently engage with one another as citizens of nation states. They experience this co-belonging on the grounds that they share a common heritage, customs and traditions, and endeavour to realise their aspirations in an atmosphere of mutuality and interdependence. However, this does not necessarily mean that their co-belonging would oblige them to pursue transformative action of benefit to all. It is decolonisation that urges them to enhance their co-belonging towards the cultivation of just action—that is, action of a transformative kind or, more specifically, to cultivate *ubuntu* justice. It is not sufficient that people merely co-belong without any realisation that their co-existence and interdependence have actually consolidated their mutual dependence and, hence, do not consider the need to confront their complacency due to certain societal privileges that they might enjoy. Currently, in South Africa, many people living in informal settlements have become satisfied with the basic social provisions they might enjoy— the right to education, equal treatment and franchise—yet, their inadequate housing and sanitation facilities do not always prompt them and government to change people's appalling living conditions. It is very much as if people have citizenship but do not really enact it. What decolonisation does is to prompt people to transformative action so that they can effect constructive change in their lives. Through decolonisation, humans are urged to act in the quest to ensure that liberation and freedom come their way. Citizenship affords people rights and responsible action towards co-living. However, it is decolonisation that extends humans' co-living into acts of empowerment and emancipation.

Third, whereas democratic citizenship invokes people's aspiration to be attentive to their deliberative concerns and co-belonging and rights, interests and aspirations, decolonisation intimates that such change ought to summon people to act reflectively and openly about their (un) known conditions. To be open and reflective about your condition is connected to what David T. Hansen refers to as having a reflective loyalty towards what is known to one (Hansen 2011). Decolonisation prompts in people not just a reflective and open loyalty to the known, but also to show, in Hansen's words, a reflective openness to the new (Hansen 2011)—that is to be reflectively open to what is still to come. Moreover, when people are summoned by themselves to exercise their reflective and open thinking in the pursuit of that which is both known and yet to come, they are well on their educational path towards decolonisation. Such an understanding of decolonisation immediately challenges the complacency that might characterise democratic citizens as they make sense of the social surroundings in which they live. Being summoned to act reflectively and openly about your social conditions and to think of a better future take democratic citizenship beyond the idiosyncratic view of just being concerned about your immediate common interests. Being reflectively open in a decolonised way about one's rights and sense of co-belonging immediately alerts one towards a recognition of obstacles that may stand in one's way when one is attempting to enact one's rights, responsibilities and sense of co-belonging. It could be that one reflectively exercises one's openness to those actions that might inhibit one in charging one's citizenship, and one would counteract such obstacles associated with racism, exclusion and marginalisation. In a similar way, one also extends one's reflective openness to that which is yet to come, such as thinking through the unexpected, the unpredictable and the unknown.

The question arises: How does the aforementioned notion of decolonised education potentially affect pedagogic university encounters among students and educators and, by implication, curriculum renewal?

9.4 Decolonised Education and the Enactment of Just Pedagogic Encounters

In the first place, any form of decolonised education that invokes people's critical and independent (autonomous) self-understandings with the intent to enact transformative change in their societal and educational situations, implies that people have to act justly. Just action in turn evokes in people an autonomy whereby they want to do things for themselves without always being told what to do. Simply put, people would earnestly be reflexive about issues that confront them without being instructed to respond to the challenges lying ahead. In Teaching for Change, there are numerous contributions of students where their autonomy is accentuated. They came up with the most thoughtful and reflective understandings as they expressed what Jacques Rancière (1991) refers to as their equal intelligence on the MOOC platform. It is as if they were summoned to articulate their equal intelligences by coming up with narratives to which some of us have not given any thought before. This expression of students' equal intelligence on a platform where criticality and reflectiveness were very prominent is a vindication that open classrooms have the potential to cultivate autonomous and, by implication, intellectually reflexive and equal beings. Of course, not all student narratives were equally enriching and thoughtful. However, at least, the platform afforded students the opportunity to express their intellectual equality as they reflectively and openly came to reason. In this regard, it would not be too exuberant to claim that Teaching for Change offered students and educators an opportunity to articulate their intellectual equality and, as a corollary, it confirmed the presence of decolonisation. Participants' pedagogical action has become embellished with decolonisation as a corollary of their willingness to engage deliberatively with one another, take issue with one another, and to come up with meanings that participants might not have thought of before. In several ways, their meanings were connected to starting anew and to seeing the other side of the metaphoric coin. Also, for the latter to happen, they were prepared to take risks within the pedagogic encounters. The risks that participants were prepared to take invariably involved expressing their resistance to any form of action that would hold them captive in a morally unjust way. They had to take a stand against that which they found unpleasant and condescending to human actions whether in the form of genocide, terrorism or even human trafficking or child labour.

Moreover, considering that Teaching for Change dealt with content in and about African ways of being, acting and thinking, it is not unexpected to observe how positively students responded to notions that accentuated the idea of Africanness. Being African implies that one not only reflects openly on how the African condition has been subjected to colonisation and oppression but also how such debilitating living conditions ought to be deconstructed and given new meanings—a matter of decolonisation being put to work. Small wonder that Kwase Wiredu calls for the Africanisation of knowledge (including science and technology) in African cultures, what he refers to as the harmonisation of African insights with knowledge that originates elsewhere (Wiredu 2005). Such a move in itself is a decolonised one, in the sense that one desires and aspires to be in a better societal condition without remaining subjected to the tortures of colonisation. Likewise, N'Dri Assié-Lumumba calls for the formation of African (philosophy of) education along the lines of an African ethos, culture and modes of knowledge construction vis-à-vis other dominant ideas but not at the expense of African education (Assié-Lumumba 2005). In other words, decolonisation does not simply mean wishing away anything that is not from Africa, for example. Rather, decolonisation intimates that African priorities are given consideration on the grounds that African knowledge could influence discoveries made elsewhere and not just buried in obscurity as if African education is insignificant. In addition, when such decolonised knowledge contributes to redressing human suffering and humiliation, decolonisation will have strengthened African identity in scholarship (Wiredu 2005: 16).

Moreover, with reference to Teaching for Change, the notion of *ubuntu* justice especially gained careful consideration as many students thought it apposite to reimagine a different African educational experience along the lines of *ubuntu* (human co-belonging and deliberative engagement) and justice for all people living on the continent. What is evident about participants' interpretation of *ubuntu* justice is that the notion has the potential to enact reconciliation and nation building together with affirming people's rights and responsibilities towards one another and just forms of human living. Here we specifically think about acting justly in relation to contentious practices such as tolerance, forgiveness and hatred. First, to tolerate does not mean that one uncritically accepts or tolerates, say, reprehensible forms of human behaviour. Rather, tolerance implies that one acts with a form of rupturing whereby one momentarily sits back and listens to what has transpired even if what one listens to happens to be repugnant and reprehensible. Then one would be obliged to act in defence of just human action. In a pedagogic encounter, tolerance therefore does not mean that one merely allows students to speak their minds without any sort of justification. Instead, tolerance implies that an educator momentarily withholds his or her judgement in order to give students an opportunity to say something different—which could be abhorrent—before the educator responds. That is, the rupturing does not happen during the articulation phase, but after students have spoken. The point is that judgements are not rendered prematurely. This kind of pedagogic tolerance would go some way to resolving unjust expressions in the sense that judgements are withheld for the sake of letting the articulations through. In another work, we posited:

> [A] tolerance of dissent is not one whereby [university] teachers just permit anything and everything that passes them by. Rather, in the moment, judgment is withdrawn to allow fractured articulations to remain in potentiality. The recognition that a student's articulation is wrong, yet in that fleeting moment a teacher reserves judgment without being subservient to ill-conceived articulations. (Davids and Waghid 2017: 173)

Second, like tolerance—a pedagogic act in the moment—forgiveness is also a momentary act of oblivion whereby one suppresses derogatory thoughts of someone else to allow for more rethinking and later pedagogic rebuttal. If one does not forget momentarily, such actions could hamper progress rather than encourage it. One does not forgive by forgetting the injustices perpetrated against humanity. Rather, one temporarily finds oneself in a state of oblivion to allow the injustice to be examined and spoken about. If not, we might not resolve the deep-rooted crisis about dilemmas such as crimes against humanity and other human rights violations. The idea of forgiveness is to allow people to be in a state of oblivion temporarily in order to deal more justifiably with inhospitable moments. Third, hating someone is a strong human act. However, it is an acknowledgement that someone's actions were of such a nature that resentment and rejection are the only means to combat the injustice. To hate someone is a denial of that person's human right (although he or she might have acted monstrously) to be respected as a human being. Thus, practising hospitality would imply that a person recognises the faults of others but does not see it fit to resent the other in his or her entirety. There has to be a moment of reconciliation where the one who hates will restrain such human anger towards another. In addition, if hatred is subdued, the possibility that humans will reconcile and perhaps find new hospitable ways of co-living might just be possible. This is impossible when hatred holds sway.

Moreover, through Teaching for Change, Africanness was clearly espoused and from our analyses of the students' comments, Africanness accentuated the importance of non-alienation, non-repression and inclusion. Non-alienation, non-repression and inclusion are human practices that work against exclusion and subjugation. If the latter happens, the possibility of human co-belonging and co-living might not ensue. It is important, therefore, for any form of curriculum renewal that advances inclusion and non-discrimination to become facets of any reimagined curriculum. In a way, students wrote their own texts and were not always reliant on what exists in the cannons of knowledge, as if to say that learning is a situated experience. This does not mean that Plato, Socrates and Aristotle have no intellectual place in African curriculum renewal. Rather, curriculum renewal also has to foreground knowledge pertaining to the context within which people find themselves and those same contexts that they endeavour to improve. It is in the latter regard that Wiredu (2005: 16) posits the following about decolonised knowledges and education:

> Attention to foreign sources of *insight* cannot compromise African identity. If there is an important truth in the Buddha or Kant or Dewey or Heidegger or Quine, you can take it and add to it the truths that you have obtained

from your own African tradition of thought. As the Akans of Ghana say, truths cannot conflict. (*nokware mu nni abra*)

Finally, a decolonised educational experience is a just human action. Throughout two presentations of Teaching for Change, we have not encountered any form of dismissal of the views of others. This does not mean that all the views articulated have been persuasive and reasonable—of course not. But then, unreasonableness and unconvincingness are not reasons to undermine and insult people. Also, it does not mean that a lack of belligerence and distress were not present. At times, students responded strongly to inarticulate views and often provoked others to proffer more convincing viewpoints. But then, the practice of belligerence was never meant to marginalise and exclude, but rather to provoke students to refine their thoughts and to produce more eloquent arguments. Again, Teaching for Change opened students up reflectively, critically and transformatively. This is what decolonised university education ought to involve without dismissing and excluding views that might be truncated or inarticulate, yet, hold the potential to become persuasive.

9.5 Towards Decolonised Curriculum Renewal

Nowadays, certainly at the institutions where we work, the concept of curriculum renewal has emerged as a potential panacea for the decontextual dilemma that confronts universities and, more specifically, university education. By the decontextual dilemma, we mean curricula at universities that are unresponsive to societal contexts and disconnected from the life experiences of those whom such curricula envisage to educate. Of course, situating curricula is important for the decolonised education agenda on the African continent. But such an agenda would mean very little if the equal intelligence of students and educators cannot be evoked. Assié-Lumumba (2005: 52) aptly reminds us of the following in defence of her view on decolonisation of university education:

> Even if Europeans in Africa had imagined a fully benevolent colonial administration with policies genuinely designed for the benefit of Africans, they would not have been successful in fully understanding and responding to the educational needs and imperatives of a free people in a colonial context. For they could not have responded appropriately to the educational needs of Africans by using their own European ethos as point of reference instead of an African one … Even if the Europeans could have succeeded in trying to use an African ethos to design their colonial education, it would have taken away agency, self-definition and self-determination from Africans.

Furthermore, when students and university educators articulate their intellectual equality they will have been summoned to speak and reimagine curricula openly and reflectively. Similarly, when curricula are not geared towards actuating lasting change on account of the predicament of colonisation and racial exclusion on the African continent, then any attempt to decolonise education might just prove to be futile. As Jane Roland-Martin (2013) aptly reminds us, education that does not invoke the potentialities of people's cultural and societal experiences together with their knowledge and skills ought to be reconfigured as it fails to address the human condition within such communities.

Thus, as we have encountered with Teaching for Change, curriculum renewal ought to be cultivated by those who take curriculum and educational change seriously. Curriculum renewal is not just a tick-box exercise whereby people look out for technical compliance to some contrived curriculum initiative. Curriculum renewal always ought to be present within the presence of those who initiate and engage with the practice. This implies that such renewal, in the first place, should involve the scholar who understands, reconceptualises and enacts the curriculum. For too long, African universities have relied on the technical competence of individuals and agencies to actuate change. Deliberative change only happens on account of people's presences within a community of co-belonging without any condition of belonging. It is not as if curriculum renewal will happen when external advisers are appointed to oversee processes of technical compliance. These initiatives have failed in the past and, as African universities would claim, technical compliance has merely confirmed curricula disconnected from the life experiences of those who matter—the agents of curriculum change—that is, those people who actually embark on curriculum renewal have taken criticality, reflectiveness and openness seriously.

In sum, Teaching for Change has taught us that reconceptualising a curriculum depends overwhelmingly on the critical and reflexive voices of people—our students—who offer critical comments and reflective openings as to why and how change ought to happen. Not taking the voices of students seriously in any form of curriculum renewal will merely perpetuate existing misunderstandings of the curriculum that have permeated (South) African universities for some time. Curriculum renewal has a real chance to bring about meaningful change if enacted along the lines of decolonised scrutiny that concomitantly invokes the practices of reflective, critical and open thinking. African universities can ill afford to ignore the legitimate call of decolonisation.

9.6 Summary: Decolonisation or Decoloniality?

Thus far, our argument has been in defence of Teaching for Change that can engender *ubuntu* justice. In the main, we contend that the cultivation of *ubuntu* justice seems to be commensurate with an enactment of global citizenship education (GCE) for the following reasons. First, *ubuntu* justice, like GCE, is mostly concerned with humans enacting their social responsibility towards others and the environment. That is, Africans enact their social responsibility out of a deep concern for others—both on the continent of Africa and elsewhere—on the grounds that they recognise their human interdependence and co-existence. In this regard, Sehoole and De Wit (2014: 231) posit that social responsibility is key to the enactment of humans' GCE. Second, the enactment of *ubuntu* justice is in consonance with a recognition that people ought to engage openly with one another as they seek to understand one another's cultural norms and expectations, thus responding to other's knowledge interests—a matter of genuinely engaging with others and their socio-environmental contexts (Sehoole and De Wit 2014: 231). Third, when people enact *ubuntu* justice, their predispositions and civic-minded actions manifest in their volunteerism, political activism and community engagement (Sehoole and De Wit 2014: 231)—a matter of enacting their GCE. The point about *ubuntu* justice, as corroborated by MOOC participants, is its alignment with an enactment of GCE in relation to that whereby students are prepared to act as informed citizens capable of engaging with complex local and global concerns.

With the aforementioned understanding of *ubuntu* justice in mind, we now want to consider whether such a notion of *ubuntu* justice can most appropriately be enacted through decolonisation or decoloniality. By now it can be argued that *ubuntu* justice is a liberatory, humanising and politico-pedagogic notion of human action that could counteract dystopic actions such as racism, xenophobia, violence, torture, child labour, human trafficking, colonialism and imperialism. On the one hand, whereas decolonialism delineates the politico-economic sovereignty a more powerful and dominant nation or society exerts over a less powerful and subjugated nation or society, decoloniality signifies the cultural and aspirational patterns internalised by colonised peoples (Maldonado-Torres 2007: 243). Also, as aptly put by Chinua Achebe, decoloniality is that human action in pursuit of epistemic justice (*ubuntu* justice, we would argue) that could redress and counteract human and non-human injustices such as genocide, human trafficking, ethnic conflict, wars of terror and environmental degradation, such as deforestation and climate change (Achebe 1989: 85). Our argument is that decoloniality seems to be an apt pedagogic and political response to rehumanise society towards "globalectical imagination"—that is, to be seriously concerned with the struggles of the marginalised and concomitantly the future of the global world (Wa Thiongo 2012: 8).

Teaching for Change is not just a pedagogic curricular activity concerned with the cultivation of human freedom and the liberation of the mind, but also an inquiry of decoloniality in the quest to cultivate a humanity that is both reflexively open to local and global aspirations. Teaching for Change is at once concerned with opening up pedagogic spaces where participants are always in the making through their deliberative engagements with thought and practice. Teaching for Change participants are required to be deeply reflexive about their learning to the extent that they might see things as they could be. In addition, by far the most poignant pedagogic act of learning they represent is one through which they embark on acts of *ubuntu* justice in relation to which they confront injustices, humiliation and struggle. In short, it behoves universities in Africa to work towards decoloniality in the quest to undermine racism, exclusion, humiliation, deforestation and other forms of human and non-human injustice. In our view, *ubuntu* justice has the potential to deal with the unexpected and unjust. Also, an African philosophy of education to cultivate *ubuntu* justice can enhance curriculum renewal and transformative change in Africa. As universities on the African continent become more open and reflective about their pedagogic practices, and as the concerns for decoloniatity begin to intensify, the need to reconceptualise teaching and learning also amplifies. It is with transformative—decolonial—pedagogic encounters of teaching and learning that African universities could become more responsive to the predicaments on the continent. This is an opportunity that African universities cannot let slip away as, through transformative teaching and learning, the possibility is always there for social, political, moral and environmental change to become more intense. The practices of teaching and learning espoused throughout this book, in particular criticality, openness, reflexivity, autonomy and imaginativeness, are never distant from liberatory pedagogic encounters. If universities ever thought about becoming flagship institutions on the African continent, considering that a lot is now being made of such a classification (Teferra 2017), the time is opportune to buttress their teaching and learning practices with emancipatory concerns of freedom, autonomy, openness, criticality, deliberation and imaginativeness.

References

Achebe, C. (1989). *Hopes and Impediments: Selected Essays*. New York: Anchor Books.

Assié-Lumumba, N. (2005). African Higher Education: From Compulsory Juxtaposition to Fusion by Choice—Forging a New Philosophy of Education for Social Progress. In Y. Waghid (Ed.), *African(a) Philosophy of Education:*

Reconstructions and Deconstructions (pp. 19–53). Stellenbosch: Department of Education Policy Studies.

Davids, N., & Waghid, Y. (2017). *Tolerance and Dissent Within Education.* New York: Palgrave Macmillan.

DoE (Department of Education). (2006). *National Curriculum Statement.* Pretoria: Government Printers.

DoE (Department of Education). (2012). *Curriculum and Assessment Policy Statement.* Pretoria: Government Printers.

Hansen, D. T. (2011). *The Teacher and the World: A Study of Cosmopolitanism as Education.* New York: Routledge.

Horsthemke, K., & Enslin, P. (2005). Is There a Distinctly and Uniquely African Philosophy of Education? In Y. Waghid (Ed.), *African(a) Philosophy of Education: Reconstructions and Deconstructions* (pp. 54–75). Stellenbosch: Department of Education Policy Studies.

Maldonado-Torres, N. (2007). On the Coloniality of Being: Contributions to the Development of a Concept. *Cultural Studies, 21*(2/3), 240–270.

Pinar, W. F. (2004). *What Is Curriculum Theory?* Mahwah: Lawrence Erlbaum.

Rancière, J. (1991). *The Ignorant Schoolmaster: Five Lessons in Intellectual Emancipation* (K. Ross, Trans.). Stanford: Stanford University Press.

Roland-Martin, J. (2013). *Education Reconfigured: Culture, Encounter, and Change.* London: Routledge.

Sehoole, C., & De Wit, H. (2014). The Regionalisation, Internationalisation, and Globalisation of African Higher Education. *International Journal of African Higher Education, 1*(1), 217–241.

Teferra, D. (Ed.). (2017). *Flagship Universities in Africa.* Dordrecht: Springer.

Wa Thiongo, N. (2012). *Globalectics: Theory and the Politics of Knowing.* New York: Columbia University Press.

Waghid, Y., & Davids, N. (2014). On Hospitality, Responsibility, and *ubuntu:* Some Philosophical Remarks on Teaching and Learning in South Africa. In J. E. Petrovic & A. M. Kuntz (Eds.), *Citizenship Education Around the World: Local Contexts and Global Possibilities* (pp. 165–179). New York: Routledge.

Waghid, Y., & Davids, N. (Eds.). (2018). *African Democratic Citizenship Education Revisited.* New York: Palgrave Macmillan.

Wiredu, K. (2005). Philosophical Considerations on the Africanisation of Higher Education in Africa. In Y. Waghid (Ed.), *African(a) Philosophy of Education: Reconstructions and Deconstructions* (pp. 6–18). Stellenbosch: Department of Education Policy Studies.

Postscript: Reflecting on Ruptured Pedagogic Moments in Teaching for Change

Introduction

HEIs have a rich history promoting the sharing of knowledge. In the contemporary era, this idea of sharing knowledge has come under increased strain due to the adoption of commercialised and market-driven practices driving education delivery (King et al. 2014). Despite MOOCs requiring considerable human and capital resources, the prospect of being able to address issues of scale and access to higher education exists (King et al. 2014). At its core, MOOCs reaffirm the HEI history of sharing knowledge, enabling individuals from potentially disadvantaged backgrounds to have access to higher education, as long as they have Internet access. For the case study in question, offering a MOOC was of strategic importance for our institution. It afforded the institution the opportunity to reaffirm its position as a leading research-intensive institution, attract international students and contribute to the knowledge economy of the world in a distinctly African way.

MOOC pedagogy has evolved much since the days when MOOCs were mainly steered by full lectures placed in an online environment. This "instructivist" model of a MOOC sees the course presenter as the custodian of all knowledge, and as all information is rendered asynchronously,

© The Author(s) 2018
Y. Waghid et al., *Rupturing African Philosophy on Teaching and Learning*,
https://doi.org/10.1007/978-3-319-77950-8

there exists little opportunity for student–teacher interaction. In an attempt to democratise these educational practices, MOOC companies have encouraged course developers to adopt what is commonly referred to as a "connectivist" approach. Learning designers make use of a combination of videos, articles, quizzes and forums in an attempt to maximise the potential for students to construct their own knowledge, but also to share their constructions of knowledge. This approach, however, necessitates students to be intrinsically motivated and technically competent to navigate a MOOC platform.

Norton (2013) provides a useful exploration as to why students are motivated to pursue MOOCs, namely enhancing vocational knowledge, improving employment prospects through new credentials and evidence of achievement, and general broadening of the mind. For the case study in question, the course was presented on the British-based FutureLearn platform, wholly owned by the UK-based Open University. Established in December 2012, FutureLearn develops MOOCs with 109 local and international institutions in almost every conceivable subject area. Thus far, it has attracted close to 7 million students from around the world. FutureLearn encourages their partner universities to produce as many courses as possible. They do, however, have an appropriate course portfolio. Their research of the market indicates that there is a strong demand for continual professional development (CPD) courses, falling under the course portfolio. CPD courses are characterised by subject areas, including healthcare, business and management, and education. Individuals who enrol for these courses are typically post-graduate students looking for ways to improve their vocational knowledge and career prospects. The case study in question can be deemed a CPD course in the subject area of education. Titled "Teaching for Change: An African Philosophical Approach", students are encouraged to learn more about this philosophy, its relevance and its capacity to respond to teaching and learning problems in a just manner. The age demographic for "Teaching for Change", indicated in the figure below, further affirms its status as a CPD course, as most students enrolled fall in the 26–35 age group. As discussed earlier, CPD MOOCs afford participants the scope to exchange ideas and experiences from their institutional contexts around the world (Laurillard 2014).

As a CPD MOOC, "Teaching for Change" focuses on pedagogic encounters (more specifically, teaching and learning) to address societal problems endemic to the African continent. Though deemed an "African philosophical approach", the course encourages participants to engage with the course content, while situating themselves within their own educational contexts. The course presenter argues that although "African", the philosophical principles are not endemic to Africa alone, but that any individual, irrespective of his or her context, can participate and share his or her contextualised understandings of knowledge. The course trailer, used to market the course, particularly emphasised the notion of learning together. Subsequently, the course has demographic data indicating a large proportion of students stemming from the United Kingdom, the United States, Australia and South Africa. There were also a few individuals from more remote areas such as Ecuador and Afghanistan, among others. The student distribution graphic seems to indicate that, although the course is deemed an "African philosophical approach", students were not deterred from enrolling for Teaching for Change.

Throughout the four weeks, students engage with subject matter pertaining to:

- African thinking and doing: a way of practicing philosophy of education
- educational encounters as forms of human engagement through an examination of case studies
- moral, compassionate and restorative justice in relation to defensible African education
- teaching and learning in the context of change
- ethno-philosophy and communitarian philosophy of education in relation to *ubuntu* and justice.

Learning Design and Reflections on Learning Through Teaching for Change

Standard MOOC pedagogy postulates a range of activities encompassing video presentations, discussions and automated assessments (Laurillard 2014). This pedagogy negates the variable teaching costs associated with supporting students while a course is running, allowing for large-scale enrolments (Laurillard 2014). "Teaching for Change" adopted a similar pedagogy with an emphasis on students being self-reliant and able to support one another.

Although there are many theories regarding teaching and learning, Laurillard's (2012) book *Teaching as a design science: Building pedagogical pattern for learning and technology* provides an overview of the main theories regarding teaching and learning, from which the learning design underpinning "Teaching for Change" draws. Laurillard's book provides a framework for considering teacher and learner activity, individual and social aspects of learning and the interplay between theory and practice (King et al. 2014). Additionally, the book refers to numerous learning experiences. For instance, learning through *initiation* (reading/watching/listening), *inquiry, practice, production, discussion and collaboration* (Laurillard 2012). The first four of these learning experiences focus primarily on individual learning, whereas learning through *discussion* and *collaboration* refer to social learning.

An *initiation* experience, encompassing reading, watching or listening, focuses primarily on the actions of the teacher, such as the teacher explaining a concept (Laurillard 2012). This does not necessitate a student providing any articulation, although the FutureLearn MOOC platform affords a student the opportunity to add commentary on what is presented by the course presenter (Laurillard 2012).

In Teaching for Change, an *inquiry* learning experience typically follows *initiation*, encompassing reading, watching or listening. During such a learning experience, a student can modulate his or her conceptual understanding through an investigation of texts, documents and other resources. Laurillard (2012: 12) commonly refers to this as "learning through finding out". With an *inquiry* learning experience, there also exists an opportunity for intrinsic and extrinsic feedback (Laurillard 2012). Extrinsic feedback was in the form of *discussion* posts.

Learning through *practice* experiences pertains to a student's application of theory. Students use their developing conceptual understandings towards the realisation of a goal, generating action to achieve. These actions are consequently used to modulate their emerging conceptions intrinsically (Laurillard 2012). Examples of how technologies would be able to facilitate this type of learning would be case studies, modelled answers, simulations, adaptive worlds and micro worlds (Laurillard 2012).

Laurillard (2012) terms learning through *production* a consolidation and an account of a students' learning of *initiation, inquiry* and *practice* experiences. Learning through *production* is simply an articulation of a student's current conceptual understanding that may be in the form of an essay, report, presentation, video, photo, blog or discussion post, to mention but a few. Through such a *production*, the student avails him- or herself of extrinsic feedback from not only a teacher or lecturer, but also peers engaged in all the teaching and learning activities. A *production* learning experience in Teaching for Change was again possible through comment posts. Comment posts in Teaching for Change were manifestations of students developing their understanding.

Regarding the social learning experiences, Laurillard (2012) refers to two types, namely learning through *discussion* and learning through *collaboration*. According to her, learning through *discussion* requires an initial impetus from the teacher in the form of a question or issue. Students are afforded the opportunity to modulate their understandings further, generate ideas and to pose additional questions. Technologies that support this form of learning are asynchronous online discussion forums, synchronous chats and seminars (Laurillard 2012). In Teaching for Change, there were close to 5000 comments posted.

Learning through collaboration differs to learning through *discussion* as it incorporates aspects of learning through *practice, production* and *discussion*. Simply put, as learners engage they may exchange their products of learning through *practice* towards the production of a joint product. Educational technologies, such as wikis and other online knowledge-building platforms may serve as a deliberative sphere through which students are able to engage with one another, sharing different conceptual understandings and the applications thereof. Through this deliberative process, the opportunity exists for students to reach some form of consensus in the form of a joint product. In Teaching for Change, this took the form of a *discussion* thread.

The FutureLearn platform afforded the Teaching for Change learning design team the latitude to create a MOOC encompassing a range of learning experiences. Students' productions in the form of comments served as points of *discussion* and potential points for *collaboration* throughout the course.

As discussed earlier, MOOC pedagogy is characterised by videos, articles, quizzes and discussion forums. Teaching for Change is no different in that it incorporates many of these characteristics but strives to promote a rich social learning experience as well. Themes dealt with include giving thought to African philosophy of education, examining different approaches (genres) to African philosophy of education, exploring a communitarian understanding of African philosophy of education, and African philosophy of education and the cultivation of justice. At the onset of the individual themes in Teaching for Change, there is an initiation experience. As discussed by Laurillard (2012), these *initiation* experiences typically constitute students *reading, watching* or *listening*. In the case of Teaching for Change, a video is used to explain a concept or to provide a brief overview. This does not necessitate a student providing any form of articulation, but encourages a student to modulate his or her own conceptual understanding intrinsically based on what is presented (Laurillard 2012). The videos in Teaching for Change incorporated a plethora of pictures and animations to help support learning experiences to follow.

As a CPD MOOC, there were several reasons for students enrolling in Teaching for Change, as outlined. Although enrolled students were sufficiently motivated and the course marketed as a collective endeavour, it was still important to *initiate* learners to engage in the learning experiences that were to follow. Here, the introductory videos in Teaching for Change played an important role. Students watching the videos could get an overview of the current research in the field of an African philosophy of education. These videos were used to evoke students' intellectual curiosity. Laurillard (2012) argues that enabling students with existing ideas is fundamental to formal education and the progressive development of new ideas. Videos as *initiation* experiences could therefore be viewed as an attempt to foster active learning. These videos were accompanied by a range of different questions for students to consider. Students were encouraged to share their initial comprehension about what constitutes an African philosophical approach before engaging with the rest of the course content and learning activities that followed. An example of a question posed by the course presenter would be (all quotes are reproduced verbatim and unedited):

> Like I am working in analytical philosophy of education, I am interested to know your own educational interests. My interest in African philosophy of education is stimulated by a concern for more deliberative educational encounters amongst students and educators. And what are yours? (Waghid 2017a, b).

To which a student replied:

> As a teaching assistant at one of African universities and in my personal opinions African philosophy of education encompasses all what we do daily (theoretically and practically) in our settings. It entails what we should be doing to respond to the nature and more importantly to critically solve our encounters upon our nature and experiences. This latter means African philosophy of education is uniquely Africanizing the education in imparting skills and knowledge. For years African philosophy was not credited. It was refuted and devalued. But denying this philosophy means there are no humans and life Africa. So, African Philosophy has all so long we accept that Africa has its system. (Elias 2017)

The above response may serve as a validation of how students were motivated to engage in the learning activities that followed.

Following an initiation step in Teaching for Change, there was an *inquiry* learning experience step. This was in the form of a reading or suggested reading, provided by the course presenter. Through an investigation of these readings, a student was afforded the opportunity to modulate his or her conceptual understanding, facilitated by the course presenter (Laurillard 2012). For a learning experience to be effective, it would necessitate a high level of student motivation and self-efficacy, as students investigate and reflect on such readings (King et al. 2014). Teaching for Change, as discussed earlier, can be categorised as a CPD course, typified by post-graduate students, looking for ways to improve their vocational knowledge and career prospects. It is, therefore, assumed that students who enrol for this MOOC are sufficiently motivated to engage with the content and peers.

Access to digital resources, online guidance and software tools, may result in a more effective approach to learning through *inquiry*, according to Laurillard (2012). As mentioned earlier, access to digital resources in the form of links to open educational resources were provided. These open educational resources such as *A companion to African philosophy* (edited by Kwasi Wiredu, 2004), were opportunities for students to work independently from the course presenter and to understand the course presenter's conceptual understanding of the aforementioned philosophy in relation to education. Laurillard (2012) defines this learning through *inquiry* as an attempt to empower students to control their own knowledge and skills development, in contrast to teacher-centred learning activities. It is, however, noted that providing students with such an *inquiry* learning experience, for instance, providing a link to an open educational resource, may not be enough for students to approximate whether their understanding was indeed improving. Here, the course presenter and peers played an important role. The course presenter's role in this regard encouraged students to provide reflections in the form of comment posts on the FutureLearn platform. Students also played a prominent role in the learning design, challenging peers' ideas posted on the platform. As already mentioned, the course presenter was not able to respond to every commented post on the Teaching for Change discussion forums. Therefore, throughout the inquiry learning experiences, comments posted by the course presenter, such as the one below, ensured that students would be stimulated to engage in the learning activities to follow.

> Welcome to you all! I am excited to know that you are engaging with the text and one another. Yes, this is a course about African thinking and doing – that is, think about and of problems or ideas related to Africa then try to uncover reasons for such situations. When one does so, you are thinking and reflecting about issues. This is my understanding of African philosophy of education! (Waghid 2017a, b)

Through an *inquiry* learning experience in Teaching for Change, students were encouraged to adopt a critical and analytical approach, engaging with content, towards a greater sense of ownership that would hopefully develop throughout the course.

Laurillard (2012) describes learning through *production* as a consolidation and an account of a student's learning in terms of the initial learning through *initiation, inquiry* and *practice* experiences. Learning through *production* is simply an articulation of a student's current conceptual understanding that may be in the form of an essay, report, presentation, video, photo, blog or discussion post, among others. Through such a *production*, the student avails him- or herself of extrinsic feedback from not only a teacher or lecturer, but also from peers engaged in the teaching and learning activities. According to the analytics provided by FutureLearn, each student produced approximately 10 comments per week. The comments were posted in the range of different learning experiences throughout the 4-week course amounting to a total of over 5000 comments.

Learning through *practice* experiences pertains to a student's application of theory. Students developed conceptual understandings towards the realisation of a goal generating action to achieve. These actions were consequently used to modulate their emerging conceptions (Laurillard 2012). Examples of how technologies would be able to facilitate this type of learning would be case studies, modelled answers, simulations, adaptive worlds and micro worlds (Laurillard 2012). Teaching for Change makes use of five case studies as modelled responses. These modelled responses, presented as videos, show how an African philosophy of education could be used to address problems endemic to the African continent. Case studies include food security and insecurity, military dictatorships, terrorism, the Truth and Reconciliation Commission (TRC) and the South African student protests due to the hike in tuition fees. To ensure authenticity and to make sure that the case studies are true to life in nature, news footage was acquired from an ITN Source. ITN Source libraries house footage from Reuters, ITN, ITV Studios, Fox News and Fox Movietone, UTV, Asian News International and other specialist collections. For each case study video, an audio narration was provided by the course presenter.

For the first case study, pertaining to military rule, an African philosophy of education framework is applied. This relates to identifying the problem of military rule, ascertaining the reasons why military rule is a problem and finally looking at the educational implications or consequences thereof. Using criticism, an examination of women's farming knowledge is conducted in the second case study. This examination yields potential reasons for why women engage in farming practices. The case study suggests that through women drawing on their lived experiences, using both local and global understandings of crop production, adopting an integrationist approach, there is scope to enhance agricultural practices. For the case study reflecting on the South African student protests, the framework for an African philosophy of education is again used. The course presenter first identifies the reasons behind the protests; second, examines the historical and cultural perspectives of the student protesters; third, discusses the inequity with regard to higher education access; and last, elucidates the implication of these protests for university education. For the case study on combating terrorism, the course presenter uses *ubuntu* as a means to address terrorism. The case study argues that *ubuntu* could serve as a means to promote human co-existence, the recognition of the other, and deliberative engagement to resolve any potential instance of terrorism. The final case study in Teaching for Change deals with the Truth and Reconciliation Commission (TRC) of South Africa as an example through which *ubuntu* justice—moral, compassionate and restorative justice—can be practised. Through this exploration of the TRC, the course presenter discusses how *ubuntu* justice, through compassion and forgiveness, is a means of enacting a moral concern for human beings, compassion and healing, contributing to a culture of respect for human rights and dignity for all citizens of the country.

As mentioned, these case studies, presented in the form of videos, were accompanied by questions setting out specific goals for students. For instance, pertaining to the case study on the South African student protests, the course presenter provided an in-depth analysis of how the adoption of an African philosophical approach could be used to address student protests, with the accompanying question following:

> Now that you have some idea of what a critical discourse means, can you think of a problem in your environment that can be addressed on the basis of some of the features of criticality explained thus far? (Waghid 2017a, b)

In this way, by using FutureLearn *discussion* forums, students were able to share their developing understanding with reference to their own practices. Although the course presenter did not provide a commentary on every comment posted there, analytical responses served as a reference point for students to determine whether they were applying the concept appropriately within their own context. Consequently, using such responses, students could become self-reliant through intrinsic feedback opportunities. An example of this independent learning includes the following comment post:

> In my country the Black Lives Matter, Women's March, and NODAPL (No Dakota Access Pipeline) social movements are all examples of African American, women's, and Native American marginalization. However, through the eyes of critical discourse, these movements present much broader macro problems-how to end institutionalized violence, a persistent gender inequality across race and class, and the degradation of the environment. By reflecting and mobilizing citizens in a democracy toward greater advocacy and social justice work, the consciousness of the public is raised by protests, marches, social media documentation, etc., that are, therefore, positively disruptive because they force people to question long-held views or prejudices they might have had about people and ideas and why change is necessary for progress. (Chandler 2017)

Through such posts, students demonstrated their ability to improve their learning independently from the course presenter. Nevertheless, due to the social nature of FutureLearn courses, there are many instances of students obtaining extrinsic feedback from the course presenter and peers. As students situated their cognition in real-world contexts, the course presenter posted comments such as:

> Thank you, some of the comments have been highly provocative and is at times needed to keep the conversation going! Yet, as Hannah Arendt so aptly reminds us in her famous book *On Revolution*, 'violence only breeds more violence' and when the voices of reason disappear a different form of totalitarianism (domination of one by the other) emerges! (Waghid 2017a, b)

This *practice* learning experience ensured that the Teaching for Change curriculum became meaningful for students. Such authentic learning experiences ensured that the philosophical concepts, which may initially have been viewed by a student as being abstract, could be contextualised within any given context. The effectiveness of such a *practice* learning experience is aptly summed up by the following comment by a student:

> That case study was brilliant. My understanding is therefore that the goals of African philosophy of education are clearly defined. The strength of their unity is clearly seen in the harmony with one another, the result a crop that feeds a nation.

At the SEC/DigiFest 2017 conference, the chief executive officer of FutureLearn, Simon Nelson, described FutureLearn as the "world's premier social learning platform". FutureLearn puts a strong emphasis on *discussion*, where *discussion* is the reciprocal criticism of ideas leading towards the development of deeper conceptual understanding (Laurillard 2012). A major theorist is often cited as the source of the idea that peer *discussion* should play a prominent role in all learning interventions. Peer *discussion* is an effective strategy to negate teacher-centred transmission models, but requires careful orchestration for students to develop their cognitive understanding. Educators have embraced Vygotsky's ideas that peer *discussion* could serve as an impulse for productive internal *discussions* leading to learning. For Teaching for Change, it was our aim to move away from teacher-centred transmission approaches towards social constructivist approaches, where the course presenter is primarily seen as a moderator, rather than as the sole source of knowledge.

The wide-ranging demographic of MOOCs, characterised by students scattered across multiple continents, confirmed that asynchronous online *discussions* were the only viable option to pursue in online education Fortunately, asynchronous online *discussions* offer several didactic benefits. For instance, students are not limited by length or frequency of posts; students are afforded the time to reflect and consequently to change their contributions; the degree of anonymity afforded by an online space affords students the self-confidence to engage online; and it takes less time to read a message than it does to listen to an individual's argument

(Laurillard 2012). The FutureLearn platform afforded students the opportunity to produce a comment post at every step in Teaching for Change. As already mentioned, these posts represented students' comprehension having engaged in prior learning experiences. The feedback that students provide to peers serves as a point of *discussion*. However, the value of these posts rests primarily on whether learners are indeed challenged and are able to respond to criticism with evidence and justification (Laurillard 2012).

Laurillard suggests that, if discussions are to have clear pedagogic value, parameters should be set as to what indeed makes *discussions* valuable. Educators should play prominent roles motivating students to engage. For Teaching for Change, it was important for the learning designers to establish a context conducive to online *discussion*. As with many online courses, this was established by providing students with suitable multimedia and text resources together with clear guidelines indicating what is to be expected from students; however, CPD MOOCs are often characterised by students who are suitably motivated and holding the intellectual prowess to engage online (Laurillard 2012).

Further to the establishment of such a context, Laurillard (2012) suggests that an educator should play a prominent role in creating opportunities for students to apply their understandings to a real-world context, as discussed in the *practice* learning experience. Additionally, open-ended questions were also used to provoke *discussion* among students. The creation of an encouraging, relaxed and supportive environment, by which students' contributions could be affirmed and constructive feedback provided, was encouraged.

Research suggests that for peer *discussions* to be effective, students need to be able to:

- hold a particular stance to a concept or conjecture;
- provide justification for their stance;
- share and criticise points of supposition;
- reflect on their own perspectives;
- work towards an agreed understanding; and
- apply what is learned (Bonk and King 1998).

Throughout Teaching for Change, students were able to adhere to the above criteria by using more than 50 questions posed throughout the course. Students were challenged to adopt a stance in relation to the philosophical topic discussed. They were then encouraged to provide justifications for their points of view and to contextualise their ideas and experiences within their responses. Moreover, their posts represented the consolidation of their learning. Laurillard (2012) refers to this consolidation of *initiation, inquiry* or *practice* experiences as a *production* learning experience. Thus, a deliberative sphere was established encouraging the sharing and criticism of ideas. Moreover, as students negotiated meaning with peers, there was an opportunity to apply what they had learned through the aid of responses, as discussed in the *practice* learning experience. Laurillard (2012) suggests that *discussions* of such a nature will drive internal dialogue and consequently richer understanding of concepts in students.

Researchers in the field of social constructivism often argue that even if online *discussion* occurs on forums, it may not be indicative of a *discussion* forum learning potential (Dysthe 2002). Researchers often argue that merely providing a *discussion* forum does not confirm that meaningful discussion will occur, but that students need to be provided with structure to scaffold their learning (Wu and Hiltz 2004). Earlier, we explored aspects which may result in effective *discussion*, such as encouraging students to hold a stance to a concept or conjecture; provide justifications; share ideas and embark on criticism of points of supposition; reflect on perspectives; work towards an agreed understanding and apply what was learned to a given context (Bonk and King 1998). Expanding on this, Laurillard (2012) proposes two methods in which structured interactions can be scaffolded: first, by initiating students into a particular type of intervention; and second, assigning students to play particular roles. In utilising the first method in Teaching for Change, students were encouraged to make use of interventions such as posing questions, explanations, conjectures, comments and criticism.

Through the above interventions, the course presenter ensured that students could contribute by questioning one another regarding a point of view, provide justifications for their points of view, and proffer conjectures, comments and criticism regarding their understanding as they engaged with the course content. Laurillard (2012) argues that when students make use of such interventions, reflect on and subsequently modulate their understanding, we can begin to distinguish between what is merely discussion from opportunities for *learning through discussion*.

Towards a Conclusion

Throughout Teaching for Change, students were exposed to a range of learning experiences namely *initiation, inquiry, production, practice* and *discussion*. In many instances, there were overlaps in the learning experiences, as discussed earlier. Arguably, the most difficult learning experience to design for was learning through *collaboration*. This learning experience differs from the other learning experiences in that it aims to build a shared conception negotiated through deliberation (Laurillard 2012). There were many instances of students demonstrating learning through *collaboration* in Teaching for Change, with students taking on different roles in the online debates that ensued. In Teaching for Change, learning through *collaboration* was confirmed by deliberations in the form of *discussion* threads on Teaching for Change. Laurillard (2012) argues that it is these shared outputs that distinguish collaborative learning from learning through *discussion*.

Despite there being indications of collaborative learning in Teaching for Change, questions often arise about whether this form of learning holds pedagogic value. It is often asked why the imperfect understandings of students should be of value if the teacher is not present. Slavin (2004) argues that learning through *collaboration* holds its worth if it incorporates three learning activities. For a MOOC with thousands of students, these learning activities would need to be sufficient to motivate students to work towards a shared goal in Teaching for Change. The first of these motivating features used in Teaching for Change was what Slavin (2004) refers to as peer modelling. Peer modelling in Teaching for Change involves students sharing their ideas in the form of comments on the FutureLearn platform. As ideas are shared in the form of comments, there is an opportunity for the reciprocal articulation and criticism of these comments. For "peer modelling" to be effective, listening, explaining, questioning, summarising, speculating and hypothesising skills are important to pursue in learning encounters (Boud et al. 1999). Slavin (2004) refers to this as cognitive elaboration. The deliberative sphere through which students engaged in criticism served as a motivating feature, what Slavin (2004) refers to as practice with one another. Slavin (2004) adds that practice with one another is more likely to occur in group learning than in individual learning experiences.

Schwartz (1999) emphasises that it is ultimately the productive agency of an individual that enables learning through *collaboration*. Students should demonstrate the intention and willingness to collaborate with one another (Schwartz 1999). Schwartz (1999) furthermore maintains that if these social values are adhered to, then students will be sufficiently motivated to engage in negotiation, learning and producing a shared output. This was indeed evident in Teaching for Change, where students, in a sphere of mutual respect, continually supported one another towards a shared African philosophical understanding. As a student produced a comment, it would be open to criticism. It was through such formative feedback comments that students could adapt their understanding. Through this iterative process, students continually provided alternative solutions to a given comment, which resulted in students modulating their understanding and, consequently, generating a new jointly revised understanding, expressed through a comment posted on the Teaching for Change forums. Given the large student numbers that this course attracted, the course presenter could not be expected to address every comment posted on the forums. This formative feedback, therefore, served as an integral component supporting students through the weeks of the course running.

At the advent of Teaching for Change, the course presenter clearly stipulated his role as that of a moderator, as he explained that he would not be able to address every comment posted on the forums. As discussed earlier, he encouraged students to "come to speech". Towards learning through *collaboration*, the course presenter intermittently joined in *discussions*, especially where students were showing an inclination towards learning through *collaboration*, to produce a joint product or understanding. His role was not to provide any form of validation or verification, but to put it as he refers to in the course trailer, as "learning together".

His presence in the *discussion* forum, therefore, served as a motivating factor facilitating learning through *collaboration*. Podcasts at the end of every week also served as a motivating factor for supporting learning through *collaboration*. Many students posted comments acknowledging the course presenter's efforts for reading their comments and addressing the comments in the form of an audio recording or podcast.

A synopsis of research in the field of collaborative learning provided by Laurillard (2012), proposes the following guidelines towards fostering meaningful interaction among students:

- encouraging students to contribute, based on clear argumentation;
- argumentation should be derived from course content; and
- contributions should reflect a theoretical underpinning.

With Teaching for Change, open questions at the end of every philosophical concept discussed were used to corroborate meaningful pedagogic interactions. Students were encouraged to provide statements and reflections while scaffolding one another in developing philosophical understandings. This was indicative of meaningful *collaboration*, as discussed by Laurillard (2012). The learning design underpinning Teaching for Change attempted to provide students with a range of learning experiences, encompassing learning through *initiation, inquiry, practice, discussion*—referred to by Laurillard (2012), as learning through *collaboration*.

References

Bonk, C. J., & King, K. S. (1998). *Electronic Collaborators: Learner-Centered Technologies for Literacy, Apprenticeship and Discourse*. Princeton: Lawrence Erlbaum.

Boud, D., Cohen, R., & Sampson, J. (1999). Peer Learning and Assessment. *Assessment and Evaluation in Higher Education, 24*(4), 413–426.

Chandler, R. (2017). *Futurelearn Comment*. Retrieved from https://www.futurelearn.com/courses/african-philosophy/2/steps/134926/comments?filter=everyone&sort=most_liked&#fl-comments. Accessed 28 Sept 2017.

Dysthe, O. (2002). The Learning Potential of Web-mediated Discussion in a University Course. *Studies in Higher Education, 27*(3), 339–352.

Elias, S. (2017). *Futurelearn Comment*. Retrieved from https://www.futurelearn.com/courses/african-philosophy/2/steps/134901#fl-comments. Accessed 28 Sept 2017.

King, C., Kelder, J.-A., Doherty, K., Phillips, R., McInerney, F., Walls, J., & Wickers, J. (2014). Designing for Quality: The Understanding Dementia MOOC. *Electronic Journal of e-Learning, 12*(2), 161–172.

Laurillard, D. (2012). *Teaching as a Design Science*. New York: Routledge.

Laurillard, D. (2014). *UNESCO Institute for Information Technologies in Education*. Retrieved from http://www.iite.unesco.org/files/news/639194/Anatomy_of_a_MOOC.pdf. Accessed 28 Sept 2017.

Norton, A. (2013). *The Online Evolution: When Technology Meets Tradition*. Melbourne: Grattan Institute.

Schwartz, D. (1999). The Productive Agency that Drives Collaborative Learning. In P. Dillenbourg (Ed.), *Collaborative Learning: Cognitive and Computational Approaches* (pp. 197–218). New York: Elsevier Science/Pergamon.

Slavin, R. E. (2004). When and Why Does Cooperative Learning Increase Achievement? In H. Daniels & A. Edwards (Eds.), *The RoutledgeFalmer Reader in Psychology of Education* (pp. 269–293). London: RoutledgeFalmer.

Waghid, Y. (2017a). *Futurelearn Comment*. Retrieved from https://www.future-learn.com/courses/african-philosophy/2/steps/107918#fl-comments. Accessed 28 Sept 2017.

Waghid, Y. (2017b). *Teaching for Change: An African Philosophical Approach*. Retrieved from https://www.futurelearn.com/courses/african-philosophy/2/. Accessed 28 Sept 2017.

Wu, D., & Hiltz, S. R. (2004). Predicting Learning from Asynchronous Online Discussions. *Journal of Asynchronous Learning Networks, 8*(2), 139–152.

Index

A

Acknowledgement, 8, 34, 35, 45, 47, 48, 54, 59, 147, 158
   public, 57
Act
   autonomously, 79, 81, 135, 142
   reflexively, 135
Acting
   African way of, 156
   critical, 129
Action(s)
   autonomous (*see* Autonomous, action)
   compassionate, 47, 90
   deliberative, 56, 58, 59, 65
   disruptive, 100, 123
   emancipatory, 59
   human, 5, 6, 8, 17, 22, 42, 45, 48, 49, 76, 91, 98, 136, 157, 159, 162
   just, 4, 48, 155
   pedagogical, 3, 23, 36, 49, 75, 113, 140
   politico-economic, 40
   post-colonial, 40
   reflexive, 84
   responsible, 84
   restorative, 87
   risk-oriented, 49, 51, 52, 64, 65, 67–69, 71–73
   socio-cultural, 40
   transformative, 59, 153
Activity
   of the mind, 5, 84
   pedagogic, 40, 78
Acts
   of deliberation, 59, 60, 67, 70
   of genocide, 93
   of responsibility, 67
   of virtue, 71

184   Index

Africa, 4, 8, 11, 12, 15, 19, 24, 27, 28, 30, 40, 43, 51, 53, 68, 83, 84, 86, 87, 92, 95, 96, 113, 117, 119, 123, 131, 134, 136, 139
  central, 93
  community, 8
  post-colonial, 120
  sub-Saharan, 92
Africanness, 156, 158
Africans, 4, 5, 7, 8, 22–24, 44, 51–53, 67, 73, 83–86, 96, 121–123, 135, 137, 161, 165, 167
  condition, 1, 84, 156
  continent, 6–13, 15, 24, 27, 33, 35, 36, 40, 43–45, 47, 72, 83–85, 87–90, 93, 95–99, 120, 129, 133, 134, 137, 138, 150, 159, 160, 163, 167
  ethic of care, 19
  experience, 15, 85
  identities, 86
  issues, 16
  life, 13, 57, 62
  people, 8, 9, 11, 12, 43, 86, 122, 123
  philosophical literature, 85
  philosophy, 1–7, 15, 16, 39, 40, 85–87
  philosophy of education (*see* Philosophy, of education, African)
  proverbs, 13, 14
  societies, 5, 20, 47, 85, 90
  university, 4, 90, 96, 127, 131–132, 134, 160, 161, 163, 171

Agreement, 9, 20, 21, 80
Agricultural
  capacity, 92
  development, 12
  economy, 11
  education, 92
  practices, 12
  predicament, 92
  sector, 92
Alienation, 95, 148, 158
Analysis, 10, 12, 24, 40, 54, 87, 88
  framework of, 77
  of the problem, 88, 90, 91
  three-pronged, 128
Antagonism, 42, 47
Apartheid, 3, 41
  crimes, 46
  educational aims, 149
  post-, 94
Approach
  decolonised, 150
  post-humanist, 124
Arguments, 23, 54, 55, 58, 59, 65, 162
Artefacts, 13, 97, 135
Assemblages of learning, 73, 75, 81, 82
Autonomous, 18, 63, 86
  action, 12, 33, 64, 84, 123
  being, 11, 155
  citizens, 150
  encounter, 124
  engagement, 135
  expression, 18
  force, 118
  learning, 71, 77
  respect, 79
  self, 8
  self-understanding, 155

thinking, 149
way, 130
Autonomy, 7, 36, 61, 64, 78, 79, 82, 103, 135, 155, 163
  human, 46
  individual, 18, 99
  institutional, 129
  moral, 47, 87
  narcissistic, 56
  pedagogic, 152

B

Beliefs, 13, 17, 61, 97
  ethno, 85
Belief systems, 13, 85, 86
Boko Haram, 19, 90–92

C

Capitalism
  global, 127
Capitalist, 87, 96
Caring, 19, 56, 61, 63, 64, 68, 100
Challenge, 27, 28, 120, 155
Change
  deliberative, 160
  pedagogic, 150 (*see also* Pedagogic, change)
  societal, 59, 119, 141, 142, 150
  transformative, 61, 140, 150, 155, 163
Citizen(s), 9, 15, 18–20, 28, 29, 109
  autonomous citizenry, 6
  competent, 30
  critical (*see* Critical, citizen)
  critical citizenship, 31
  critical-minded, 150
  equal citizenship, 22

free and decent citizenry, 6
  global, 114, 150
  responsibilities, 18
  rights, 18
  ubuntu citizenship, 22
Citizenship, 3, 18, 19, 21, 33, 120, 121, 151–154
  African democratic, 151, 152
  democratic, 3, 123, 154
  education
    democratic, 33, 120, 121, 151, 152
    ubuntu, 21, 22
Civic
  courage, 33
  equals, 102
Civility, 7, 8
  civilly engaged, 7
Climate change, 24, 92, 162
Co-belonging, 6, 22, 23, 42, 151–154
  human, 156, 158
Coercion, 9, 86
  political, 94
Co-existence, 7, 8, 21, 94, 98, 153
  human (*see* Human, co-existence)
Co-living, 22, 154, 158
Colonial, 5, 27, 40, 87, 93, 160
  powers, 134
Colonialism, 34, 53, 96, 123, 162
  violence of, 122
Coloniality, 34, 96, 123, 124
  patterns of, 123
Colonisation, 148, 152, 153, 156, 160
  decolonisation, 4, 5
Colonised
  curricula, 33
  societies, 35

186 Index

Comments, 76, 78, 80, 81, 116, 117, 119, 134, 137, 138, 141, 158
  critical, 161
  of engagement, 138
  students, 140
Common good, 60, 61
Communication, 57, 58, 95
  technology, 133
Communitarianism, 52, 53, 56, 58–60, 62–64
Community/communities, 8, 12–14, 18, 19, 36, 45–47, 53, 55–58, 60–68, 72, 83, 86, 97, 98, 107, 109, 114, 129, 130, 135, 160
  of co-belonging, 160
  engagement, 90, 162
  farming, 92
  global, 129
  global learning, 129
  of learners, 79
  learning, 129
  religious, 109
  of thinkers, 86
  of thinking, 2, 131
Compassion, 45–48, 60, 61, 67, 87
  compassionate actions, 2
  compassionate responsibility, 46
Compliance
  technical, 160
Concerns
  ethical, 19
  moral, 19
  societal, 5, 56, 149
Contemporary, 4
  African society, 52, 59–61, 63, 68–73

era, 129, 165
living, 3
living experiences, 3
societies, 134
university, 127–129
Contexts
  societal, 149, 150, 159
Continent
  African (see African, continent)
Contributions, 58, 116
  constructive, 80
  individual, 57, 77
  knowledge, 77
  meaningful, 57, 80
  multiple, 80
  pedagogic, 143
  students, 116, 155
Conversation, 7, 9, 18, 54, 55, 57, 60, 70, 143, 148, 175
  complicated, 148
Cooperation, 67, 135
  human, 19, 48
  respectful, 71
Cosmopolitanism, 114, 115
Courage, 52, 65–69, 71, 72
Course, 20, 23, 45, 48, 52, 76–82, 118, 135, 139
  activities, 80
  content, 81, 140
  design, 136
  materials, 80, 81, 139–141
    online, 135
  texts, 130
Crimes, 93
  against humanity, 43, 98, 158
  apartheid, 46
  war, 43
Critical

citizen, 29
person, 28
scrutiny, 23, 34, 77, 91
thought, 33, 132
Criticism, 2, 11, 15, 16, 31, 36, 54,
59, 85, 133, 136–138, 142
commencement, 29–30
framework of, 11
Cultural
commonalities, 17
concerns, 97, 123
connections, 15
contexts, 97
differences, 7, 18, 57, 114
experiences, 97, 135
hegemony, 124
phenomenon, 14
realties, 97
spaces, 128
stock, 97
wisdom, 15
Culture, 6, 7, 17, 32, 55, 83, 97,
102, 114, 121, 123, 127,
132, 156
African, 13, 18, 72, 156
cosmopolitan, 121
dominant cultural orientation,
116
knowledge, 97
national, 127
oral, 13
of respect, 47
Curriculum, 9, 27, 31, 34, 76, 118,
143, 147–150, 152, 153,
158, 160, 161
apartheid, 148
decolonised, 151, 159
dominant, 148
online, 133

post-apartheid university, 149,
150
renewal, 147, 154, 158–161, 163
statements, 149, 150
university, 147, 148
unresponsiveness, 27, 33
Customs, 13, 17, 97, 153

D
Decolonial, 34, 35, 124, 136, 163
Decolonialism, 162
Decoloniality, 4, 5, 15, 40, 96, 113,
122–124, 134, 136, 139,
143, 147, 162, 163
enactment of, 124
Decolonisation, 4, 5, 15, 40, 96,
134, 139, 143, 147–150,
152–156, 159, 161, 162
agenda, 134
pedagogy of, 136
Deconstruction, 10, 14, 24
opportunities for, 9
problems, 6
understandings of meanings, 10
Deliberation, 51, 54–59, 69–72, 86,
118, 152, 153, 163
act of, 152, 153
Deliberative, 54–59, 73, 77, 81, 91,
99, 114, 118, 120, 141,
142, 152, 153
action, 49, 51, 56, 58, 59, 65, 68
concerns, 154
educational encounters, 99
encounters (*see* Encounters,
deliberative)
engagement (*see* Engagement,
deliberative)
ethics, 153

188   Index

Deliberative (*cont.*)
exchanges, 59
inquiry, 152, 153
interaction, 139
skills, 57
Democracy, 3, 33, 34, 57, 59, 94,
103, 108, 141
democratic iterations, 98
democratic spaces, 99
political and social, 39
radical, 108
Democratic
citizenship education (*see*
Citizenship, education,
democratic)
consensus, 142
inclusion, 59, 116
rule, 94, 95
university, 130
Democratisation, 5, 15, 148
Deterritorialisation, 75, 117
Dialogue, 21, 54, 55, 60, 132
Differences, 7, 8, 20, 22, 34, 47,
114, 116, 131, 152
Dignity, 35, 47, 48, 68, 123, 153
human, 68
Discourse, 4, 5, 7, 24, 29, 56, 83,
85, 115
dominant Western discourses, 1
educational, 24
emancipatory, 113
hegemonic, 108
higher education, 76
less dominant discourse, 1
of meaning making, 29
pedagogic (*see* Pedagogic,
discourse)
rational, 58

Discrimination, 41, 99, 101, 102
Discussion, 8, 11, 13, 16, 31, 42, 44,
48, 57, 68, 77–80, 82–85,
88, 106, 107, 117, 133,
138–140
forums, 77–79, 138
posts, 48, 79, 80, 130, 138, 140
Disruption, 113, 120, 123, 124
art of, 139
expressions of, 124
Disruptive, 100, 103, 110
action, 100, 123
agents of change, 119
encounters, 110, 124, 133, 139,
142
pedagogic encounters, 99
speech, 99, 100, 102–104, 108
way, 99, 142
Dissent, 9, 15, 20, 31, 36, 100, 157
Doing
way of (*see* Way, of doing)

E
Economic
hegemony, 124
interests, 96
spaces, 128
Education, 1–5, 9, 13–17, 19,
22–24, 32, 33, 39, 40, 48,
49, 57, 58, 77, 83–90, 92,
94–98, 102, 103, 108,
113–124, 135, 138–141,
143, 148–156, 158–160,
165
act of, 152
in Africa, 2, 86, 96, 117
African, 86, 140, 160

agenda, 92, 96
agricultural, 92
aims, 152
anti-Western, 90
change, 163
colonial, 163
concerns, 24, 96
cosmopolitan, 116, 121
cultural, 97
decolonised, 154, 155, 158, 159
democratic, 100–103, 108, 109,
    113, 115, 120, 122–124,
    141, 143
democratic African, 51
democratic citizenship (*see*
    Citizenship, education,
    democratic)
discourse, 91, 120
encounters, 5, 97, 99, 127
equal access to, 90
ethno-philosophy (*see* Ethno-
    philosophy of education)
experiences, 4, 8, 9, 13, 22, 71,
    83, 159, 160
form of, 110
global citizenship, 161
higher (*see* Higher education)
implications, 10–12, 21
institution, 72, 96, 100, 134
liberal democratic, 108
moral dimension, 98
needs, 160
outcomes-based, 149
political, 96
practice, 13, 134
predicaments, 15
problems for (*see* Problems, for
    education)
pursuit, 120

relations, 10, 11, 13
right to, 90, 153
system, 69, 149
teacher, 120
theory on, 95, 96
understanding of, 119, 122, 124
university (*see* University,
    education)
view of, 114
views on, 117
Western (*see* Western, education)
Educators, 9, 32, 34–36, 40, 55, 56,
    59, 64, 68, 69, 71, 72,
    76–78, 81, 82, 99, 100,
    103, 104, 106, 107, 110,
    114, 118–120, 122, 135,
    137, 141–143, 148, 150,
    152–155, 157, 159, 160
MOOC, 139
roles as, 118
university, 72, 136, 137, 141,
    148, 150, 160
Emancipation, 16, 24, 59, 95, 96,
    154
Encounters, 141
deliberative, 31, 54, 56, 77, 81,
    115, 118
online, 141
pedagogic (*see* Pedagogic,
    encounters)
Engagement, 2, 20, 21, 103
collective, 20, 99
critical, 91, 132, 135, 137, 139,
    140
deliberative, 2, 15, 20–22, 54–56,
    59, 68, 69, 73, 114, 120,
    124, 135, 151, 152, 156,
    162, 174
democratic, 71, 103, 141

190   Index

Engagement (*cont.*)
  engaging, 20, 22, 32, 114, 116,
      133, 152, 161, 162
  engaging questions, 77
  mutual, 20
  open, 54, 129
  societal, 129
Equality, 32, 33, 41, 42, 47, 48, 62,
      108, 119–124, 132, 155
  civic, 101
  democratic, 113, 120, 122–124
  expressions of, 124
  human, 121
  intellectual, 117, 119, 160
  moral, 41, 42
  political, 122
Equal opportunities, 61, 90
Ethical
  agency, 101
  concerns, 19
  development, 11
  possibilities, 143
  stand, 103
  thoughts, 39
  values, 60
Ethics, 2, 56, 153
  of responsibility, 153
Ethnic
  conflict, 47, 93, 94, 162
  groups, 47, 68, 93
Ethnicity, 101
  ethnicities, 7, 47
Ethno-philosophy of education, 13,
      14
  African, 22
Exclusion, 16, 17, 47, 69, 86, 87,
      94, 99, 101, 102, 119, 154,
      158, 160, 163

  racial, 160
Experience
  democratic, 142, 143
  human, 85, 108
  lived, 11, 17, 22, 40, 42, 97
Exploitation, 44, 122
  economic, 53
  human, 44
Expression
  excessive, 102
  free, 102

F

Famine, 12, 53, 138
Feedback, 80
  student, 143
Folklore, 13
Food
  insecurity, 89, 92, 95, 134
  predicament, 92
  production, 11, 92
  security, 92
Forgiveness, 45–47, 157, 158
Free, 32, 42, 118
  articulation, 85
  association, 18
  atmosphere, 138
  of charge, 80
  citizenry, 6
  discussions, 85
  elections, 9
  individuals, 101
  inquiry, 128
  pedagogic encounters, 104
  processing of topics, 58
  speech acts, 143
  will, 85

Index   191

Freedom(s), 6, 9, 30, 32, 33, 41, 42, 48, 67, 71, 81, 85, 94, 96, 100–104, 108, 116, 132, 154, 162, 163
   academic, 129
   equal, 101
   of expression, 20
   expressive, 100, 101
   legitimate, 96
   manifestation of, 104
   of speech, 18, 67
   of thought, 120
   unconstrained, 102
Friendship, 60, 65–68

G

Gender, 24, 41, 103
   stereotyping, 103
Genocide, 24, 43, 44, 93, 94, 104, 122, 138, 156, 162
Globally informed citizen, 28
Global-minded, 28
Goals, 10–13, 53, 61, 77, 135, 148, 151, 168
Graduate attributes, 28, 96

H

Hatred, 42, 103, 109, 157, 158
Higher education, 17, 27, 28, 32, 33, 36, 76, 134, 136, 139, 165, 174
   in Africa, 140
   African, 137, 138
   discourses, 27
   institutions, 30, 135
   landscape, 133
   South African, 90, 133

Human
   activities, 58
   agency, 45, 69, 70, 132
   antagonism, 47
   co-existence, 8, 21, 42, 48, 67, 93, 94
   condition, 8, 39, 98, 122, 160
   dilemma, 99
   experiences, 98, 100, 142
   flourishing, 56, 58
   human conditions, 8
   interdependence, 18–21, 52, 109, 135, 161
   predicament, 69, 99
   relations/relationships, 4, 23, 36, 56, 65, 68, 103, 141
   responsibility, 43
   rights, 33, 43, 47, 158
   rights violations, 158
   trafficking, 24, 162
   value, 68
Humanely
   act, 35, 36
Humaneness, 19, 35, 48, 52, 121, 123, 135
Humanity, 7, 35, 36, 42, 43, 46, 47, 67, 87, 98, 108, 109, 116, 121, 122, 130, 153, 157, 158, 162
   crimes against, 43
   cultivation of, 42
Humiliation, 45, 49, 105, 156, 163
Hunger, 12, 42, 88, 92, 97

I

Identification, 12, 97, 109, 137
Ideologies, 53, 61, 83
   consumerist, 127

192   Index

Imagine, 5, 6, 12, 35, 149
Imperialism, 162
  Western, 35
Inclusive, 33, 34, 59, 100, 104,
    107–110
Inequality, 16, 34, 39, 41, 48, 62,
    67, 89
  civic, 101
  social, 119
Inequities, 16, 17, 67, 120
Inhumanely
  act, 35
Inhumanity, 15, 39, 41, 86, 122
  inhumane treatment, 41
Initiating, 36
Initiation, 30
Injury, 105–107, 110
  vehicle of, 110
Injustice, 16, 35, 36, 41, 45, 51, 67,
    73, 97, 100–102, 143, 157,
    162, 163
  social, 119, 120
Inquiry
  deliberative, 156
Institutional
  responsibility, 90
  space, 129
Interaction, 8, 48, 59, 65
  reflexive, 143
Interconnectedness, 2, 18, 48, 68
Interconnections, 8
Interdependence, 19, 53, 57, 60, 62,
    63, 67, 94, 98, 153
  human (*see* Human,
    interdependence)
Interest
  collective, 12
  individual, 12
Internal goods, 52, 53
Issues

contextual, 80
societal, 149

J

Judgement, 34, 132, 148, 157
  critical, 142
  evaluative, 55
  intellectual, 148
  own, 34
  students, 34
Justice, 2, 4, 23, 41, 43–49, 54
  compassionate, 39, 43–45, 47, 48
  conversational, 51, 52, 54–59,
    69–72
  cosmopolitan, 84, 87–99, 110,
    114
  democratic, 84, 87
  epistemic, 162
  moral, 39–42
  pedagogic, 51–73, 84, 87, 114
  restorative, 39, 45, 47
  social, 128, 150
  ubuntu, 23, 39–47, 49, 51–54,
    58, 59, 61, 64, 67–69, 73,
    76, 77, 82, 84, 87–90, 94,
    99, 110, 113, 115, 119,
    120, 127, 130, 135, 136,
    140, 149, 153, 156,
    161–163
Justification, 5, 9, 15, 36, 55, 56, 60,
    78, 79, 92, 98, 117, 138,
    151, 152, 157

K

Knowledge, 5, 7, 8, 10–14, 20, 30,
    32, 33, 36, 62, 67, 77, 79,
    86, 87, 89, 91, 97, 118,
    123, 134, 160, 161, 167

academic, 148
construction, 120
cultural, 97
decolonised, 158
interests, 148
local, 12
quest for, 95
and skills, 160
sources of, 13, 91
spaces, 117
traditional, 22
traditions, 30, 32

L
Language, 8, 17, 19, 47, 97, 104–106,
108–110, 118, 123
life, 105
Learners
school, 140
Learning, 1, 14, 27–36, 59, 70, 71,
73, 75, 76, 78, 90, 103,
108, 114, 120, 123,
140–142, 147, 150–152,
158, 163, 167, 168
approach to, 137
autonomous (*see* Autonomous,
learning)
context, 78
course, 141
critical, 141
environment, 116
experiences, 141
globalised, 129
online, 127
outcomes, 149
place of, 114
platform of learning, 1
pre-packaged, 96

self-, 79
self-directed, 77, 78
transformative, 155
vision of, 86
Liberation
decolonial, 123
Liberty, 101, 102
Lines of flight, 75, 82, 117, 130,
136, 137
Listening, 22, 46, 55, 59, 69, 70,
130–132, 138, 152
Literature
Western, 86
Western scientific, 85

M
Maathai, Wangari, 39, 40, 43, 44
Mandela, Nelson, 2, 39, 40, 43
Map, 75, 136
Marginalised, 21, 44, 70, 105, 121,
162
Massive open online courses
(MOOC), 1, 2, 77, 79, 83,
133, 134, 139, 140, 155,
162, 165–167
on African philosophy of
education, 1
learners, 134
platform, 117, 135, 138, 155
site, 137, 139
on Teaching for Change, 23, 27,
76, 81, 87, 113, 115–120,
122–124, 127, 133, 176
Meaning
co-construct meanings, 82
constructing, 29
construct meanings, 10
deconstructing, 10, 29

194 **Index**

Meaning making
  deconstructive, 14
  reflective, 15
Military
  dictatorships, 89, 94, 95
  rule, 9, 94
Militia, 43, 93
Moral
  concern, 41, 47
  conduct, 14
  identity, 14
  imaginations, 100
  issues, 98
  responsibility, 46
Morality, 47, 62
Mutuality, 18, 64, 86, 153

N

Narcissistic, 18, 53
Narratives, 30, 36, 54, 55, 83, 113,
    116, 155
  oral, 13
  of racial injustice, 128
  of terror, 128
Non-discrimination, 102, 158

O

Online
  course, 1, 79, 83
  students, 78, 79
Oppressed, 42, 45, 49, 61, 121
Oppression, 45, 53, 69, 70, 86, 87,
    99, 119, 121, 122, 156
Oppressor, 42, 45
Oral tradition, 2, 15

P

Passive recipients of knowledge, 36
Paths to learning, 141
Pedagogic, 44, 49
  act, 163
  activities, 68, 78, 118, 133, 135,
      137, 141, 142
  advantages, 142
  assumptions, 82
  autonomy, 152
  change, 135
  concerns, 91
  contributions, 143
  courses, 142, 143
  curricular activity, 162
  deliberative pedagogic encounters,
      141
  dilemmas, 27
  discourse, 1
  disruptive pedagogic encounters,
      133, 139, 142
  encounters, 4, 9, 23, 36, 49, 51,
      53, 70, 71, 73, 76–78, 81,
      86, 89, 99, 100, 102–104,
      106–110, 115, 118–120,
      123, 124, 133–143, 153,
      155–159, 163, 167
  engagements, 76
  exchanges, 138
  experiences, 141
  initiatives, 119, 133
  invitation, 77
  justice (*see* Justice, pedagogic)
  lenses, 24
  notions, 75
  online moments, 137
  opportunity, 143

Index   195

practices, 30, 163
preoccupation, 124
procedures, 40
spaces, 33, 129, 142, 162
success, 140
tolerance, 157
unresponsiveness, 27
Pedagogical
  action, 3, 23, 36, 51–73, 75, 113, 140, 162
  initiative, 36
  practices, 31
Pedagogy, 1
  of critical engagement, 32
  democratic, 132
  untamed, 103
People's rights, 90, 154
Perpetrators, 46
  of injustices, 45
Philosophical inquiry, 15
Philosophy, 1, 2, 4–8, 10–13, 15–21, 23, 24, 36, 39–47, 49, 51–73, 77, 83–96, 98, 100, 101, 103–110, 115–117, 119, 133–137, 140, 151, 163
  African communitarian, 23
  African critical, 23
  critical African, 15–17
  of education, 3, 4, 6, 11, 12, 23, 24, 36, 135
    African, 1, 2, 4–8, 10–13, 15–21, 23, 24, 36, 39–47, 49, 51–73, 77, 83–96, 98, 100, 101, 103–110, 115–117, 119, 133–137, 140, 151, 163
  indigenous, 4

traditional, 3
  Western, 85
Platform, 1, 78, 117, 155
Podcasts, 77, 79, 80, 135
Point of view, 9, 21, 34, 54–56, 59, 60, 65, 67, 70, 92, 101, 115, 139, 142, 152
Political, 9, 11, 17, 19, 39, 43, 44, 47, 53, 56, 57, 61, 72, 94–96, 98, 99, 122, 124, 134, 138, 143, 148, 162, 163
  activism, 162
  dimension, 95
  elites, 94
  existence, 95
  hegemony, 124
  preoccupation, 124
  response, 105
  selves, 98
  situatedness, 96
  spaces, 128
  stand, 103
  way of being, 148
Politico-pedagogic, 162
Politics
  democratic, 32, 95, 103
Population, 92–94
  voice of, 94
Post-apartheid, 107, 149, 150
Post-colonial, 40, 93
  paradigm, 134
Poverty, 16, 24, 39, 41, 48, 53, 63, 87, 88, 92
Power, 44, 67, 72, 106, 109, 116
  colonial, 134
  corrupting, 72
  effects of, 34

196 Index

Power (*cont.*)
 hegemonic forms of, 87
 political, 44
 relations, 34
 to respond, 109
 of the social web, 139
Practical reasoner, 54, 56, 60
Practices
 communal, 18
 cultural, 14
 educational, 4
 ethnic, 14
 historical, 14
Prejudice, 42, 71
 racial, 121
Problems, 6, 9, 10, 12, 16, 17, 42,
  91, 93, 94, 134
 African, 16
 analysis of (*see* Analysis, of the
  problems)
 deconstructing, 10
 for education, 10, 13, 88, 89
 educational, 15
 human, 98, 99
 identification of, 12, 137
 major, 8, 9, 21, 88, 89, 92
 political, 56
 practical, 55
 responsive to, 11
 societal, 134, 138, 142
 socio-economic, 56
Programme
 academic, 134
 online, 129

Q
Qualification, 16, 95
 university, 134

R
Racism, 42, 70, 106, 154, 162, 163
Radicalisation, 79, 108
Rationality, 55, 63, 91
Recognition, 3, 7, 8, 22, 41–43, 46,
  47, 55, 64, 82, 86, 109,
  110, 114, 133, 150, 152,
  154, 157, 161
 art of, 138
Reconciliation, 45–48, 59, 89, 93,
  95, 134, 157, 158
Reflect
 critical reflection, 31, 91
 opportunities for reflection, 14
 reflecting, 11
 reflecting on, 10, 12, 13, 120–121
 reflection, 6, 8, 10, 14, 15, 24,
  40, 71
Reflective
 knowledge traditions, 30
 openness, 14, 114, 120, 154
 practice, 80
 thinking, 32
Reflectiveness, 14, 24, 114, 155, 161
 critical, 114
Reflexive, 6, 20, 121, 135, 138, 139,
  141, 150, 155, 161, 163
 capacities, 150
 criticism, 142
 encounters, 143
 imagination, 5, 6
 intellectually, 155
 interactions, 141
 reasoning, 70
 re-evaluation, 58
 thoughts, 113, 115–120,
  122–124
 views, 138
 voices, 161

Index 197

way, 17, 81
Reflexivity, 6, 56, 58, 59, 113, 163
  cosmopolitan, 113–115, 120, 121
  expressions of, 124
Relations
  human (*see* Human, relations/
    relationships)
Relationships
  democratic, 101, 116
  human, 65, 68
  social, 14, 18, 53, 60
Religion, 101, 105–107
Resentment, 42, 69, 158
Resistance, 35, 104, 105, 110, 156
Respect, 5, 6, 21–23, 41, 47, 48, 57,
    59, 79, 98, 101, 102, 114
  autonomous (*see* Autonomous,
    respect)
Responsibility, 2, 6, 11, 18–20, 32,
    34, 36, 41, 43, 45, 48, 51,
    52, 60–64, 71, 72, 87, 90,
    129, 131–132
  humane, 20
  social, 161
Responsiveness, 87, 129, 140, 150
Restoration, 45, 47, 61, 90
Restorative responsibility, 46
Rhizomatic, 117, 133, 136
Rights
  communal, 19
  individual, 18
  moral, 98
  political, 9, 19
  religious, 19
Risk taking, 65, 66, 98
Rules
  guiding, 13
  less formal, 55

S
Scepticism, 34–36
Scholars, 9
  academic circles, 4
  African, 3, 4, 84
  Western, 4
Self-determination, 9, 69, 70, 123, 160
Self-development, 69, 70
Self-education platform, 78
Self-realization, 148
Self-reflexivity, 148
Skills, 28, 31, 32, 71, 95, 96, 132
  cooperative, 58
  deliberative, 57
  development, 31
  interpersonal, 58
Social
  change, 32, 72
  justice, 31, 33, 119
  practices, 17, 32, 52, 70, 132
  spaces, 128
  upliftment, 72
Socialisation, 28–30, 95
  tersocialised, 29, 30
Socialising, 36
Society, 5, 12, 34, 44, 57, 60, 62–64,
    66, 67, 69, 70, 96, 101,
    102, 107, 117, 120, 127,
    129, 131, 132, 140, 148,
    150, 162
  African, 20, 21, 52, 55, 57, 59,
    61–63, 67–73
  contemporary, 134
  democratic, 41, 120
  democratic South African, 46
  humane, 123
  non-African, 130
  service to, 129

198   Index

Solidarity, 60, 61, 63, 67
South Africa, 17, 31, 46, 89, 94,
  107, 133, 148, 153
South Africans, 107
Speaking
  critical, 129
Speech, 106, 143
  acts, 102, 104–106, 109, 110,
    143
    illocutionary, 106
    perlocutionary, 106
  counter-speech, 99, 100,
    102–104, 106, 108, 110
  equal, 99, 123
  excitable, 104, 107
  hate, 99, 102–110
  injurious, 105–107, 110
  insurrectionary, 105
  offensive, 102, 103, 107
  reasonable, 100
Starvation, 88
Stereotyping
  gender, 103
Student(s), 1, 9, 16, 17, 27–36, 39,
    51, 54–56, 58, 59, 64, 65,
    68–72, 76–82, 89, 90, 93,
    96, 99, 100, 103, 104,
    106–110, 114, 116–120,
    122, 129, 132–143,
    148–150, 152, 154–161,
    165–168
  fees, 90
  protests, 17, 89, 95
  university, 135, 136
Subjectivity, 91, 95, 148
Suffering, 39, 41, 156

T
Teaching, 140, 141
  for change, 83, 84, 114, 132, 133
Teaching and learning, 1, 3, 4, 23,
    27, 28, 30–36, 100, 103,
    123, 134, 135, 140, 150,
    163
  African philosophy of, 39
  challenges, 27
  critical, 32
  encounters, 1, 35
  higher education, 27, 28
  online, 36, 135
  predicament, 27
  responsive, 35
  spaces, 33
  strategies, 150
  transformative, 163
Terrorism, 89, 95, 130, 134, 156
Themes, 23, 76, 77, 136
Thinking, 71
  absence of, 132
  African, 76, 134
  African way of, 156
  authentic, 71
  autonomous (*see* Autonomous,
    thinking)
  critical, 129, 148, 150
  dominant, 150
  enacting, 11
  modes of thought, 138
  rational, 58
  rhizomatic, 117, 133
  way of, 10, 11, 22
Thought
  deconstructive, 14

Index   **199**

Tolerance, 157
Traditions, 13, 30, 83, 84, 95–97, 153
  existing, 95, 96
Transformation, 72, 81
Truth and reconciliation, 134
Truth and Reconciliation
      Commission (TRC), 46
Truthfulness, 52, 60, 61, 63, 69, 72
Tuition fees, 89, 90
Tutu, Desmond, 39, 40, 45, 46

U

Ubuntu, 2, 19, 21–23, 41, 44–46, 52, 53, 58, 68, 81, 135
  justice (*see* Justice, *ubuntu*)
Ukama, 8
Undemocracy, 34
Understanding, 10
  common, 10, 70
  global, 11
  human, 12
Unequal power relations, 34
Universals, 128–131
University, 96
  African (*see* African, university)
  contemporary, 127–129
  education, 16, 33, 36, 90, 150, 159
  listening, 130

V

Value(s), 13, 17, 24, 32, 53, 68, 72, 95–97, 131
  cultural, 85
  ethical, 60

  human (*see* Human, value)
Vectors of escape, 117
Victims, 45, 46
  of terror, 91
Views
  critical, 138
  local, 11
  reflexive, 138
Violence, 2, 16, 24, 42–44, 47, 69, 87, 91, 93, 94, 97, 122, 130, 162
  prevention of, 48
  state, 128
Virtue(s)
  of courage, 65, 68, 72
  of human dignity, 68
Voice
  critical, 150
Vulnerability/vulnerabilities, 5, 9, 12, 43, 44, 46, 47, 87, 109
  human vulnerability, 44

W

Way, 20, 76, 117, 149, 156
  being
    African, 20, 156
  of doing, 10, 11, 15
  thinking
    African, 76, 117, 149
Western
  education, 19, 20, 91
  imperalism, 35
Wiredu, Kwasi, 2–6, 8, 84

X

Xenophobia, 22, 70, 71, 162

CPSIA information can be obtained
at www.ICGtesting.com
Printed in the USA
LVOW13*1020060518
576151LV00009B/108/P